CHRISTOLOGY

SECOND EDITION

CHRISTOLOGY

A Global Introduction

VELI-MATTI KÄRKKÄINEN

Baker Academic

a division of Baker Publishing Group
Grand Rapids, Michigan

Published by Baker Academic
a division of Baker Publishing Group
P.O. Box 6287, Grand Rapids, MI 49516-6287
www.bakeracademic.com

Printed in the United States of America

Library of Congress Cataloging-in-Publication Data
Names: Kärkkäinen, Veli-Matti, author.
Title: Christology : a global introduction / Veli-Matti Kärkkäinen.
Description: Second edition. | Grand Rapids, MI : Baker Academic, 2016. | Includes bibliographical
    references and index.
Identifiers: LCCN 2015045923 | ISBN 9780801030888 (pbk.)
Subjects: LCSH: Jesus Christ—Person and offices. | Jesus Christ—History of doctrines.
Classification: LCC BT203 .K37 2016 | DDC 232.09—dc23
LC record available at http://lccn.loc.gov/2015045923

In keeping with biblical principles of creation stewardship, Baker Publishing Group advocates the responsible use of our natural resources. As a member of the Green Press Initiative, our company uses recycled paper when possible. The text paper of this book is composed in part of post-consumer waste.

16 17 18 19 20 21 22   7 6 5 4 3 2 1

Contents

Acknowledgments

For some time I had felt a need to revise this textbook, written more than a decade ago. My initial plan was to correct some inaccuracies and poor formulations as well as update the references and make documentation more detailed. However, having started planning for the work, it became clear to me that a thorough revision and to some extent rewriting would be necessary and useful because of the flood of scholarly literature in relevant fields of biblical, historical, and doctrinal studies. Furthermore, my recent major monograph on Christology, *Christ and Reconciliation: A Constructive Christian Theology for the Pluralistic World* (Eerdmans, 2013), gave me an opportunity to deepen my understanding and clarify some issues in this rapidly developing field. At the same time, continuing to teach theology students not only in the United States (Fuller Theological Seminary, Pasadena, CA) and Europe (University of Helsinki, Finland) but also in various locations in the Global South further helped me think about how to best communicate these lessons to students and other interested readers.

In addition to having revised the whole text, including taking stock of recent literature and adding a plethora of references, I have also added whole new sections: part 4 focuses on perceptions and interpretations of Jesus Christ among four living faith traditions (Jewish, Muslim, Hindu, and Buddhist). All-new discussions on postcolonial Christologies and queer Christologies have been added to part 3. Furthermore, throughout the text I have used insights and contributions from recent research. As it now stands, the text provides a concise introduction to biblical and historical developments in Christology as well as a wide survey of contemporary global diversity in both the Global

North and South (and, as mentioned, among some living faith traditions). It seems to me that no other christological textbook attempts such a wide reach.

I am deeply grateful to Robert Hosack at Baker Academic, who helped me gain this opportunity for revision. Throughout the final editorial process, Baker Academic editor Eric Salo's attention to details and need for clarity helped make the text more precise and user-friendly. My Korean doctoral student, Jongeock Shin, checked all the bibliographic references. Susan Carlson Wood, the technical editor and writer at Fuller, who also edited the original version of the manuscript, again helped transform my writing into proper American English. The index was prepared by Viktor Toth.

As always I am grateful to my wife of over three decades, Anne-Päivi, who always supports my writing tasks and helps make life so much easier and happier.

Abbreviations

ANF	*The Ante Nicene Fathers*. Edited by Alexander Roberts and James Donaldson. 1885–1887. 10 vols. Repr., Peabody, MA: Hendrickson, 1994.
COQG	Christian Origins and the Question of God series
DJG (1992)	*Dictionary of Jesus and the Gospels*. Edited by Joel B. Green, Scot McKnight, and I. Howard Marshall. Downers Grove, IL: InterVarsity, 1992.
DJG (2013)	*Dictionary of Jesus and the Gospels*. Edited by Joel B. Green, Jeannine Brown, and Nicholas Perrin. 2nd ed. Downers Grove, IL: InterVarsity, 2013.
DPL	*Dictionary of Paul and His Letters*. Edited by Gerald F. Hawthorne, Ralph P. Martin, and Daniel G. Reid. Downers Grove, IL: InterVarsity, 1993.
ET	English translation
NPNF[2]	*Nicene and Post-Nicene Fathers*. Series 2. Edited by Philip Schaff and Henry Wace. 1886–90. Repr., Peabody, MA: Hendrickson, 1996.

Introduction

What Is Christology? Why Does It Matter?

Jesus's question to his first disciples—"Who do you say I am?"—is addressed also to us. Just as his early followers tried to answer this question in the context of their times, we today must try to give as adequate an answer as possible in the context of our times. "In every generation Christian theology is faced with the task of articulating the intuitions of the biblical tradition about the significance of Jesus Christ in a way that engages its own cultural context."[1] How should we speak of Jesus at the beginning of the third millennium?

Different and diverse interpretations of Christ coming from theologians from all continents and Christian traditions reveal the continuing task of Christology: to interpret the significance and meaning of Jesus Christ for our own times in light of biblical and historical developments. Beginning in the biblical period and traveling through two thousand years of winding theological roads, Christian theology has tried to make sense of the person and work of Jesus Christ. Every generation of theologians and Christians has responded to Christ's person and influence in the context in which it has found itself.

The person of Jesus Christ stands at the center of Christian faith and theology. For this reason, the study of Christology needs no particular justification per se: "While no theology can confine itself exclusively to Christology, no Christian theology would be complete without serious reflection

1. F. LeRon Shults, *Christology and Science* (Grand Rapids: Eerdmans, 2008), 1.

1

on Jesus Christ."[2] Jesus's brief life on earth, his death on the cross, and his disciples' claims regarding the resurrection and ascension lay the historical and religious foundations for Christianity. "Over the years Christology has been a perennial object of fascination, for it is the keystone of theology for serious Christians."[3]

The Spectrum of Christologies

From the beginning of Christianity there arose a variety of interpretations of who Christ is. At no time was one picture of Jesus dominant. In fact, the New Testament itself contains several complementary interpretations of Jesus Christ. The existence of four Gospels provides an everlasting reminder of the plurality of the Christian canon. Moreover, the pictures painted by Paul and other New Testament writers should be added to the distinctive testimonies of the evangelists of the New Testament. The New Testament, therefore, contains a myriad of pictures, silhouettes, and appropriations of Jesus Christ. What binds them together is the common core, a conviction that something crucial happened in the person of this One who is confessed as the Lord and Savior by all Christians of all times.

Along with the establishment of the biblical canon in the fourth century, Christian theology, in the form of the classical creeds, attempted to formulate a definitive understanding of Christ in light of the existing philosophical, cultural, and religious milieu. Much was achieved by the exact formulations concerning Christ's divinity and humanity, but even more was left open. Basically, what the early creeds said was in the negative. In other words, they combated views regarded as heretical. During the subsequent centuries up until our own time, theology has taken its point of departure from these early formulations and has refined them. Still, the work continues.

The blossoming of christological study and reflection beginning at the turn of the twentieth century and culminating in the emergence of so-called contextual or intercultural Christologies in the 1960s and since has produced a fascinating rainbow of christological interpretations. Indeed, one of the most exciting features in contemporary theology is the rise of contextual and/or intercultural Christologies that attempt to speak to specific local needs (for example, in Africa or Asia) or needs of specific groups of people (such

2. J. P. Galvin, "Jesus Christ," in *Systematic Theology: Roman Catholic Perspectives*, ed. Francis Schüssler Fiorenza and John P. Galvin (Minneapolis: Fortress, 1991), 1:251.
3. William J. LaDue, *Jesus among the Theologians: Contemporary Interpretations of Christ* (Harrisburg, PA: Trinity Press International, 2001), vii.

as women or the poor).[4] Some Christologies are also linked with specific philosophical or worldview movements, such as process philosophy. The most recent challenge to—as well as opportunity for—Christian interpretation of Christ is to compare it with other faith traditions. As is well known, Islam regards Jesus highly and has developed its own "Christology." Other living faith traditions have also commented on Jesus's meaning.

What is Christology more specifically? How is it done? Is there a particular method to it? Let us clarify first those orientational questions by looking briefly at two interrelated sets of questions: Is there a distinction between the "person" (identity) and "work" of Jesus Christ? And if so, what might be the relationship? Furthermore, should we begin the inquiry into who Jesus is from the known theological proclamation on the basis of biblical study, or is there a way to investigate based on the historical background and claims? How do these two avenues (routinely called Christology "from above" and "from below") relate to each other?

The Person and Work of Christ Belong Together

In works of Christology written before the twentieth century, there was often a sharp distinction between "the person of Christ" (Christology proper) and "the work of Christ" (soteriology, the doctrine of salvation). Nowadays the distinction is less clear, and there are both philosophical and practical reasons for a less sharp division (though a clear distinction is helpful for educational purposes).

Just consider one early Eastern church father, Athanasius, who argued that Christ had to be both human and divine in order to be our Redeemer: divine in order to save and human in order to identify with us. His insight into the full divinity and humanity did not grow out of sustained abstract philosophical reflection but out of Jesus's role as Savior. Usually it is the salvation and healing brought about by Christ that leads a person to ask about the person of Christ. When Jesus of Nazareth healed a crippled man in John 5, the man did not know who the healer was. He had to go seeking after Jesus at the temple in order to find out who the man was who had cured him. This is what Philipp Melanchthon, a colleague of Martin Luther in the Protestant Reformation, meant with his oft-cited saying: "To know Christ means to know his benefits."[5] That is, apart from soteriology, the doctrine

4. See, e.g., Volker Küster, *The Many Faces of Jesus Christ: Intercultural Christology*, trans. John Bowden (Maryknoll, NY: Orbis, 2001).
5. Philipp Melanchthon, *Loci Communes Theologici*, in *Melanchthon and Bucer*, ed. Wilhelm Pauck (Philadelphia: Westminster, 1969), 19:21.

of salvation, there is no access to the person of Christ. That is the approach of the Bible. The New Testament nowhere enters into a sophisticated philosophical discussion about Christ's person but rather focuses on the salvation brought about by Christ.

Famous philosopher of the eighteenth century Immanuel Kant, who inquired into the conditions of our knowledge, maintained that in general we cannot know things directly but only insofar as we can perceive their impact. The identity of Jesus, therefore, is known through his impact on us. In the same spirit, Albrecht Ritschl, one of the founders of classical liberalism, argued that it is improper to separate Christology and soteriology because the only way to receive knowledge of something is to observe its effects on us.

These foundational perspectives concerning the integral link between the person and the work of Christ have led theologians to a growing realization of the connection between "functional" (what Christ has done for us) and "ontological" (who Christ is in his person) Christologies. Yet at the same time, works of Christology tend to focus on one or the other, and this book is no exception. The focus here is on the person of Christ, and therefore soteriological questions will be addressed only insofar as they are intertwined with that inquiry.

But should we speak of "Jesusology" rather than "Christology"? After all, Jesus is the first name of the divine-human person. This question takes us to the most foundational methodological question in Christology.

Christology "From Below" and "From Above"

There are two options, in principle, for inquiry into the person and work of Christ. Conveniently, these have been labeled "from above" and "from below." Christology from above begins with the confession of faith in the deity of Christ as expressed in the New Testament. Christology from below begins with an inquiry into the historical Jesus and the historical basis for belief in Christ. In other words, the approach from above takes the theological interpretation of Jesus Christ as found in the New Testament as its point of departure for determining the meaning of Christ for our own times. Theologians who use the approach from below go behind the theological interpretation of the evangelists, Paul, and other New Testament writers and attempt to ascertain for themselves the historical and factual foundation of christological claims. It is important to note that this is not a distinction between "conservative" and "liberal" but one of method. (Although most conservatives work from above, many notable theologians in the from above category are liberal. Other theologians advocate a from below method but still hold to a "high" view of Christ as truly divine.)[6]

Understandably, from above was the dominant orientation of the earliest centuries. There was no question about the historical reliability of the Gospel records. The development of christological tradition before the time of the Enlightenment was simply an interpretation of the New Testament confession of faith in Christ and an attempt to express it in precise philosophical and theological terms. The from above method also had its proponents in the twentieth century, though their motivation was vastly different from the pre-Enlightenment orientation. Theologians associated with neo-orthodoxy (a movement examined in part 3), such as Emil Brunner and Karl Barth, and those with existentialist leanings, such as Rudolf Bultmann, argued that the basis for understanding Christ is not the historical Jesus but the *kerygma* (Greek, "preaching," "proclamation"), the church's proclamation of Christ. In other words, these modern from above advocates did not necessarily believe in the content of the New Testament and the early church's confession of faith, but neither did they see a reason to check its historical reliability (or, as with Barth, they considered checking its historical reliability harmful in some way). In some real sense, that approach is fideistic (from the Greek term for "belief"—in other words, valuing faith over reason). Whatever one believes about the earthly, historical Jesus is secondary to one's own existential view of Christ.[7]

The main orientation of Christology since the time of the Enlightenment, however, has been from below. This is understandable given the intellectual developments associated with the Enlightenment, particularly the centrality of critical reasoning and the individual's freedom to make judgments (part 2 discusses in detail the implications of the Enlightenment for Christology): out of that desire to judge for oneself rose the highly influential quest of the historical Jesus. Theologians involved in this quest attempt to go beyond the biblical authors' confessions and ascertain for themselves who Jesus of Nazareth was. In this sense, the nineteenth-century searches for the historical Jesus were "Jesusologies" rather than Christologies because they focused on the human person Jesus rather than on the divine Christ confessed by the early church.[8]

---

6. For basic discussion and sources, see Kärkkäinen, *Christ and Reconciliation: A Constructive Christian Theology for the Pluralistic World* (Grand Rapids: Eerdmans, 2013), 37–42.

7. See the useful discussion in chap. 32 of Millard J. Erickson, *Christian Theology*, 3rd ed. (Grand Rapids: Baker Academic, 2013).

8. For an accessible, nontechnical discussion of historical, philosophical, and language-related problems and challenges facing contemporary Christology, see chap. 1 in Gerald O'Collins, SJ, *Christology: A Biblical, Historical, and Systematic Study of Jesus*, 2nd ed. (Oxford: Oxford University Press, 2009).

Not all from below advocates, however, agreed with a "Jesusology" orientation. A notable exception is late German systematician Wolfhart Pannenberg, who named his approach as "from below to above."[9] His Canadian Baptist pupil, the late Stanley Grenz, followed his teacher.[10] Pannenberg maintains that the task of Christology is to offer rational support for belief in the divinity of Jesus. Since the from above approach presupposes rather than argues for it, it cannot be judged as valid. A from above approach tends to neglect the history of Jesus and therefore avoids tackling the obvious question of the reliability of the sources on Jesus. Pannenberg argues that historical inquiry is both necessary and possible. But he also contends that a critical scholar should be open to "supernatural" events such as the miracle of resurrection. If resurrection can be shown to be historically true (or at least likely), it may lead to a "high" Christology, that is, the confession of Jesus's divinity. In other words, differently from the typical from below approach, Pannenberg's approach seeks to lead to the confession of faith on the basis of critical study; and differently from the typical from above approach, faith follows critical study rather than being merely (or primarily) an existential choice.[11]

In contemporary theology, the from below and from above template is used only heuristically, and many theologians do not even appreciate it particularly. As a general principle, the distinction is not either-or but rather both-and; they are complementary.[12] It is rather a matter of methodologically beginning from below toward constructing a high Christology.[13] The obvious danger of from above divorced from the history of Jesus is the violation of the biblical insistence on Jesus as the way to the knowledge of God (John 14:6). The danger of a one-sided from below method is that the church's faith may be contingent on ever-changing results of human inquiry without any basis in authoritative revelation and tradition.

As said, the discussion on christological method is hardly at the center of christological prolegomena anymore. New ways of constructing a more dynamic, relevant, and appropriate Christology are continuously sought for the sake of the pluralistic world. Let us briefly register those impulses and

9. Wolfhart Pannenberg, *Systematic Theology*, trans. Geoffrey W. Bromiley (Grand Rapids: Eerdmans, 1994), 2:279.

10. Stanley Grenz, *Theology for the Community of God* (Grand Rapids: Eerdmans, 1994), chaps. 9, 10, 11.

11. Pannenberg's own, quite technical account can be found in vol. 2, chap. 9 of his *Systematic Theology*. See chap. 5 below for discussion of his Christology.

12. Pannenberg, *Systematic Theology*, 2:289. So also Donald G. Bloesch, *Jesus Christ: Savior & Lord* (Downers Grove, IL: InterVarsity, 1997), 57.

13. Pannenberg, *Systematic Theology*, 2:289.

then take a more careful and detailed look at them in the exposition of contemporary views in the book.[14]

Toward Dynamic and Relevant Ways of Doing Christology

Although theology is always based on and ruled by biblical revelation and growing Christian tradition, it is also deeply embedded in the local worldview and cultural-religious as well as socioeconomic and political realities. The worldview of the beginning of the third millennium is radically different from the static, semi-mechanistic view of reality during earlier periods of Christian history, when the contours of classical Christology were hammered out. Not only more dynamic and elusive but also robustly relational, the contemporary view of reality offers new ways of giving account of traditional biblical, and traditional formulations of, Christology.[15] Because of criticism against tradition's framing the Christian confession of Christ in a way that leads to a static and abstract account (particularly with regard to so-called two-nature Christology, to be explained below), new, complementary, and often also competing ways of conceiving the task of Christology have emerged.

The title of Reformed German Jürgen Moltmann's celebrated *The Way of Jesus Christ* points to a more dynamic way of doing Christology, that is, away from a static two-nature approach of tradition to one in which Jesus Christ is grasped "dynamically, in the forward movement of God's history with the world."[16] Consequently, the outline of the discussion is not structured according to the typical dogmatic topics—divinity, humanity, and natures—but rather according to a developing process or various moves on the way of Jesus Christ from his birth to earthly ministry to cross to resurrection to current cosmic role to parousia. It is an eschatological Christology, pointing to the future, and hence is based on God's promise.[17] Moltmann also reminds us that unless Jesus's earthly life is rediscovered in theology, what he calls "christopraxis" will be lost. Christopraxis—"christological theory which is concerned with the knowledge of Christ in his meaning for us today"—leads to discipleship and the appreciation of community

---

14. For details, see Kärkkäinen, *Christ and Reconciliation*, 42–51.

15. For a careful historical-philosophical retrieval of the rise of relationality, see F. LeRon Shults, *Reforming Theological Anthropology: After the Philosophical Turn to Relationality* (Grand Rapids: Eerdmans, 2003), chap. 1.

16. Jürgen Moltmann, *The Way of Jesus Christ: Christology in Messianic Dimensions*, trans. Margaret Kohl (Minneapolis: Fortress, 1993), xiii.

17. Ibid., xiv.

in which the practical reflection on the teaching and life-example of Jesus is practiced.[18]

Moltmann's approach echoes key concerns of liberation Christologies and Christologies from the Global South. Their approach is from below but not in the sense previously explained: rather, instead of focusing on abstract speculations about themes such as preexistence or two natures, they seek insights and guidance for the sake of equality and liberation. Just consider the agenda of some womanist (African American female) theologians, whose main interest is in the "deeds of the historical Jesus and not the idealized Christ, in keeping with the liberative traditions of the religious community."[19] Similarly, senior African American theologian James H. Cone critiques the classical Christology of the creeds for neglecting the grounding of the "christological arguments in the concrete history of Jesus of Nazareth." Consequently, Cone surmises, "little is said about the significance of his ministry to the poor as a definition of his person."[20]

As much as this shift from the "old" to "new" approaches is needed, Moltmann reminds us that the "transition does not have to be a breach. Transitions can also place traditions within wider horizons, and preserve older perceptions by translating them into new situations."[21] That is, while the contours of contemporary Christology may differ quite significantly from the approach of the past, it does not mean leaving behind what is sometimes called the metaphysical Christology of Chalcedon. Rather, a careful and detailed consideration and reworking of traditional Christology is a continuing task.

A Brief Synopsis of the Book

This book seeks to offer a comprehensive—even if not exhaustive—introduction to Christology in four different moments. Part 1 surveys the main biblical approaches to the person of Christ as they are presented by the Gospel writers and Paul. Part 2 inquires into historical developments, focusing on two crucial, defining phases: early developments during the first five centuries that laid the foundation for the rest of Christology, and the quest of the historical Jesus, which in conjunction with the radical transformation of the intellectual climate as a result of the Enlightenment definitively changed the study of

18. Ibid., 41.
19. JoAnne Marie Terrell, *Power in the Blood? The Cross in the African American Experience* (Maryknoll, NY: Orbis, 1998), 108.
20. James H. Cone, *God of the Oppressed*, rev. ed. (Maryknoll, NY: Orbis, 1997), 107.
21. Moltmann, *Way of Jesus Christ*, xvi.

Christology. Part 3 examines the current landscape of international Christology in its various forms: contemporary interpretations in the West and several contextual approaches that have been developed not only in Europe and North America but also in Asia, Africa, and Latin America. The final part (4) further widens the domain of the discussion by engaging four living faith traditions (Jewish, Muslim, Hindu, and Buddhist) with regard to their perceptions of Jesus Christ and his meaning to those traditions.

While this work claims no originality (in the sense that several highly useful introductory manuals have been produced in recent years, which also have helped shape the current one), its distinctive nature is the intentional and wide engagement of not only mainline christological traditions in the past and present but also the above-mentioned contextual and intercultural ones. Part of that orientation is also the opening up of theology to religious plurality and types of pluralisms.

PART 1

CHRIST IN BIBLICAL TESTIMONIES

Diversity in Unity

The foundational document for the Christian church is the Bible, the canonical books of the Old and New Testaments. Even though it is the task of Christian theology, especially systematic theology, to go beyond the Bible when inquiring into the meaning and significance of Jesus Christ for people living in various contexts in the third millennium—asking many questions the Bible did not ask—the importance of the biblical testimonies should in no way be thereby diminished.

In the Bible there is of course no systematic theological or doctrinal explanation of Jesus the Christ. Instead, there are a number of testimonies, stories, metaphors, and other such accounts. Moreover, Jesus's own teachings are given through symbols and stories, and the accent is on his deeds. In this sense, we could perhaps describe biblical Christology as a sort of "lived" Christology rather than a schematized doctrine.

The Gospel Silhouettes of Jesus

The Rich Plurality of the Biblical Testimonies

That the New Testament contains various complementary faces of Christ is illustrated most aptly by the existence of four Gospels. Why four Gospels? Why not just one? This fact has been acknowledged and pondered by Christians for centuries. Already in the second century, attempts were made to harmonize the four Gospels into one whole in order to make the story of Christ more coherent. Even the first Bible readers noticed that having four stories not only added to the richness of the overall story but also created problems such as contradictions between various details related to the same story. The church and Christian theology, however, decided in favor of a plurality of testimonies at the expense of harmony in every detail.

How much do we know of the history of Jesus? A dramatic shift happened in theologians' estimation at the time of the Enlightenment. While until then the Gospel records' testimonies were taken at face value, after the advent of modernity, skepticism became the default position. That put the historical question at the center.[1]

---

1. For a detailed, well-documented, and accessible account of the "history of Jesus," that is, how much and with what certainty we can know historical details of Jesus's life in reference to non-theological sources, see chap. 2 in Hans Schwarz, *Christology* (Grand Rapids: Eerdmans, 1998). For nonbiblical sources and opinions about Jesus of Nazareth, see C. A. Evans, "Jesus in Non-Christian Sources," in *DJG* (1992), 364–68.

The most popular approach to biblical Christology has involved focusing on the various titles given to Jesus Christ. There is an old Latin saying, *nomen est omen*, which means "name is an omen." In ancient cultures, as well as many cultures in today's two-thirds world, the name given to a person reflects either a distinctive personal characteristic or significant events related to that person. Clearly, various titles given to Christ serve that function. Although no longer at the center of New Testament Christology, the theological implications of the titles should be properly considered.

The more recent method of New Testament Christology involves reading each book as it stands without necessarily trying to pull all the differing materials into a coherent whole. In other words, the specific contribution of each of the Gospels is appreciated on its own terms. Thus, there is a Christology of Matthew, of Mark, of Luke, and of John. Before looking at these, however, two preparatory tasks lie ahead of us. First, in order to locate the Jewish Messiah in his own milieu, we take a short look at the Jewish background. Second, in order to orient the reader to the thought forms and ways of naming Jesus in the Gospels, a brief look at the titles of Christ will be provided. Thereafter, the bulk of the chapter is devoted to profiling each Gospel's distinctive account of the Messiah.

The Jewishness of Jesus the Messiah

Until recently, Christian theology in its discussion of Christology neglected its most obvious background, namely, the Jewish messianic milieu. Although it is true that precritical exegesis often added notes on the Old Testament prophecies and allusions to the Messiah, the implications of Jesus's Jewishness were not allowed to shape Christian theological understanding. Even worse, more often than not the Jewish religion was conceived in negative, "legalistic" terms as opposed to the religion of "grace." This development started early and was evident already in much of patristic theology. This misconception divested theology of its messianic dimension.[2]

Happily, the most contemporary Jesus research as conducted by biblical scholars shows a wide and variegated interest in the Jewishness of Jesus.[3] What has hindered the integration of these discoveries into systematic and

2. See further Jürgen Moltmann, *The Way of Jesus Christ: Christology in Messianic Dimensions*, trans. Margaret Kohl (Minneapolis: Fortress, 1993), 69–70; chap. 2 in Gerald O'Collins, SJ, *Christology: A Biblical, Historical, and Systematic Study of Jesus*, 2nd ed. (Oxford: Oxford University Press, 2009).

3. "Twentieth-century [New Testament] scholarship has at least one great advantage over its predecessors. . . . It has been realized that Jesus must be understood in his Jewish context."

constructive theologies is that too often biblical and systematic disciplines have not engaged each other in a way that we would hope for.[4] This omission, however, is in the process of being slowly corrected even among doctrinal theologians.

Differently from most systematicians, Moltmann begins his major monograph on Christology with a careful investigation of "Jewish messianology."[5] Note that the subtitle of his book is *Christology in Messianic Dimensions*. Moltmann takes Old Testament messianic hopes and metaphors as the presupposition of Christian theology of Christ as Israel's Messiah.

The religious categories of the Jewish faith provide the explanatory framework for New Testament Christology. Christian hopes for Christ are based on the development of the hope for the Messiah and the figure of the Son of Man (especially in Dan. 7:14) in the Old Testament.[6] It can safely be said that, on the one hand, behind much of Jewish messianic expectations is the distinctive Jewish apocalypticism that, as is routinely mentioned, laid the framework for the Gospels' presentation of Jesus;[7] on the other hand, as current scholarship also knows well, there are a number of types of messianic expectations in Second Temple Judaism, rather than one generally held.[8] As a result, it is highly important for Christian theology, both for its proper self-understanding and its relation to the Jewish people, to reflect carefully on the Jewish roots of its faith.

This book seeks to be sensitive to the Jewishness of Jesus in more than one way. First, in discussing the meaning of Jesus's person and work (as manifested, for example, in the many "titles" stemming from the Old Testament), Jewish and Old Testament background will be carefully noted. Second, when looking at Christology in the context of the contemporary pluralistic world, Jewish interpretations of Jesus Christ will be included as well.

N. T. Wright, *Jesus and the Victory of God*, COQG 2 (Minneapolis: Fortress, 1996), 5; see also 91–98, with numerous references to current scholarship.

4. Among biblical scholars, N. T. Wright particularly has been keen on the *theological* implications of his massive scholarship on the origins of Christian faith. Other such figures include J. D. G. Dunn and R. Bauckham in their respective ways.

5. Moltmann, *Way of Jesus Christ*, xv. Chap. 1 as a whole deals with Old Testament background. In this orientation, Moltmann follows the program he introduces in *Theology of Hope* and further develops in many other publications, such as his *Trinity and the Kingdom*, implying that Jewish/Old Testament expectations and metaphors laid the presuppositions for all of Christian theology.

6. Wright, *Jesus and the Victory of God*, 486; for a careful theological analysis, see Moltmann, *Way of Jesus Christ*, 5–27.

7. See William C. Placher, *A History of Christian Theology: An Introduction* (Philadelphia: Westminster, 1983), 28–31.

8. For a detailed discussion and literature, see Wright, *Jesus and the Victory of God*, chap. 11.

How Jesus Is Named in the Biblical Record

The Message of the Kingdom of God

Before anything else, the student of the Christologies of the Gospels should be reminded of the center and major theme of Jesus's proclamation—which came mostly in the form of the parables—that is, the kingdom of God. While many historical questions are under dispute among Gospel scholars, no one disputes that talk about the righteous rule of God (which is what the kingdom means) lies at the heart of the Nazarene preacher's proclamation.[9]

Although Jesus did not address his Father as "king," a favorite designation in the Old Testament (particularly in Psalms but also elsewhere), the language of God's "kingdom" was frequently on Jesus's lips. Although—as the ensuing historical discussion will reveal—much ink has been wasted among biblical scholars as to the exact meaning of the concept of the kingdom, it is safe to say the following in light of mainstream biblical scholarship: on the one hand, the kingdom had already arrived in the person and ministry of Jesus (Matt. 12:28; Luke 11:20, and so forth), and, on the other hand, it was yet to appear in its final eschatological consummation (Mark 1:15; 9:1; Matt. 4:17; Luke 11:2, and so forth). To the proclamation of the advent of God's rule belongs the summons to repentance and change of mind and behavior. It "was a warning of imminent catastrophe, a summons to an immediate change of heart and direction of life," first to Israel and then to others.[10]

If parables were the teaching device to illustrate various facets of the dawning rule of the righteous God, miracles and powerful deeds were another integral way of reference. Just recall this saying: "But if it is by the Spirit of God that I cast out demons, then the kingdom of God has come to you" (Matt. 12:28 NRSV). All four Gospels narrate numerous healings and miraculous cures,[11] and the Synoptic Gospels add to the picture acts of deliverance and exorcisms. Indeed, "among all the activities ascribed to Jesus in the New Testament gospels, exorcism and healing are among the most prominent."[12]

Each of the Synoptic Gospels highlights different aspects of Jesus's proclamation and embodiment of God's kingdom. Although in John the concept hardly appears, he speaks of God's presence and salvation in the world using other terms,

9. For a detailed discussion, see C. C. Caragounis, "Kingdom of God/Heaven," in *DJG* (1992), 54–59.

10. Wright, *Jesus and the Victory of God*, 172.

11. A reliable, nontechnical discussion is Harold Remus, *Jesus as Healer* (Cambridge: Cambridge University Press, 1997).

12. Amanda Porterfield, *Healing in the History of Christianity* (New York: Oxford University Press, 2005), 21.

such as "life" and "glory." Although, curiously, kingdom language becomes marginal in Pauline theology, it is safe to say that "the idea of the kingdom of God or kingdom of Christ is certainly foundational to the whole" of his theology.[13]

Christ/Messiah

One of the most important christological titles is "Christ," which appears over five hundred times in the New Testament.[14] It seems at times almost that "Christ" functions as a proper name in the New Testament. Theologically we may say that it means "'Jesus is the Christ' or 'Jesus is the Messiah.'"[15] "Christ" (*Christos*) is the Greek equivalent of the Hebrew "Messiah" (*mashiach*), which means literally "the anointed one." Several key persons in the Old Testament were anointed for a task appointed by Yahweh, particularly kings (Saul in 1 Sam. 9–10), prophets (Elisha in 1 Kings 19:16), and priests (Lev. 21:10–12).

In Jesus's times, there were also a number of self-made messiahs who sought political deliverance or a position in earthly society. Jesus declined that role (see John 6:15). Jesus did not want to identify with this primarily political messianic expectation and wanted to avoid conflict with the political and religious establishment until the time had come for him to die. That context may help us understand a curious aspect of Jesus's messiahship, what William Wrede, nineteenth-century pioneer of research into the Gospels, called the "messianic secret" in his *Messianic Secret in the Gospels* (1901). Rather than encouraging his followers to spread the good news of the Messiah who had come, Jesus forbade those he healed to tell anyone (Mark 7:36).

An important locus for the Christ/messianic sayings has to do with Jesus's sufferings. Indeed, "Messianic themes emerge most clearly in the accounts of Jesus' death to the extent that 'we cannot ignore that the Messiah questions [*sic*] runs through the Passion story of all the gospels like a red thread.'"[16] Recall that at the turning point of Mark's Gospel (8:29) stands Peter's confession of Jesus's Christhood: from there on the shadow of the cross guides the narrative. Importantly, the very last occurrence of "Christ" in Mark also appears in the context of the cross.[17] Similarly to the Gospels and Paul, especially in 1 Peter the title Christ is connected with the sufferings of Jesus (1:11; 2:21; 3:18, and so forth).

13. L. J. Kreitzer, "Kingdom of God/Christ," in *DPL*, 524.
14. This discussion is based on M. F. Bird, "Christ," in *DJG* (2013), 115–25; see also O'Collins, *Christology*, 25–29.
15. Bird, "Christ," 115.
16. Ibid., 119; the citation is from M. Hengel, *Studies in Early Christology* (London: SCM, 1995), 45 (emphasis in original removed).
17. See Bird, "Christ," 119–20.

It is worth noting that while all the Gospel writers, each in his own distinct way, appropriates the title "Christ," Paul uses the term by far the most frequently; more than half of all New Testament occurrences are found in his writings.[18] The heavy concentration of the term in Paul's letters, the earliest New Testament writings, suggests that very early the term became an important part of the vocabulary of Christian faith. *Christ* is undoubtedly Paul's favorite title for Jesus.

Even though Jesus fulfilled the hopes of Israel's Messiah in a way incompatible with the dreams of a majority of the people, he still was and is Israel's Messiah, not merely the Messiah of the gentiles (in biblical terminology, all non-Jews are gentiles). As said, Christian theology has too often lost sight of this perspective throughout history, resulting in unfortunate implications for Christian-Jewish relations.

Son of God

Two parallel names have become part of Christian theology's vocabulary from the beginning: Son of God and Son of Man. Naturally, one would assume that the former refers to Jesus's divinity and the latter to his humanity. This was, indeed, taken for granted until the twentieth century, when a more careful exegesis of biblical texts created ambiguity regarding these two titles. In fact, exegetically, both assumptions—that Son of God denotes divinity and Son of Man denotes humanity—are inaccurate.

In the Old Testament, the concept of the son(s) of God is elusive, as it may refer to the people of Israel (Exod. 4:22), or the king (particularly David and his successors [2 Sam. 7:14]), or even angels. Reference to kingship, particularly Davidic, is the main New Testament background. Yet, in Israel (differently from some surrounding nations), sonship does not mean divinity. The Old Testament does not speak explicitly of the Messiah or of a specifically messianic figure as the Son of God.[19]

Jesus used the term rarely, but according to the Synoptic Gospels he did understand himself and his mission according to the idea of divine sonship. Some scholars have questioned the authenticity of those rare passages in which Jesus refers to himself as the Son, but the majority of scholars think that at least some of the sayings come directly from Jesus (Matt. 11:27; Mark 12:6; 13:32; Luke 10:22).

Examination of the authentic sayings of Jesus regarding the "Father" and the "Son" reveals the following emphases. First, Jesus claimed personal

18. For details, see Ben Witherington III, "Christ," in *DPL*, 95–100.
19. Main sources are Adam Winn, "Son of God," in *DJG* (2013), 886–94; and L. W. Hurtado, "Son of God," in *DPL*, 900–906.

intimacy with the Father. This comes to the fore especially in the *abba* sayings of Jesus (Mark 14:36); this Aramaic term denotes a warm, close address similar to "daddy." Second, the use of "Son" signified obedience to the will of God, as is evident especially in Jesus's prayer in Gethsemane (Mark 14:32–42). Finally, "Son" referred to the uniqueness of his status. Jesus's relation to the Father as Son is exclusive. This becomes evident in the distinction Paul makes between Jesus's sonship and our sonship, using two different Greek terms: believers are adopted and called sons or children (*tekna*), but Jesus is the Son (*huios*).

For Paul, the divine sonship of Christ is a major christological category; it also plays an important role in Hebrews. According to Romans 1:4 he was "designated Son of God in power according to the Spirit of holiness by his resurrection from the dead, Jesus Christ our Lord" (RSV). At the same time, the term's use indicates not only Jesus's divinity but also his intimacy with God, similar to the Gospels, particularly John. While exclusive to Christ, for Paul and the Gospel writers, Jesus's relationship to the Father applies to believers as well in a derivative sense.

One of the concerns of our day is the question of inclusive language: should "son" be replaced by "child" in order to be inclusive? The New Testament usage of "son" is not sexist: it includes both sexes. The discussion of feminist and other female interpretations of Christ in chapter 7 delves into this problem.

Son of Man

No other title comes even close to "Son of Man" as Jesus's self-designation. Indeed, it is used only by Jesus himself (except in John 12:34, though in reference to him). A regular term in all four Gospels, curiously it disappears in the rest of the New Testament (except for Acts 7:56).[20]

In Aramaic, Jesus's native language, it is less a title and more a description—and can often be translated as "the human one." The Old Testament term *ben adam*, "Son of man," refers to both the proper name "Adam" and the noun denoting the human person. The Hebrew term is used in three contexts. First, in the book of Ezekiel, the term appears over one hundred times as a form of address to Ezekiel. Second, it is used to emphasize the frailty of human nature, as in the famous saying in Psalm 8:4. Third, christologically, the most significant usage is that of Daniel 7:13–14, which speaks of "one

---

20. The main source here is D. L. Bock, "Son of Man," in *DJG* (2013), 894–900. Among the Gospel passages the following are representative (as listed on p. 896): Matt. 8:20; 9:6; 10:23; 13:37, 41; 17:9, 12; 26:2, 24, 45, 64; Mark 2:10, 28; 8:31, 38; 9:9, 12, 31; 14:21, 41, 62; Luke 5:24; 6:5, 22; 7:34; 9:22, 26, 44, 58; 18:8, 31; 19:10; 24:6–7; John 1:51; 3:13, 14; 5:27; 8:28; 9:35; 12:23, 34; 13:31.

like a son of man . . . [who] came to the Ancient of Days and was presented before him. And to him was given dominion and glory and kingdom" (RSV). Christian theology has seen in Daniel's Son of Man the Messiah, who came in the person of Jesus of Nazareth.

It is customary to classify the Son of Man sayings under three interrelated categories. The expression is used in much the same way in each of the Synoptic Gospels. New Testament scholarship basically agrees that as a christological title, "Son of Man" in the Synoptic Gospels is related to the following:

1. Jesus's present ministry and authority (e.g., Mark 2:10, 28, and par. in Matthew and Luke)
2. Jesus's suffering and resurrection (e.g., Mark 8:31; 9:9; 10:33, and par. in Matthew and Luke)
3. Jesus's glorious coming (e.g., Mark 8:38; 13:26, and par. in Matthew and Luke)

Remarkably, in the authority sayings the Son of Man assumes for himself the authority of God, for example, over the Sabbath, the divinely sanctioned holy day. With regard to suffering, the sayings make it clear that Jesus as the Son of Man came to serve others and to give his life as a ransom for many. The sayings that refer to the future coming of the Son of Man "in clouds with great power and glory" (Mark 13:26) are associated with his being seated at the right hand of God.

The title "Son of Man" has a distinctive usage in John's Gospel: it is used with the expression "be lifted up," which may refer either to the cross or to Christ's exaltation (John 3:14; 8:28; 12:34). Perhaps the author preserved the ambiguity on purpose, wanting his readers to make both connections. John also contains the unique sayings about the Son of Man coming down from heaven (3:13) and ascending to where he formerly was (8:28).

Lord

The early Christian confession was "Jesus is Lord" (Rom. 10:9; 1 Cor. 12:3; Phil. 2:11).[21] Surprisingly, this attributes to Jesus the same name that in the Old Testament was applied to God: *kyrios*, "Lord."[22] At the same time, in the Roman context it challenged the "lordship" of the emperor. Not infrequently,

21. This section is based on B. Witherington and K. Yamazaki-Ransom, "Lord," in *DJG* (2013), 526–35; L. W. Hurtado, "Lord," in *DPL*, 560–69.
22. *Kyrios* is the Greek translation of the Hebrew word for "Lord," used when reading to render the written Hebrew term YHWH, the tetragrammaton that denotes the name of God.

the emperor was worshiped as a semi-god. Various mystery religions also used the term *kyrios*. In other words, in both Jewish and secular contexts the use of "the Lord" by Christians in relation to Jesus was daring and bold.

The most explicit passage in which Jesus applies the title *kyrios* to himself is Mark 12:35–37, which is based on Psalm 110:1: "The LORD says to my lord: 'Sit at my right hand.'" If this passage is an authentic saying of Jesus—and there is no compelling reason to deny that it is—it means that Jesus considered himself equal to the Old Testament Lord, Yahweh; sitting at the right hand is the place of highest status and honor.

A noteworthy observation about the use of *kyrios* with regard to Jesus in Matthew is that only the disciples use this address; outsiders prefer the neutral term "teacher" or "rabbi." It took spiritual insight to see who Jesus was. The title "Lord" was not loosely used.

The main passage in the Pauline corpus is Philippians 2:10–11, which most scholars believe is a pre-Pauline hymn. The passage says that as a result of his obedience to the Father, Christ was granted the title "Lord," which implies equality with God.

Other Titles of Jesus

Son of David

The christological title "Son of David" naturally links Jesus to the royal Messiah in the line of David, Israel's king.[23] In his person and ministry, Jesus fulfills the promises of God given to the Davidic dynasty in the Old Testament (2 Sam. 7:12–16). Rejecting popular royal expectations, as the Suffering Servant Jesus laid down his life for the sake of others and their salvation. Among the Gospel writers, the title plays the greatest role in Matthew, as he writes with a Jewish audience in mind; Matthew begins his Gospel with the Davidic lineage (1:1–17).

Logos

This title is the transliteration of a common Greek word that generally means "word," "speech," and "wisdom."[24] As a christological title, it occurs only in John, with the main references in the beginning of the Gospel (1:1; 1:14). With roots in both pagan philosophy (Plato) and the Old Testament

---

The Greek translation of the Hebrew Old Testament is called the Septuagint, literally "seventy," and abbreviated LXX.

23. Y. Miura, "Son of David," in *DJG* (2013), 881–86.
24. B. E. Reynolds, "Logos," in *DJG* (2013), 523–26.

concept of the "word" of Yahweh, it was relevant in both contexts. John 1:1 contains an obvious allusion to the beginning of the Old Testament, to the creative word of Yahweh. John says that in the beginning of creation the *Logos* existed. The *Logos* was not only with God but also was God. John 1:14 describes the incarnation of the *Logos*.

Having discussed the main christological titles in the New Testament, we turn next to the distinctive features of Christology in each of the four Gospels. The main method of current New Testament scholarship and theology is to appreciate the specific contribution of each of the New Testament books in general and the Gospels in particular in order to do justice to the rich pluralism of the biblical witness to Christ. The rest of the chapter follows the order in which scholarship believes the Gospels were written: Mark, Matthew, and Luke, which are the Synoptic Gospels, and then John.

The Suffering Servant in Mark

Routinely dated now as the first Gospel, on which the other two Synoptics (Matthew and Luke) built,

> the Gospel of Mark is a case study in paradox. On the one hand, it leaves its readers breathless in its presentation of Jesus the Messiah (Mark 1:1) as one who comes teaching with authority, driving out powerful demons and performing spectacular miracles. On the other hand, there is no other Gospel in which Jesus remains so misunderstood and so fiercely resisted by all manner of people, including at times his most devoted followers. If the kerygma—the proclamation of the early church—was essentially a narrative about divine triumph despite and indeed through human suffering, then arguably there is no other text in which this paradox comes into crisper expression than the Gospel of Mark.[25]

Mark's Jesus narrative is fast-paced, beginning with the appearance of John the Baptist, the forerunner of Christ, and climaxing in the conflict between Jesus and the religious and political leaders. Its narrative nature should be properly acknowledged: "the Christology of Mark's Gospel is in the story it tells."[26] The story identifies Jesus as the Messiah, the Son of God, whose destiny is to suffer, die, rise from the dead, and return as the glorious Son of Man to gather the elect.

25. N. Perrin, "Mark, Gospel of," in *DJG* (2013), 553. In addition to Perrin (553–66), this section draws mainly from Frank J. Matera, *New Testament Christology* (Louisville: Westminster, 1999), 5–26; Schwarz, *Christology*, 119–20.
26. Matera, *New Testament Christology*, 24.

From the very first sentence, Mark's Gospel is christologically focused, starting the narrative with "the beginning of the gospel of Jesus Christ, the Son of God" (1:1 RSV). Until 8:29, Jesus's public ministry, with teaching, healings, exorcisms, and pronouncements of forgiveness, is on the ascending scale, so to speak, despite much opposition. Thereafter, the shadow of the cross dominates the narrative.

Jesus's role as the Messiah is confirmed at his baptism with the voice from heaven (1:11). Echoing the royal coronation psalms (see Ps. 2:7), the Father's voice from heaven also declares Jesus to be the Suffering Servant whom God equips with the Spirit (see Isa. 42:1).

More than any other Gospel writer, Mark highlights the role of Jesus as miracle worker and healer. Beginning from the first three chapters, Jesus appears as exorcist, healer, and overcomer of infirmities that bind people. After he teaches in chapter 4, Jesus continues his ministry of deliverance. In the words of Frank Matera:

> The Messiah is the Spirit-anointed Son of God who proclaims the arrival of God's kingdom in word and deed. He heals the sick, expels demons, and even extends his ministry to Gentiles. Most important, he gives his life as a ransom for the many. Having suffered, died, and risen from the dead, he will return as the glorious Son of Man.[27]

The presence of miracles and wonders in Jesus's ministry, however, is ambiguous. After encountering initial enthusiasm, the Messiah faces increasing opposition. No amount of miracles will stop people, especially the religious leaders, from getting angry at his person and claims. Consequently, it is not the miracles and authority but rather the suffering and death of the Messiah that are the ultimate focus of Mark's story of Jesus. In this light it is understandable that it is only after Jesus has explained what kind of Messiah he is that he dares to confess to be the Messiah. The title "Messiah," therefore, becomes visible in the latter part of the Gospel, where the approaching death looms over the narrative. In fact, after the opening words of 1:1, *Christos* does not appear in Mark until 8:29–30. Thereafter, it is used more frequently, especially with regard to Jesus's approaching clash with the religious leaders and the cross.

While Jesus is reserved in his use of "Christ" and "Son of God" as self-designations, he freely uses the designation "Son of Man" publicly. Why did Jesus prefer this title, which is at best ambiguous? Perhaps the reason lies in

27. Ibid., 24–25.

the ambiguity: Jesus did not want his audience to understand his role clearly until he was ready to suffer and die. Recall the term "messianic secret," mentioned above. Matera summarizes in a helpful way the distinctive Markan picture of Jesus:

> For Mark, Jesus is the Messiah, the Son of God, because he fulfills the destiny of the Son of Man. Were Jesus not to fulfill this destiny, he would not be God's messianic Son. Markan Christology, then, can be summarized in the terms "Messiah," "Son of God," "the Son of Man." And yet, none of these can be understood adequately apart from Mark's narrative; for the Christology is in the story, and through the story we learn to interpret the titles.[28]

The King of the Jews in Matthew

Matthew's audience is Jewish.[29] For that purpose, Jesus's Davidic genealogy in the beginning of the Gospel makes a great contribution. Indeed, the infancy narratives (chaps. 1–2) not only identify Jesus as the Son of David but also link Jesus with the whole history of Israel going back to Abraham. No wonder Matthew emphasizes the fulfillment of the Old Testament prophecies and frequently cites Scripture.

Matthew labors to paint his portrait of the Jewish Davidic Messiah, making significant additions to the Markan outline, particularly the five great speeches of Jesus: the Sermon on the Mount (chaps. 5–7), the sending of the Twelve (chap. 10), the parables (chap. 13), and speeches on the church (chap. 18) and on eschatology (chaps. 24–25). To accommodate to Jewish sensibilities, the "kingdom of God"—his main theme—translates into "kingdom of heaven" in order to avoid mentioning God's name.

To speak to Jews, tutored under the instruction of the Torah, the teaching ministry of Jesus is the focus of Matthew, as distinct from Mark's interest in miracles. The main form this rabbi's teaching ministry takes is parables. In light of the centrality of Jesus's teaching ministry, it is highly ironic that only non-disciples describe Jesus as teacher (8:19; 9:11; 19:16, etc.). The disciples of Jesus never call him "teacher" but rather "Lord" and similar titles.

The emphasis on his teaching ministry, however, is not to say that healings, exorcisms, and other wondrous deeds do not play a role in Matthew's presentation of the Christian Messiah. In fact, he records a myriad of healings,

28. Ibid., 26.
29. This section draws mainly from the following: J. K. Brown, "Matthew, Gospel of," in *DJG* (2013), 570–84; Matera, *New Testament Christology*, 26–48; Schwarz, *Christology*, 120–22.

exorcisms, and nature miracles (such as walking on the sea and multiplying food). For example, in chapters 8 and 9, he recounts no less than eight healings and several other miracles. But even these have ultimately a pedagogical aim, along with showing compassion.

Against the backdrop of Matthew's Gospel, the centrality of the idea of the kingdom of heaven, Jesus acts as the inaugurator of the kingdom. This he accomplishes in three moments: his public ministry, his passion, and his vindicating resurrection. After the resurrection, the disciples of Christ are sent into the world to preach the good news and to invite all nations to obedience to the master, teacher, and king (28:18–20). This emphasis on the universal scope of Jesus's ministry culminates in the last verses of the Gospel, but it runs through the narrative as a dominant theme, beginning with the visit of the gentile magi to the newborn king of the Jews in chapter 2.

The Friend of All in Luke

If Mark is the dynamic, fast-paced story of Jesus, and Matthew a carefully constructed Jewish portrait of the Messiah, then, "from the early church to the present, Luke's Gospel has functioned like a warehouse of scenes and stories from which favorites might be drawn, whether in discussions of the virginal conception or of everyday ethics, whether by preachers or theologians or artists."[30] Luke's narrative comes in two parts, the Gospel, with the focus on Jesus, and the book of Acts, centering on Jesus's people, the church. When it comes to his Gospel, somewhat similarly to Mark's (but differently from Matthew's five-part template), it is divided into two parts: beginning from the latter part of chapter 9, Jesus sets his eyes toward Jerusalem with the anticipation of suffering, death, and resurrection. Whereas Mark writes to gentiles and Matthew to Jews, Luke's portrait of Jesus is meant for both of these groups. Here is the plot:

> The Messiah of God comes to his people Israel as the Spirit-anointed Son of God with a gracious offer of salvation: the forgiveness of sins. Despite this gracious offer, Israel does not repent. Nonetheless, its rejection of the Messiah paradoxically fulfills God's plan that the Messiah must suffer in order to enter into his glory so that repentance and forgiveness can be preached in his name to all nations.[31]

30. Joel B. Green, "Luke, Gospel of," in *DJG* (2013), 540. In addition to Green (540–52), this section draws mainly from Matera, *New Testament Christology*, chap. 2 (which includes both Luke and Acts); Schwarz, *Christology*, 122–25.
31. Matera, *New Testament Christology*, 51.

Although writing to gentiles as well, Luke also makes explicit the connection between Jesus and Israel; just consider the narrative in 2:25–32 about Simeon and the "consolation of Israel" when dedicating the infant Jesus. The Gospel ends with the identification of the resurrected Jesus as Christ (24:26–27, 44–47).

The idea of Jesus as a prophet emerges in his inaugural sermon at Nazareth, his hometown (4:16–30), based on the messianic passage in Isaiah 61. This messianic figure is sent to preach the good news, offer forgiveness, heal the blind, and set captives free. Old Testament prophets Elijah and Elisha are depicted as parallels to Jesus (4:25–27), and people soon recognize Jesus as a prophet (7:16; 9:7–9, 19). A special concern for the poor, widows, and children characterizes this prophet. Women especially receive a great deal of attention in this Gospel (7:12, 36–50; 8:40–56; 10:38–42; 13:10–13; 15:8–10; 18:1–8; 21:1–4; 23:55–56).

Not merely a prophet among others, for Luke, Jesus is also God's Christ, the Davidic Messiah. The way Luke presents the intimate relation of the Son to the Father is with prayer. Jesus is depicted as praying at every critical turn in his ministry, beginning at his baptism (3:21). Not surprisingly, prayer characterizes also his followers' lives in Acts.

Jesus as the Son of Man is introduced as early as Luke 5:24, and the title appears frequently in Luke, as it does in Mark and Matthew. Luke highlights the role of the Son of Man in his mission to save the lost (19:10) and to suffer and die for sinners (chap. 24). This theme and Jesus's status as Lord become the focus of dispute later in the Gospel (20:41–44; 22:67–71).

It is significant that while all the Gospel writers mention the resurrection, only Luke narrates the ascension. This is of course the bridge to Pentecost and the birth of the church in Acts. The Acts narrative is carefully constructed in a manner that makes Jesus's life—from birth to baptism to ministry in the Spirit—parallel to the birth, baptism (with the Spirit), and ministry of the church. Jesus's exalted status as the ascended one is highlighted time after time in the sermons of the book of Acts, the first missionary speeches of the incipient community.

The Word of Life in John

Jesus performed many other signs in the presence of his disciples, which are not recorded in this book. But these are written that you may believe that Jesus is the Messiah, the Son of God, and that by believing you may have life in his name. (John 20:30–31)

In this passage, the purpose of the Fourth Gospel is stated explicitly, and its focus is on Christ and his ministry and significance.[32] Although the goal of the narrative is stated clearly, namely, to elicit faith, there is also ambiguity (and confusion), so characteristic of John's portrayal of people's response to Jesus: we wonder whether the Greek phrase translated as "that you may believe" refers to the hope of conversion (after which one believes) or affirms the continuing belief of the faithful.

Be that as it may, John's presentation of Jesus is dramatically different from the three Synoptics. Rather than Galilee (as in Mark, Matthew, and Luke), Judea is the center of the ministry. Jesus's public ministry seems to last three years (not one year). Among many other differences, it is highly significant that the Johannine Jesus does not cast out evil spirits. The number of healings is meager: three altogether and one resuscitation (Lazarus, chap. 11). His actions are called "signs" and have an obvious symbolic importance. The Jesus of the Fourth Gospel does not teach in parables, in contrast to the Synoptics; Jesus delivers seven "I am" oracles. Even the structure of the Gospel of John is unique compared to the other Gospels: after the prologue about the Word (1:1–18), the first part, the "Book of Signs" (1:19–12:50), contains miracles and speeches, and the second part, the "Book of Glory" (chaps. 13–20), tells about the farewell speeches of Jesus, his suffering on the cross, and his subsequent resurrection. A later appendix is attached to the Gospel (chap. 21).

Whereas Mark begins his Jesus narrative from baptism as the gateway to public ministry, Matthew connects Jesus's pedigree with Abraham, and Luke goes all the way back to Adam, John links Jesus with creation and unity with God (1:1). The prologue (1:1–18) introduces many of the main themes of the Gospel's portrayal of Jesus, such as light, life, truth, Word, and incarnation. The most distinctive feature is the application of the title *Logos* to Christ, which connects Jesus with both the Old Testament beginning—the Word as creative force in Genesis 1—and the Greek concept of wisdom. His unique intimacy with the Father is depicted in these terms: "No one has ever seen God; the only Son, who is in the bosom of the Father, he has made him known" (v. 18 RSV). Indeed, intimacy becomes one of the central themes; just consider chapter 5.

Typical of John is his dual emphasis on the humanity and the divinity of Jesus. John's Gospel is in many ways the most human portrayal of Jesus: Jesus experiences fatigue (4:6) and anguish (12:27); he weeps (11:33) and changes his mind (7:1–10). On the other hand, Jesus is "God's Word," the

---

32. The main sources are C. S. Keener, "John, Gospel of," in *DJG* (2013), 419–36; Matera, *New Testament Christology*, 215–37; Schwarz, *Christology*, 125–29.

Logos. He speaks as no man has ever spoken (7:46); he is the one who reveals the Father (1:18).

A number of unique metaphors, titles, and symbols are used by John in describing Jesus, including the Lamb of God (1:29, 36), Rabbi (1:38), Messiah (1:41), "the one Moses wrote about in the Law, and about whom the prophets also wrote—Jesus of Nazareth, the son of Joseph" (1:45), Son of God and King of Israel (1:49). Then there are the seven "I am" sayings: the "bread of life" (6:35, 48), "light of the world" (8:12; 9:5), "gate for the sheep" (10:7), "good shepherd" (10:11), "true vine" (15:1), "resurrection and the life" (11:25), and "way and the truth and the life" (14:6). The epithet "I am"—which also appears a few times without an attribute (4:26; 6:20, among others)—invokes the "I am" of Yahweh in the Old Testament. Furthermore, Johannine symbolism is also enriched by names (1:42) and numbers (2:1; 21:11), especially the number seven, which denotes perfection.

In keeping with the ambiguity and symbolic presentation of Jesus in John, even Jesus's death and resurrection are put in ambiguous, mysterious terms: John talks about Jesus "being glorified" (7:39; 8:54, etc.) and "being lifted up" (12:34)—yes, lifted up on the cross but also put down to death, to be raised to life immortal! Similarly, miracles, described as "signs"—curiously seven in number, perhaps corresponding to the seven days of the new creation—are depicted in a highly ambiguous way with regard to their reception: the more Jesus performs these signs, the more confusion he creates. Indeed, from early on the people start asking, "What sign can you show us to prove your authority?" (2:18) and "What sign then will you give that we may see it and believe you?" (6:30). In the midpoint of the Gospel, it has become clear to the author (confirming Isaiah's experience in Isa. 6:10) that Jesus's signs did not lead to belief in him (12:40).

The existence of four Gospels in the canon provides an everlasting testimony to the richness and legitimate plurality of the biblical picture of Jesus Christ. While they all share a common historical and theological basis, they do not have a forced uniformity. Rather, like a rainbow with many colors, the four Gospels highlight various aspects of the life, death, and resurrection of the one who was and is confessed as Lord and Savior.

2

Pauline Interpretations of Christ

The Matrix of Pauline Christology

The Pastoral-Missional Setting of Pauline Christology

The sequence of discerning the New Testament testimonies to Jesus Christ does not follow chronological but rather canonical order. Key Pauline letters are routinely dated as the earliest Christian literature, although their placement in the canon follows the evangelists. This means that Paul's interpretations represent an earlier authoritative strata. As the title of this chapter implies, Paul is far less interested in Jesus of Nazareth per se—although he undoubtedly assumes the outline of the Gospel narratives; his interest is in the theological implications of the crucified and risen Christ. Recall his note to the church of Corinth (1 Cor. 1:22–23; 2:2): "For Jews demand signs and Greeks seek wisdom, but we preach Christ crucified, a stumbling block to Jews and folly to Gentiles. . . . For I decided to know nothing among you except Jesus Christ and him crucified" (RSV). As contextual as that statement may be—in response to some Corinthians' excitement over worldly, perhaps esoteric, wisdom—the general message is still applicable in a wider sense.

Although Paul's interests are theological, they are so in a pastoral setting. Paul is not a "systematic" theologian, nor are his epistles primarily doctrinal treatises. They are scripturally (Old Testament) based, theologically grounded pastoral-missional responses to and reflections on issues facing emerging Christian communities in the matrix of Jewish religion and Greco-Roman philosophy, thought forms, and mystery cults.[1]

From what did Paul's Christology stem? On what sources did he base it? The answers to these questions shed light on the shape and content of his thinking about Christ. Understandably, several proposals have been presented among scholars. Because Paul was a Jew, even a Jewish Pharisee, a religious teacher, it would be most natural to locate the origin of his Christology in Judaism. However, even though Pauline theology, like the rest of the New Testament, is embedded in Judaism for the simple reason that the Bible of the early church was the Old Testament, the origin of Paul's Christology lies elsewhere. The so-called history of religions school maintained that the Christology of Paul stems from ideas in the Greco-Roman world, particularly those found in its various forms of pagan religions, but this proposal has not met with much acceptance.

There is no doubt that part of Paul's Christology originates from his Judaic background and that he occasionally borrowed from the secular or religious environment of the Greco-Roman world. Yet the most viable origin of Paul's Christology is his conversion experience, his subsequent call, and early Christian tradition. In his conversion and call to preach the gospel, Paul received what he calls "the gospel of Christ" (Gal. 1:7, 11–23 is the most extensive account of Paul's call and subsequent events). Paul says that "God . . . was pleased to reveal his Son in me" (Gal. 1:15–16). As a result of his conversion and call, Paul learned that Jesus was risen from the dead and exalted at the right hand of the Father. He claims to have seen the risen Lord (1 Cor. 9:1).

In Romans 1:4 Paul testifies that Jesus was vindicated as the Son of God in power by his resurrection from the dead. Paul argues that while we once viewed Jesus from a purely human point of view, we do so no longer (2 Cor. 5:16). In other words, he and all those "in Christ" now view Jesus as the Son of God.

---

1. Traditionally, all "Pauline" letters were regarded as written by Paul. Current New Testament scholarship agrees that some letters in the Pauline corpus represent the thought forms of Paul's theology but most likely were not written by him. They were perhaps written by his students and younger colleagues. Letters that most scholars consider authentic (meaning they were written by Paul himself) are Romans, 1 and 2 Corinthians, Galatians, Philippians, 1 Thessalonians, and Philemon. A majority of scholars also believe that Colossians and Ephesians were written by Paul, even though Ephesians was most likely a circular letter rather than a letter addressed specifically to the church in Ephesus. The Pastoral Epistles (1 and 2 Timothy and Titus) and 2 Thessalonians are regarded as later literary products in the line of Pauline theology. The main source for this section is Ben Witherington III, "Christology," in *DPL*, 110–15; I have also gleaned from Frank J. Matera, *New Testament Christology* (Louisville: Westminster, 1999), chaps. 3 and 4; and Hans Schwarz, *Christology* (Grand Rapids: Eerdmans, 1998), 129–35.

Paul appropriates in his writings early christological confessions, for example, the famous Christ hymn in Philippians 2:5–11. But even the sections in his writings that are not based on previously existing hymns and confessions reveal a Christology growing out of the emerging tradition among Christian churches.

Whereas much of earlier discussion and study of Pauline Christology focused on the titles, contemporary New Testament theology combines and qualifies that with the narrative approach and pays attention to the distinctive contribution of each letter. Furthermore, Paul's interests are deeply soteriological and often tackle issues such as justification, sanctification, liberation, and forgiveness. A good case can be made for the claim that for Paul, his own personal story, the story of Israel, and the story of God's saving plan for the world are intertwined with the story of Christ. In other words, this is "the story of God's dealings with Israel and the Gentiles in light of what God has done in his Son, Jesus Christ."[2] Each of Paul's letters offers a distinctive, context-related response to an aspect of this story in light of the needs and problems faced by a young first-century church.

It has been suggested that there is a "fourfold narrative," a story in four aspects:[3] (1) "The Story of Christ" accounts for the coming, service, suffering, and exaltation of Christ as presented (Phil. 2:6–11; Col. 1:15–20; see also Heb. 1:2–4). Here there are material similarities with John's story in his Gospel's prologue (1:1–18). (2) Christological narrative is part of "the story of Israel" as the Messiah was born under the conditions of Israel and her Torah (Gal. 4:4). Thus Christ fulfills Israel's expectations and promises (Rom. 9:4–5). (3) More widely, the christological narrative also happens in the context of the "story of the world"; although the current form of the world will pass away (1 Cor. 7:31), Christ's saving work aims at nothing less than the renewal of all creation (Rom. 8:20–22; 2 Cor. 5:17). (4) Ultimately, it is "the story of God": "Transcending the story of the world is the story of the Son as part of the ongoing life of God. This is a story of the interrelationship of Father, Son and Spirit."[4]

Theological Implications of Naming Christ in Paul

Having considered above the key ways the Gospels name Jesus Christ, let it suffice here to highlight more robustly the distinctive Pauline contributions. An especially dear title for him is "Christ." As mentioned above, it seems to function virtually as the second name to Jesus.[5] The frequent appearance

2. Matera, *New Testament Christology*, 85.
3. Witherington, "Christology," 104–5.
4. Ibid., 105.
5. Ben Witherington III, "Christ," in *DPL*, 95–100.

of this title in the salutations of Paul's letters suggests both an exalted state and unity with God; just consider Philippians 1:2: "Grace to you and peace from God our Father and the Lord Jesus Christ." A distinctive Pauline way of using the name is to speak of the crucified Christ (1 Cor. 1:23, rather than the crucified Jesus of Nazareth): "The phrase must have had some shock value for Jewish listeners since there is no conclusive evidence that early Jews expected a crucified Messiah."[6] Crucifixion was for blasphemers, those cursed by God (Deut. 21:23; see Gal. 3:13). Although for Paul "Christ" clearly signifies not only what "Messiah" means for the Jews—namely, a divinely anointed (but not divine) figure—but also the divinity of the crucified and risen One (Rom. 1:3–4; Phil. 2:11), he additionally links the title "Christ" with his human nature (Rom. 5:17–19; Phil. 2:7).

The almost technical formula *en christō*, "in Christ," serves as a main soteriological category in Paul. Although often read individualistically, for Paul it is a deeply communal conception: it denotes the whole body of Christ, the church. Both individuals and (local) churches can be found to be in Christ. The formula's frequent usage in Paul is striking in light of its virtual absence elsewhere in the New Testament. Theologically, the most pregnant statement is 2 Corinthians 5:17—"Therefore, if any one is in Christ, he is a new creation; the old has passed away, behold, the new has come" (RSV)—which clearly is not only communal but also relates to the whole of creation in eschatological anticipation of coming consummation. No wonder the title "Savior" appears more often in Pauline traditions (widely speaking, with a concentration in the Pastoral Epistles) than elsewhere in the New Testament.[7]

One of the most peculiar ways of naming Christ in Paul is "Last Adam" (in Rom. 5 and 1 Cor. 15). Here Adam clearly is not an individual but a typological representative of humanity. In the former passage, Christ and Adam contrast with regard to the "origins" and nature of the fall and sin, whereas the latter (1 Cor. 15) discusses eschatological hope based on the resurrection of Christ.[8]

Distinctive Testimonies to Christ in the Epistles

To honor the narrative and distinctive way of considering the meaning and theological implications of Christ in key Pauline traditions, let us try to

6. Ibid., 97.
7. A. B. Luter Jr., "Savior," in *DPL*, 867–69.
8. L. J. Kreitzer, "Adam and Christ," in *DPL*, 9–15; Gerald O'Collins, SJ, *Christology: A Biblical, Historical, and Systematic Study of Jesus*, 2nd ed. (Oxford: Oxford University Press, 2009), 30–35.

sketch some general portraits, roughly following the chronological order of the writings.[9]

The Eschatological Christ in 1 and 2 Thessalonians

As a way of exhorting this gentile Christian community facing affliction and perhaps persecution, Paul presents a pastoral eschatology.[10] Almost silent about the earthly life of Jesus, he focuses on the parousia—the coming of the Lord as eschatological Savior and Judge to rescue his people. These believers have turned away from idols to worship the true God and to wait for the return of his Son from heaven (1 Thess. 1:9–10); as such, the community is associated with the story of Israel as an elected community (1:4–5; 2:11–12; 5:9).

Christ as the Wisdom of God: 1 Corinthians

Both the first and the second letter to the church at Corinth are christologically pregnant pastoral responses to a charismatic church tackling divisions and immorality. While endorsing charismatic ministry and gifts, Paul builds a contrast between a semi-esoteric (perhaps gnostic) appeal to worldly wisdom and Christ as God's true wisdom. Only the crucified Christ, a "stumbling block," qualifies as true wisdom and God's power in weakness (1:23–24). In fact, the cross of Christ is the focus of Paul's preaching and faith (1:17). This wisdom, hidden from human wisdom, is found in Christ (2:1–9). By virtue of the cross, Christ is not only our wisdom but also our righteousness, holiness, and redemption (1:30). In chapter 15, Paul records the early Christian creed he had received: Jesus Christ died for our sins, was buried, was raised on the third day, and appeared to numerous witnesses. His resurrection is the basis not only for our resurrection but also for Christian faith in general. This letter also expands on the idea of Christ's preexistence (8:6; 10:4, 9).

Christ as the Reconciler: 2 Corinthians

In the meantime, the divisions have grown worse in Corinth. While grounding his Christology in profound Old Testament expositions, Paul keeps the focus of this letter on the exposition of Christ as the agent of reconciliation.

9. In addition to entries in *DPL* on each of the epistles under discussion, I am drawing from the following: Matera, *New Testament Christology*, chaps. 3, 4; Luke T. Johnson, *The Writings of the New Testament: An Interpretation* (Philadelphia: Fortress, 1986), part 4: Pauline Traditions; Schwarz, *Christology*, 129–35.

10. Second Thessalonians is routinely taken as post-Pauline. My discussion here is not dependent on the authorship issue.

In Christ, God has reconciled the world to himself—the world that because
of sin was in enmity with God—so that we may become the righteousness of
God. Christ not only bore our sin but was "made sin" for our sake (5:17–21).
This pattern of reconciliation is depicted as the model for overcoming divisions in the church (6:1–9).

Jesus as the Covenant Maker: Galatians

The pastoral issue in Galatians is faith in Christ vis-à-vis the legalism of
some Christians coming from a Jewish background. Paul argues that even
though faith in Christ, the Jewish Messiah, is based on the Old Testament,
it also surpasses and qualifies it. Religiously and socially, Christian churches
were called to live a life free from the prescriptions of the Mosaic law. Again,
Paul's christological emphasis is on the death of Christ (see the strong appeal
in 3:1), and he puts it to pastoral use, namely, urging both gentile Christians
and Jewish Christians to be united in the covenant going back to Abraham
and fulfilled in Christ. Only through Christ can true righteousness be attained,
not through the law (2:21). Similarly, Paul also reminds his readers that it is
only in and through Christ that the original promise of blessing to all nations
given to Abraham (Gen. 12; 15) comes to fulfillment, since Christ has reversed
the curse of the law, changing it into blessing (3:13–14).

Jesus as Our Righteousness: Romans

In Romans, another missionary letter rather than a doctrinal treatise per
se, Paul sets forth his understanding of Christ's gospel in order to receive support for his evangelization trip to Spain (15:14–33). To ground his appeal, he
offers the most detailed exposition of his theology and Christology, and this
time he did not have to tackle a particular pastoral problem. To put Christ's
work on the cross in the correct perspective, Paul shows the hopelessness of
the human situation—for both Jews and gentiles—as a result of sin (chaps.
1–3). In fact, so hopeless is their condition that death is the only expected
result (chap. 5). As a response, he offers the cross of Christ as the only basis
of justification (3:21–31). Taking once again the story of Abraham as his
paradigm, he argues on the basis of Christ's story that even Abraham's faith
was oriented to and fulfilled in the coming of Christ (chap. 4). Christ has
become the "end" (the Greek term *telos* also means "goal") of the law and
has opened up the doors for the salvation of gentiles (10:4). Yet the story of
Israel is not forgotten; in a masterful way, Paul relates the story of the gentiles
and the story of Israel in light of Christ's story (chaps. 9–11). In chapters

6–8, Paul gives further exposition of the possibility of life based on faith in Christ. Whatever the meaning of the highly disputed chapter 7—whether Paul is recounting his story before or after conversion—it is clear that only on the basis of the faithfulness of Christ have the demands of the law been met.

Christ as Humble Servant: Philippians

Too often the Christology of Philippians is viewed only through the lens of the liturgical hymn about Christ in 2:5–11. But this is not all that Philippians says about Christ. Philippians is a friendly letter of encouragement written from prison to a church Paul had founded. The main purposes of the letter are to admonish the Philippians to carry on with their lives in a way worthy of the gospel of Christ, to further the proclamation of the gospel, and to thank the Philippians for their gift to him. In light of the coming parousia, "the day of Christ," Paul reassures the Philippians of the certainty of their salvation (1:6). As so often, the story of these Christians is included in the larger story of Israel and the nations in light of Christ's story:

> Through Christ, God began the work of establishing the Philippians in righ-teousness, consecrating them to himself as he did Israel of old. But this work will only be completed by God at Christ's parousia. In the meantime, the sanctified Philippians must prepare themselves for that day so that they can stand pure and blameless. The primary actor of this story is God who is Father; the agent of salvation is Jesus Christ who is Lord; and the beneficiaries are Gentiles such as the Philippians who have been granted an elected status formerly reserved for Israel of old.[11]

Paul's own story is linked to that of Christ; Christ is his life and death (1:21). Paul's death and resurrection are part of Christ's (3:9–11), and knowledge of Christ is the highest goal of his life. Therefore, he is ready to forsake every-thing for Christ's sake (3:7–8).

Jesus as the Embodiment of Fullness: Colossians

According to Colossians, "Christ is all, and is in all" (3:11). The hymnic passage of 1:15–20 talks about Christ as the one in, through, and for whom all things were created and reconciled. Verses 15–18a tell us that Christ is the image of the unseen God and the beginning of all creation because all things were created in him. Christ is also the head of the church. Verses 1:18b–20 identify

11. Matera, *New Testament Christology*, 121.

Christ as the origin of everything, visible and invisible, and the firstborn from the dead, in whom the fullness of God dwells. Through Christ's blood, God has reconciled the world, the entire universe, to himself. The pastoral concern in Paul's mind is that the believers at Colossae were in danger of resorting to human wisdom and traditions (2:6–23) that were less-than-perfect foundations when compared to the fullness in Christ (2:1–5). In one of the most distinctive christological claims in the New Testament, Paul intends to show the inadequacy of all human wisdom and traditions in light of the fullness of Christ (2:6–23): Paul states that "in Christ all the fullness of the Deity lives in bodily form" (2:9; see also 1:19). Not only in his state of exaltation but also in his incarnation, Christ represented divine fullness.

Jesus as God's Mystery: Ephesians

The Christ story in Ephesians begins with an expanded story of the blessing found "in Christ" (1:3); out of that flow all the various facets of the blessing, such as election (1:4) and grace and forgiveness (1:6), as well as redemption through his blood (1:7). Furthermore, true knowledge and wisdom are found in Christ, as is adoption as God's children (1:9–12). So comprehensive is Paul's understanding of Christ and the salvation he accomplished that he uses this unique expression: God's plan of salvation is summed up (or gathered) in Christ (1:10). A similar comprehensive term appears in Ephesians 2:14, where Christ is called our "peace"; Christ not only brings peace but *is* peace in his person. This saying perhaps goes back to the Old Testament concept of *shalom*, which means not merely peace but wholeness, happiness, and well-being. The remarkable prayer at the end of the first chapter speaks of Christ "far above all rule and authority, power and dominion, and every name that is invoked" both in this age and the age to come. Christ has been put in charge and has authority over everything, including the church (1:20–23). Reference to Christ's dominion includes the cosmic victory of all resisting spiritual powers (see also 2:1–2). Indeed, the Christology of Ephesians is closely linked to ecclesiology. Paul's view of the church here is that of a new humanity, composed of Jews and gentiles alike (2:11–22), which is in the process of growing into "the fullness of Christ" (4:13).

Postscript

As a summative statement of the basic outline of Pauline interpretation of Jesus, which laid the foundation, along with Gospel narratives, for all subsequent doctrinal developments, the following "four-stage account" is useful: "Jesus Christ (1) was with God before birth, then (2) lived a life on earth, and now (3) dwells with God in heaven awaiting (4) his second coming."[12] One can easily see that this account is based on the Gospels' outline but that it also expands it doctrinally, by including preexistence and elaborating on the eschatological hope.

12. William C. Placher, *A History of Christian Theology: An Introduction* (Philadelphia: Westminster, 1983), 39.

PART 2

CHRIST IN CHRISTIAN TRADITION

Unity in Diversity

The second part of this book delves into the question of how the christological tradition emerged and developed over time. This survey of history, however, is not meant to be comprehensive but selective. Two main topics from two time periods will be examined in some detail.

The first topic focuses on christological developments during the first six centuries of the church, the time during which the canon was emerging. During this time, the main questions that have to do with the person and work of Jesus Christ were raised, and various foundational answers were offered, though these answers were not final in status. Still, all later developments of Christology, those of our time included, need to take stock of the answers offered during the first six centuries.

The second topic is the quest of the historical Jesus, which began in the eighteenth century and eventually, as a result of the Enlightenment and other worldview changes, altered the entire course of interpreting Jesus. The Enlightenment was a watershed for Christian theology—and for the intellectual milieu of the West. On the eve of modernism, nothing was left untouched by new philosophical and scientific developments. Therefore, to gain perspective on current thinking concerning Jesus Christ, knowledge of this background is absolutely necessary.

This historical part ends with a look at the continuing quests of Jesus Christ among twentieth-century scholars, most of whom are biblical experts. That will pave the way for the book's third main part, which focuses on theological interpretations of Jesus the Christ in the global theological academy.

3

The Patristic and Creedal Establishment of "Orthodoxy"

What Was at Stake in the Historical Disputes? Why Bother?

Often beginning students of theology are tempted to ask two legitimate questions: Why should we bother ourselves with an antiquarian discussion of christological issues of the past that seem irrelevant to our current concerns? And what is the point of these finely nuanced disputes—what difference do they make after all? One may also wonder why the church ever entered into disputes surrounding, for example, conceptual distinctions between Christ's divinity and his humanity. Why didn't it just stick with the Bible?

It belongs to the essence of faith and worldviews in general that we often simply accept the tenets of our faith or worldview without much explicit reflection on them. But we also have a built-in need to make sense of what we believe. Therefore, it is most natural that as the church began to establish itself and its distinctive identity apart from Judaism, out of which it arose, Christians began to ask doctrinal questions: Who is this Jesus after all? What is the nature of the salvation he claims to have brought about? How is he different from us, and how is he similar to us?

When questions such as these were asked, Christians naturally went first to the Bible. But the New Testament did not yet exist (not until the fourth century were its contents finally ratified), even though Paul's and other Christian leaders' writings began to circulate soon after the death and resurrection of Jesus Christ. Very soon, these writings and written sermons (the book of Hebrews and 1 Peter, for example, were both originally sermons) were given high regard, but even these writings did not address all the questions, especially those having to do with the exact natures of Christ's divinity and humanity and their relationship.

Thought about Christ developed in various quarters of the expanding church parallel to the establishment of the New Testament. It is significant to note that christological developments of the first six centuries—the topic that forms the first section of part 2—do not differ from the biblical Christologies. Though the Christian church gives the New Testament canon a higher status than the Christian tradition of the first six centuries, we need to remind ourselves that those who lived close to New Testament times were in a good position to offer a definitive interpretation of the Christ event.

Among theologians there have been differing assessments of the development of classical christological dogma as it has come to be expressed, for example, in creeds. Some consider the dogmatic development an aberration that replaced New Testament Christology with philosophical reflection on the person and natures of Christ. Those with this perspective have rejected the Christology of the patristic period, seeing it as a hellenization of Christianity in which Greek metaphysical speculation supplanted the biblical historical mode of thought. Great historian of theology Adolf von Harnack expressed this view clearly in his celebrated *What Is Christianity?* He regarded the development of dogma as a deterioration and a deviation from the simple message of Jesus of Nazareth.[1] Many others have concurred.

Contrary to this position is a conception that has been called the dogmatic approach to Christology. According to this view, the development of christological dogma moved from the more functional Christology (what Christ has accomplished for us, i.e., the concerns of salvation) of the New Testament to the more ontological thought (Christ in himself, i.e., the concerns of the person of Christ) of the creeds, and this movement was progress. Theologians of this persuasion believe this kind of development in thinking was both helpful and necessary, and therefore they welcome the more philosophical approach of the creeds.

Yet another position judges the early councils' doctrine to be a true expression of the reality of Christ but nonetheless finds the development of dogma

---

1. As brilliantly presented and argued in his multi-volume *History of Dogma*. The most famous statement of Harnack, often quoted and often misinterpreted, is, "*The Gospel, as Jesus proclaimed it, has to do with the Father only and not with the Son.*" Adolf von Harnack, *What Is Christianity?*, trans. Thomas Bailey Sanders, 2nd rev. ed. (London: Williams and Norgate; New York: G. P. Putnam's Sons, 1902, 1957), 154 (emphasis original).

marked by a gradual narrowing of the questions. For example, while the questions surrounding Christ's divinity and humanity are to be taken seriously, even nowadays, they are not the only questions to be considered, perhaps not even the most crucial ones. Thus, while these early developments were legitimate against their own background, they are neither exhaustive nor final formulations. Each age has to wrestle afresh with these issues and provide its own answers, even while building critically on tradition. This last view seems to be the most coherent one, and a majority of theologians have embraced it.

This brings us once again to the relevance of these questions for our own needs and contexts. Nowadays, we hear so much about the need for theology to be contextual, to relate to the questions that arise in a particular context. We have to understand that, in fact, these early christological disputes were in themselves contextual responses to the culture of the day, the Greek/Hellenistic culture, which was philosophically and conceptually oriented, in contrast to the Hebrew/Judaic culture, which was less philosophical and more holistic in its approach to divine things. Early Christian thinkers attempted to express christological convictions based on the testimony of the Old Testament and emerging Christian writings in thought forms that would be understandable even to educated people of the time.

The questions we bring to Christology today are vastly different from the questions of the early centuries, yet we also keep asking the same questions: Who is this Jesus? How does his humanity make sense in the third millennium? What does it mean to believe in this divine Savior? We also ask questions such as the following: How do men and women together confess their faith in Christ? If Christ is male, is his maleness exclusive of motherhood and femininity? How does the idea of Christ as the Liberator relate to social injustice? How do we understand creation and the world process in light of Christ being the origin and goal of creation? What is Christ's role and meaning in relation to other faiths? These questions and many others are still related to those tentative, sometimes conflicting answers that our fathers and mothers in faith proposed.

The long and winding road of the history of christological traditions is divided here into two main parts. First, we will delve into the early history, the patristic and creedal periods (which cover roughly the first six centuries of Christian history). Following that, after a brief discussion of some leading medieval and Reformation developments, the main focus of the second major part will be on the time of the Enlightenment and emerging modernity (beginning from the end of the sixteenth century with the heydays of the following two centuries). Whereas the patristic and creedal periods laid the foundation for all doctrinal affirmations, Enlightenment/modern rebuttals and challenges sought to revise or reject most of them.

The first major part in this chapter will be divided conveniently into two sections, roughly following the chronology:

    a. The Relation of the Son to the Father: On the Way to Nicaea
    b. The Divinity and Humanity of Christ: From Nicaea to Chalcedon[2]

The Relation of the Son to the Father: On the Way to Nicaea

Was Jesus a Real Human Being?

At the heart of the incipient Christian faith, stemming from and founded in the strict monotheism of Judaism, was belief in the unity and oneness of God. Therefore, the obvious "problem for theology was to integrate with it, intellectually, the fresh data of the specifically Christian revelation," which at its core claimed "that God had made Himself known in the Person of Jesus, the Messiah, raising Him from the dead and offering salvation to men through Him, and that He had poured out His Holy Spirit upon the Church."[3] Related emerging (though yet to be theologically developed) claims had to do with the preexistence of Christ and his copresence in the creation and providence of the world.[4] While these profound questions were tackled, somewhat ironically, a main debate already in the New Testament was the question of Christ's humanity. In the Johannine community, belief in Christ's humanity became the criterion for true orthodoxy, as is evident in 1 John 4:2–3: "This is how you can recognize the Spirit of God: Every spirit that acknowledges that Jesus Christ has come in the flesh is from God, but every spirit that does not acknowledge Jesus is not from God." It seems that the fact of Jesus's divinity had been settled among Johannine Christians, but the Christians to whom John wrote still struggled with Christ's true humanity and the seeming incompatibility between his divinity and his humanity.

2. In addition to J. N. D. Kelly (*Early Christian Doctrines*, rev. ed. [San Francisco: Harper, 1978]) and William C. Placher (*A History of Christian Theology: An Introduction* [Philadelphia: Westminster, 1983]), which I have used extensively in the following discussions, in the classroom I have found the following historical presentations (in the order of length and detail) reliable and accessible; they cover the whole history of Christology: G. W. Bromiley, "Christology," in *International Standard Bible Encyclopedia*, ed. G. W. Bromiley (Grand Rapids: Eerdmans, 1979), 1:663–66; Colin Brown, "Person of Christ," in ibid., 3:781–801 (highly recommended); Hans Schwarz, *Christology* (Grand Rapids: Eerdmans, 1998), 137–200; Gerald O'Collins, SJ, *Christology: A Biblical, Historical, and Systematic Study of Jesus*, 2nd ed. (Oxford: Oxford University Press, 2009), 158–228.
3. Kelly, *Early Christian Doctrines*, 87.
4. Ibid.

In the second century the christological debate centered on the question of the divinity of Christ; most early church fathers took it for granted that Christ was human. What required clarification was the way he differed from other human beings. In this discussion, the Johannine concept of *Logos* was introduced, and its implications for a more developed Christology were considered. Two heretical views concerning the specific nature of Christ's humanity were rejected. Both of these views, Ebionitism and docetism, were attempts to define Jesus's humanity in a way that was deemed inappropriate by orthodoxy.

Ebionitism: An Elevated Human Being

Ebionites (from a Hebrew term meaning "the poor ones") were primarily a Jewish sect during the first two centuries that regarded Jesus as an ordinary human being, the son of Mary and Joseph. These Jewish believers, to whom the monotheism of the Old Testament was the received tradition, could not begin to imagine that there was another god besides the God of Israel. Such a belief would naturally imply polytheism.

Our knowledge of the Ebionites and their beliefs is scattered and scanty. Consider that Justin Martyr thought Ebionites regarded Jesus as the Messiah but still as a human being, born of a virgin (but not necessarily through virginal conception). According to third-century church historian Eusebius, there were actually two classes of Ebionites. Both groups insisted on the observance of the Mosaic law. The first group held to a natural birth of Jesus, who was characterized by an unusual moral character. The other group accepted the virgin birth but rejected the idea of Jesus's preexistence as the Son of God. But what kind of Christ would that be? More than likely, most Ebionites saw Jesus as one who surpassed others in wisdom and righteousness but was still more a human being than a god.[5] Ebionitism was quickly rejected by Christian theology because it was obvious that regarding Jesus as merely a human being compromised the idea of Jesus as Christ and Savior.

Docetism: He Only Seemed to Be Truly Human

The other early view that defined Jesus's humanity in a non-orthodox way—prominent especially during the second and third centuries—is called docetism. The term comes from the Greek word *dokeō*, "to seem" or "to appear." According to this understanding, Christ was completely divine, but his humanity was merely an appearance. Christ was not a real human being. Consequently, Christ's sufferings were not real.

5. Ibid., 139–40.

Docetism was related to a cluster of other philosophical and religious ideas that are often lumped together under the umbrella term "gnosticism" (from the Greek term *gnōsis*, "knowledge").[6] This term is elusive and may denote several things. The most important contribution gnosticism made with regard to docetism was the idea of dualism between matter and spirit. It regarded spirit as the higher and purer part of creation, whereas matter represented frailty and even sinfulness. Religion in gnosticism was an exercise in escaping from the material, visible world into the haven of spirit. It is easy to see how this kind of orientation was linked to docetism: to make Christ really "flesh" (cf. John 1:14) would compromise his divinity and his "spirituality."

Christian theology denied both docetism and Ebionitism. Docetism had a divine Savior who had no real connection with humanity. Ebionitism had only a human, moral example but no divine Savior.

The first major attempt to express in precise language the New Testament's dual emphasis on Christ as both a human being and a divine figure came to be known as *Logos* Christology, for the simple reason that these early fathers adopted the Johannine concept of *Logos*.

Early *Logos* Christologies: An Explanation of the Presence of Deity in Jesus

Justin Martyr, leading second-century apologist (a Christian thinker who wanted to offer a reasonable defense of the Christian faith vis-à-vis contemporary culture and philosophy),[7] sought to establish a correlation between Greek philosophy and Judaism. The idea of *logos*, referring to wisdom, learning, philosophy, and divine insight, while originating in Greek culture, was not foreign to Jews. Philo, a contemporary of Jesus who lived in Alexandria, Egypt, and was an influential thinker and historian, wrote about Jewish writers who had made a connection between the *logos* and the Old Testament word or wisdom of God. Such a connection is understandable given the important role the word of God plays in the Old Testament. The word is instrumental, for example, in creation (Gen. 1).[8]

Justin creatively made use of contemporary intellectual elements, especially in Stoic and Platonic philosophies, for the purposes of apologetics. Taking John 1:14 as his key text, he argued that the same *logos* that was known by pagan philosophers had now appeared in the person of Jesus of Nazareth.

6. For a basic account of gnosticism, see Placher, *History of Christian Theology*, 45–49; for its influence on docetism and the meaning of docetism, see 68–70.
7. For a basic account, see ibid., 59–64.
8. See ibid., 41–42, 58; Kelly, *Early Christian Doctrines*, 9–11.

According to Justin, philosophers had taught that the reason in every human being participates in the universal *logos*. The Gospel of John teaches that in Jesus Christ the *logos* became flesh. Therefore, whenever people use their reason, Christ, the *Logos*, is already at work. "We have been taught that Christ is the firstborn of God, and we have declared above that He is the Word of whom every race of men were partakers; and those who lived reasonably are Christians, even though they have been thought atheists."[9] Through Jesus Christ, Christians know the true meaning of *Logos*, while pagans have only partial access to it. Furthermore, according to early apologists, the divine *Logos* sowed seeds throughout human history; therefore, Christ is known to some extent by non-Christians. This concept was known as *logos spermatikos* ("seeds of *Logos* sown" in the world). In his *Second Apology*, Justin explains the fullness of the Christian doctrine of Christ:

> Our religion is clearly more sublime than any human teaching in this respect: the Christ who has appeared for us human beings represents the Logos principle in all its fullness. . . . For everything that the philosophers and lawgivers declared or discovered that is true was brought about by investigation and perception, in accordance with that portion of the Logos to which they had access. But because they did not know the whole of the Logos, who is Christ, they often contradicted each other.[10]

Origen, the leading second- to third-century church father from the Eastern Christian church—building on the legacy of Irenaeus[11] and the apologists—brought *Logos* Christology to its fullest development.[12] According to his thinking, in the incarnation the human soul of Christ was united with the *Logos*. On account of the closeness of this union, Christ's human soul shared in the properties of the *Logos*. Origen brought home this understanding with the help of a vivid picture from everyday life:

> If, then, a mass of iron be kept constantly in the fire, receiving the heat through all its pores and veins, and the fire being continuous and the iron never removed

---

9. Justin Martyr, *The First Apology* 46, in *ANF* 1:178.

10. Justin Martyr, *The Second Apology* 10, quoted in Alister McGrath, *Christian Theology: An Introduction*, 5th ed. (Oxford: Wiley-Blackwell, 2011), 274. For a detailed discussion of Justin Martyr and other key figures' *Logos* Christology, see Kelly, *Early Christian Doctrines*, 9–11, 95–101.

11. For St. Irenaeus's role in and contribution to second-century christological developments, see Kelly, *Early Christian Doctrines*, 104–8, 145–49.

12. Placher, *History of Christian Theology*, 61–63; and in more detail: Kelly, *Early Christian Doctrines*, 126–32; also 154–58. As disputed a figure as he was (e.g., for his espousal of a distinctive type of universalism, that is, at the end all will be saved and reconciled to God), Origen's influence on later theology is tremendous.

from it, it becomes wholly converted into the latter. . . . In this way, then, that soul which, like an iron in the fire, has been perpetually placed in the Word, and perpetually in the Wisdom, and perpetually in God, is God in all that it does, feels, and understands.[13]

As a consequence of this union between the *Logos* and Jesus of Nazareth, Jesus is the true God. Yet to safeguard the preeminence of the Father, Origen reminded his followers of the principle of *autotheos*, which simply means that, strictly speaking, God only and alone is God. Origen did so in order not to lessen the divinity of Christ but to secure the priority of the Father.[14]

One of the most profound contributions of Origen has to do with the establishment and clarification of Christ's preexistence, a conviction that was already present among the so-called apostolic fathers[15] (the first post-biblical theological authorities at the turn of the second century). Origen taught that the Father had begotten the Son by an eternal act; therefore, Christ existed from eternity. In fact, there were two begettings of the Son: one in time (the virgin birth) and one in eternity by the Father. To make his point, Origen appealed to John 1:1, which has no definite article in the Greek expression "the Word [*Logos*] was God" and therefore could be translated "the Word was *a* God" (or perhaps "divine"). While Origen's exegetical ground is not convincing to modern interpreters, his *Logos* Christology represents a significant milestone in the development of the christological tradition. *Logos* Christology has been a dominant way of interpreting Christ's incarnation and has taken various forms throughout history.

The Unique Status of the Father in Relation to the Son

The study of theology, as with any other academic field, requires mastery of its basic vocabulary. Some terms (e.g., "person") are used in everyday speech but in theology have a different, often strictly defined, meaning. Other terms are coined specifically for the purposes of theological accuracy. One of the latter kind of terms was coined to explain the relationship among the members of the Trinity that assured the supremacy of God the Father. The term is *monarchianism*, which means "sole sovereignty." There are two subcategories of this view: dynamic and modalistic monarchianism.[16] Both emerged in the

13. Origen, *De principiis* 2.6.6, in *ANF* 4:283.
14. It is customary in the Christian East to consider the Father as the "source" of the Trinity (and the Son and the Spirit, as expressed by Irenaeus, as the "two hands of the Father").
15. For details, see Kelly, *Early Christian Doctrines*, 90–95.
16. Strictly speaking there are more than two types of monarchianisms, and their historical and theological nature is a complicated and complex issue. Furthermore, it is often rightly

late second and early third centuries and stressed the uniqueness and unity of God in light of the Christian confession that Jesus is God. Such views, similar to those of Origen, were eventually rejected by Christian orthodoxy.

Concern for the uniqueness of God the Father is understandable given that Christian theology grew out of Jewish soil. The leading theme of Judaism in the Old Testament is belief in the one God, as expressed in Deuteronomy 6:4 and a host of other passages. While these two monarchianist views were rejected, they express a noteworthy milestone in the struggle of Christian theology to retain its ties to the Jewish faith and to explicate fully the implications of Christ's divinity.

Dynamic Monarchianism: God Dynamically Present in Jesus

The etymology of dynamic monarchianism explains its meaning: the "sole sovereignty" of the Father was preserved by the idea that God was dynamically present in Jesus, thus making him higher than any other human being but not yet a god. In other words, God's power (Greek *dynamis*) made Jesus *almost* God; as a consequence, the Father's uniqueness was secured.[17]

Theodotus, a Byzantine leather merchant, came to Rome, an important city of Christianity, at the end of the second century. He taught that prior to baptism Jesus was an ordinary man, although a virtuous one; at his baptism, the Spirit, or Christ, descended upon him and gave him the ability to perform miracles. Jesus was still an ordinary man, but he was inspired by the Spirit. Some of Theodotus's followers went further and claimed that Jesus actually became divine at his baptism or after his resurrection, but Theodotus himself did not concur.

In the second half of the third century, Paul of Samosata further developed the idea of dynamic monarchianism by contending that the Word (*Logos*) does not refer to a personal, self-subsistent entity but simply to God's commandment and ordinance: God ordered and accomplished what he willed through the man Jesus. Paul of Samosata did not admit that Jesus was the Word, *Logos*. Instead, the *Logos* was a dynamic power in Jesus's life that made God dynamically present in Jesus. This view was condemned by the Synod of Antioch in 268.

Modalistic Monarchianism: No Real Distinctions in the Godhead

According to modalistic monarchianism, the three persons of the Trinity are not self-subsistent "persons" but "modes" or "names" of the same God.

---

remarked that what are now the two best-known types—dynamic and modalistic—in fact represent different kinds of heresies lumped under one umbrella. That said, for an introductory knowledge of christological history, they can be conveniently discussed together because of obvious material similarities.

17. For basic ideas and sources, see Kelly, *Early Christian Doctrines*, 115–19.

They are like three "faces" of God, with a different one presented depending on the occasion. Whereas dynamic monarchianism seemed to deny the Trinity, indicating that Jesus is less than God, modalistic monarchianism appeared to affirm the Trinity. Both, however, tried to preserve the oneness of God the Father, though in different ways.[18]

Several early-third-century thinkers such as Noetus of Smyrna, Praxeas (perhaps a nickname meaning "busybody"), and Sabellius contended that there is one Godhead that can be designated as Father, Son, or Spirit.[19] The names do not stand for real distinctions but are merely names that are appropriate and applicable at different times. In other words, Father, Son, and Spirit are identical, successive revelations of the same person. This view is sometimes called Sabellianism after one of its early proponents. A corollary idea follows: the Father suffered along with Christ because he was actually present in and personally identical with the Son. This view is known as patripassianism (from two Latin terms meaning "father" and "passion").

Modalistic monarchianism was considered heretical by the church, even though its basic motivation, to preserve the unity of God the Father, was valid. Early Christian theologians soon noticed its main problem: How can three (or two) persons of the Trinity appear simultaneously in the act of salvation if they are but three names or modes of one and the same being? The account of Jesus's baptism, during which the Father spoke to his Son and the Spirit descended on the Son, seemed to contradict the idea of modalism.

But even the orthodox position had to struggle with the question, If Christ is divine but is not the Father, are there not two Gods? Tertullian, one of the ablest early Christian theologians, coined much of the trinitarian vocabulary. He sought to clarify this problem with a series of metaphors:

> For the root and the tree are distinctly two things, but correlatively joined; the fountain and the river are also two forms, but indivisible; so likewise the sun and the ray are two forms, but coherent ones. Everything which proceeds from something else must needs be second to that from which it proceeds, without being on that account separated.[20]

By analogies such as these, Tertullian and others believed they had clarified the New Testament distinction between Father and Son without leading to belief

18. For basic ideas and sources, see ibid., 119–23.

19. Lumping together these different figures associated with modalism can be done only for pedagogical and heuristic reasons; an advanced student of theology should keep in mind their differences and perhaps also the somewhat contrasting orientations in the forms of modalism(s).

20. Tertullian, *Against Praxeas*, chap. 8, in *ANF* 3:603; for a detailed discussion of Tertullian (and his famed martyred colleague, Hippolytus), see Kelly, *Early Christian Doctrines*, 110–15, 149–53.

in two gods. But one may seriously ask whether this was the case. Metaphors such as the one depicting the Father as the sun and the Son as a ray imply subordinationism, that Christ is inferior to the Father. In fact, Tertullian admitted this: "For the Father is the entire substance, but the Son is a derivation and portion of the whole as He Himself acknowledges: 'My Father is greater than I.'"[21] In fact, these ideas and related problems associated with defining Christ's relation to the Father led to the emergence of a new set of questions.

How to Define Christ's Deity: The Challenge of Arianism

As soon as Christian theology had combated these two versions of monarchianism, it faced an even more challenging problem named Arianism, after Arius, a priest of Alexandria. Even though historically it is unclear whether Arius himself ever expressed ideas related to Arianism, it is evident that a major debate took place in the third and fourth centuries concerning the way Jesus's divinity and relationship to the Father could be expressed.

According to his opponents (on whose reports we have to depend here), the basic premise of Arius's thinking was that God the Father is absolutely unique and transcendent, and God's essence (the Greek term *ousia* means both "essence" and "substance") cannot be shared by another or transferred to another, not even the Son. Consequently, for Arius, the distinction between Father and Son was one of substance (*ousia*); if they were of the same substance, there would be two gods. Rather than sharing the same "essence" with the Father, the Son is the first and unique creation of God. A saying attributed to Arius emphasizes his main thesis about the origin of Christ: "There was [a time] when he was not." This view was problematic because it meant that Christ was begotten of God in time, not from all eternity. Christ, therefore, was a part of creation and inferior to God, even though greater than other creatures.[22]

It is easy to see the concerns and logic of Arianism. On the one hand, it attempted to secure the divinity, or at least the supreme status, of Jesus in regard to other human beings. On the other hand, it did not make Jesus equal to the Father. In a sense, Jesus stood in the middle. What was the main concern behind this reasoning? Although we are unable to go into many debated scholarly (and historical) questions behind Arianism, current scholarship believes that Arianism's problems stem from universal Hellenistic ideology, according to which it is not possible to attribute suffering, let alone death, to gods or divine beings. Although for the Greco-Roman world the idea of a human becoming

---

21. Tertullian, *Against Praxeas*, chap. 9.
22. For an accurate historical and theological discussion, see Kelly, *Early Christian Doctrines*, 226–31.

divine is not impossible at all—as it was to Jewish intuitions—the attempt to link the divine with earthly sufferings is totally impossible (unlike Old Testament passages in which Yahweh seems to be intimately engaged in the sufferings of his people).[23] As a result, the (later) Christian confession of the Messiah who suffered under Pontius Pilate and was crucified was anathema to Arian theology.

Now it can also be seen how monarchianisms and Arianism relate to each other: while the former (in keeping with Jewish intuitions) seeks to defend the uniqueness of God/Father vis-à-vis any notion of "polytheism," the latter's concern is to defend the idea of the deity free from any notions of suffering and death and, as a result, to make the Son less than divine.

Mainstream Christian theology had to respond to this challenge because it seemed to compromise the basic confession of Christ's deity. The ablest defender of the full deity of Christ was the Eastern father Athanasius. He argued in response to Arius that the view that the Son was a creature, albeit at a higher level, would have a decisive consequence for salvation. First, only God can save, whereas a creature is in need of being saved. Thus, if Jesus were not God incarnate, he would not be able to save us. But both the New Testament and church liturgy call Jesus "Savior," indicating that he is God. Worship of and prayer to a Jesus who is less than God would also make Christians guilty of blasphemy.[24]

The response of Athanasius provides a model of the way early Christian theology developed. Academic or intellectual concerns were not primary, even though argumentation was carried on at a highly sophisticated level. The soteriological concern, the question of salvation, was the driving force behind theological developments. Christology is a showcase example of this. Early Christian theologians did not sit comfortably in their studies seeking to produce something novel about Christ. They were pastors and preachers whose primary concern was to make sure that people knew how to be saved. That what was confessed in church liturgy was considered doctrinally binding shows the full force of the ancient rule *lex orandi lex credendi* ("the principle of prayer is the principle of believing"): what is believed and worshiped becomes the confession of doctrine.

---

23. Soon in Christian doctrine there arose the twin views of the "immutability" and "impassibility" of God, that is, God is "able" to neither change nor suffer. This was to defend the absolute uniqueness and transcendence of God—but its price was a somewhat distanced God. Much of contemporary theology of God revolves around this issue.

24. For a brief, accessible account, see Placher, *History of Christian Theology*, 72–75; for a detailed discussion of Athanasius and his pro-Nicene defense, see Kelly, *Early Christian Doctrines*, 240–47, 284–89.

In the spirit of Athanasius's and other mainline theologians' responses to Arius, the Council of Nicaea (as formulated in the 381 Constantinopolitan Creed)[25] defined Christ's deity in a way that made Christ equal to God the Father. The text says:

> We believe . . . in one Lord Jesus Christ, the Son of God, begotten of the Father [the only begotten, that is, of the essence of the Father], God of God, Light of Light, very God of very God, begotten, not made, being of one substance [*homoousios*] with the Father; by whom all things were made [both in heaven and on earth]; who for us men, and for our salvation, came down and was incarnate and was made man; he suffered, and the third day he rose again, ascended into heaven; from thence he shall come to judge the quick and the dead.

An appendix at the end listed Arian tenets to be rejected:

> But for those who say: "There was a time when he was not;" and "He was not before he was made;" and "He was made out of nothing," or "He is of another substance" or "essence," or "The Son of God is created," or "changeable," or "alterable"—they are condemned by the holy catholic and apostolic Church.[26]

The creed said that Christ was not created but "begotten of the substance of the Father." The key word was the Greek *homoousios*, which created great debate. It means literally "of the same substance" or "of the same essence," indicating that Christ was equal in divinity to the Father. Not all theologians were happy with that definition. Even though, as mentioned above, virtually all confessed Christ's divine nature, the question was how to define it. Especially theologians from the Eastern wing of the church, the Greek church, would have preferred the Greek term *homoiousios*. The difference is one *i*, which makes a difference in meaning: *homoi* means "similar to," whereas *homo* means "the same." In other words, this formulation would not make Christ identical with the Father but similar to the Father. Greek theologians had concerns about the stricter formulation because they believed it was not biblical and could lead to modalism. For Eastern theology, the distinctive "personhood" of the Father and the Son was important in addition to securing the privileged status of the Father. Latin-speaking theologians objected to the "similar to" interpretation,

25. The creedal text referred to as the Nicene Creed is from the 381 Constantinople Council, which gave it final formulation. Hence, often it is named the Nicene-Constantinopolitan Creed.
26. Philip Schaff, ed., *The Creeds of Christendom*, 6th ed. (1931; repr., Grand Rapids: Baker, 1990), 1:28–29. For a definitive, detailed treatment of Nicaea's theology of Christ (and the Trinity), see Kelly, *Early Christian Doctrines*, 231–37; for a nontechnical, reliable account, see Placher, *History of Christian Theology*, 75–79.

believing it could be interpreted in a subordinationist way, meaning that the Son is (in this case, slightly) different from the Father and therefore less than the Father (that is, going back to what Arianism was arguing).

This difference of opinion between the Greek- and Latin-speaking churches did not lead to a division or a permanent labeling of either side as heretical, but it did highlight a growing gulf between the Christian East and (what became later) the Christian West. Even though both traditions at least formally concurred with the Nicene formulation, they began to develop their own distinctive approaches to Christ, namely, the Antiochian and Alexandrian schools. Each school produced a distinctive Christology, which in turn gave rise to distinctive christological heresies. In a way, the heresies that arose took seriously the concerns of each of these schools and pushed the boundaries until the theological consensus came to the conclusion that they had gone too far.

The Divinity and Humanity of Christ: From Nicaea to Chalcedon

Two Christological Orientations

Up until the Council of Nicaea in 325, the main questions surrounding Christ focused on whether he was divine and how to define precisely his divinity in relation to the Father. After Nicaea these questions still loomed in the background, but the focus shifted to the corollary problem: Granted that Christ is divine, how are Christ's two natures—divine and human—related to each other? It is one thing to confess that Christ is human and that he is divine; it is another thing to determine how to hold together these seemingly opposite claims. If a person is fully divine, doesn't that by definition render that person not fully human and vice versa?[27]

Two orientations emerged among Christian churches, partly because of cultural and geographical differences and partly because of influences from the surrounding societies and religions. To point to these two orientations, it is customary in textbooks to speak of two schools in the Christian East, namely, those of Alexandria (of Egypt) and Antioch (of Syria). They were among the leading centers of Christian learning and authority (along with Constantinople, another leading Eastern center, and Rome in the West, among others). Although geographically both cities belong to the Christian East (and were thus Greek speaking), throughout the centuries they also gave impetus

27. For a detailed discussion of post-Nicene issues, debates, and solutions, see Kelly, *Early Christian Doctrines*, 237–47; for "Anti-Nicenes," see 247–51.

to the division between Greek and Latin Christianities (or the Christian East and Christian West, respectively, which formalized itself only after the formal split in 1054).

Alexandria in Egypt was the center of Greek-speaking theological learning. Alexandrian Christology emphasized soteriological questions and expressed its doctrine of salvation in terms of deification or divinization (Greek *theōsis*), that is, union between the divine and human (without blurring the distinction, that is, without succumbing to pantheism). In doing so, Alexandrians' main focus was naturally on the divinity of Christ—to the point that (while not, of course, denying the human nature) theirs was a much more "one-nature" Christology[28] (in comparison with the "two-nature" view of Antioch). Athanasius's rebuttal of Arius serves as a showcase example of the Alexandrian school. In contrast, the Antiochian school sought to hold together the divine and human natures, paying more attention to the theological significance of the latter than their Alexandrian counterparts. For Antioch, Christ's earthly life and obedience played a more important role.[29]

One can easily imagine that out of these two Eastern church orientations distinctive kinds of heretical views could emerge when taking either focus to the extreme: on the Alexandrian side, a strong leaning toward *monophysitism* led some to the virtual denial of Jesus's human nature, and on the Antiochian side, the distinction between the two natures was claimed by opponents to result in separation of the natures altogether.

Christ's Divinity and Our Deification: The Challenge of One-Nature Heresies

As said, the focus of the Alexandrian school was on redemption in the sense of human life ("flesh" of John 1:14) being taken up into the life of God (deification). If human nature is to be deified, it must be united with the divine nature. For this to happen, God must become united with human nature in such a manner that the latter shares in the life of God; this is what happened in and through the incarnation. This raised the question of the relationship between the divinity and the humanity of Christ.

---

28. Technically called *monophysitism*, from Greek terms meaning "one" and "nature."

29. The way Kelly names them is "Word-flesh" (Alexandrian) and "Word-man" (Antioch) Christologies. In the former, the emphasis is on the union of the *Logos*/Word/divine nature with human "flesh," whereas in the latter, the union links both the divine and human natures of the Savior (*Early Christian Doctrines*, 281; see the whole of chap. 11 for an authoritative, detailed discussion of all central issues involved). A short, nontechnical discussion can be found in Placher, *History of Christian Theology*, 79–84 (who names them the "Logos-flesh" Christology of Alexandria and the "two-natures" Christology of Antioch).

The explanation of Cyril of Alexandria, a leading Alexandrian theologian, emphasized the reality of the union of the two natures in the incarnation. The *Logos* existed "without flesh" before its union with human nature; after that union, one nature existed, for the *Logos* had united human nature to itself. In juxtaposition with Antioch, Cyril argued:

> We do not affirm that the nature of the Logos underwent a change and became flesh, or that it was transformed into a whole or perfect human consisting of flesh and body; rather, we say that the Logos . . . personally united itself to a human nature with a living soul, became a human being, and was called the Son of Man, but not of mere will or favor.[30]

This raised the question of what kind of human nature was assumed. Did Christ's nature encompass all of human nature? A heretical view called Apollinarianism tried to answer these questions in a less than satisfactory way. Among the many heresies faced by early Christianity, none probably outdoes Apollinarianism in sophistication and nuance. Apollinarius of Laodicea worried about the increasingly widespread belief that the *Logos* assumed human nature in its entirety. He wondered whether that conviction would lead to the belief that the *Logos* was contaminated by the weaknesses of human nature. If so, the sinlessness of Christ would be compromised. To avoid this unacceptable view, Apollinarius suggested that if a real human mind in Jesus were replaced by a purely divine mind, then and only then could Christ's sinlessness be maintained. He argued that a purely human mind and soul were replaced by a divine mind and soul, preventing contamination of the divine *Logos* by any sin from a human mind.[31]

As appealing as this idea seems, it renders the human nature of Christ incomplete. Alexandrian theologians soon noticed that the price for protecting Jesus's sinlessness in this way was too high. Apollinarianism compromised Jesus's role as Savior, as Gregory Nazianzen (a Cappadocian father, also called Gregory of Nazianzus) noted: How could human nature be redeemed if only part of it was assumed by the *Logos*?

> For that which He has not assumed He has not healed; but that which is united to His Godhead is also saved. If only half Adam fell, then that which Christ assumes and saves may be half also; but if the whole of his nature fell, it must

---

30. See Cyril of Alexandria, *The Epistle of Cyril to Nestorius* (Peabody, MA: Hendrickson, 1994); a highly useful discussion of Cyril's Christology can be found in Kelly, *Early Christian Doctrines*, 317–23.

31. For the basic theological claims of Apollinarianism, see Kelly, *Early Christian Doctrines*, 289–95.

> be united to the whole nature of Him that was begotten, and so be saved as a whole. Let them not, then, begrudge us our complete salvation, or clothe the Saviour only with bones and nerves and the portraiture of humanity.[32]

Gregory Nazianzen built on the Eastern view of Origen and others, according to which the incarnation accomplished a "recapitulation" of human history; the God-man Jesus not only experienced all phases of human life from birth to adulthood to death but also restored the history of humanity by facing Adam's temptation without sinning. Gregory maintained that if all of human nature were not assumed, taken up in the humanity of Christ, then Jesus's role as Savior was incomplete.

The logic of Eastern Christology was governed by soteriological motives. Christ had to be fully and genuinely divine and fully and genuinely human to serve in the capacity of the Savior. If Christ were less than human, he would not be able to identify with us, and even worse, our human nature would not be taken up into his deified humanity. On the other hand, if Christ were less than divine, he would not possess the power and authority to save us, even if he could sympathize with us. The Eastern church was never able to define in precise theological terms the relationship between the two natures of Christ—and as mentioned earlier, it emphasized his divinity—but it held firmly to the basic christological conviction that would secure salvation.

The proposal of Apollinarius did not meet acceptance, and other routes were taken to secure the sinlessness of Christ while focusing on his divinity even in the incarnation. Before looking briefly at another one-nature heresy of Alexandria (Eutychianism), we need to consider the "two-nature" heresy of Antioch related to the dent of Eutychianism.

Christ's Humanity and Our Obedience: The Two-Nature Heresy

"Two Natures" of Christ in Focus

The Christology of Antioch focused more on the moral aspects of the Christian life (e.g., discipleship) than on soteriology. It held Christ's human nature in view along with his divine nature. Particularly in response to Apollinarianism, there was a need for "a thoroughly realistic acknowledgment of the human life and experiences of the Incarnate and of the theological significance of His human soul." In that sense Antioch "deserves credit for

---

32. Gregory Nazianzen, *Letter to Cledonius the Priest against Apollinarius*, epistle 101, in *NPNF²* 7:440. For Orthodox responses to Apollinarianism (with the focus on the two Cappadocians, Gregory of Nyssa and Gregory of Nazianzus), see Kelly, *Early Christian Doctrines*, 295–301.

bringing back the historical Jesus."[33] It taught that on account of their disobedience, human beings exist in a state of corruption from which they are unable to save themselves. Redemption calls for obedience on the part of humanity. Because humanity is unable to break free from the bonds of sin, God is obliged to intervene. This leads to the coming of the Redeemer, who unites humanity and divinity and thus establishes an obedient people of God. This view defends the two natures of Christ: he was at one and the same time both God and a human being. Not surprisingly, the Alexandrians criticized Antioch for denying the unity of Christ. Against this criticism, the Antiochenes' response spoke of the "perfect conjunction" between the human and the divine natures of Christ.

Antioch's leading theologian, Theodore of Mopsuestia, strongly opposed the neglect of Christ's human nature by the Alexandrians, emphasizing that Christ assumed both genuine human body and "soul" (will and rationality). On the basis of biblical teaching, Theodore believed that in Jesus's case the taking on of humanity did not include a sinful nature. Theodore also states that the two natures of Christ do not compromise his unity: "In coming to indwell, the Logos united the assumed [human being] as a whole to itself, and made him to share with it in all the dignity in which the one who indwells, being the Son of God by nature, possesses."[34] That said, Theodore also adds to the confusion when he seems to distinguish the two natures of Christ in a way that leans toward separation. Indeed, as William Placher says, it looks as if he were "treating each 'nature' as a subject to which one could assign different predicates. When Christ wept or feared, that was the human nature; when he performed miracles or forgave sins, that was the divine nature."[35] Undoubtedly, Theodore "thus gives the impression of presupposing a real duality" between the two natures.[36] No wonder Alexandrians remained suspicious and attacked, believing that the

33. Kelly, *Early Christian Doctrines*, 302; for the basic teachings of Antioch, see 301–9.

34. Theodore of Mopsuestia, *On the Incarnation*, quoted in McGrath, *Christian Theology*, 279 (Theodore's *De Incarnatione* is available only in fragments, and the history of their compilations suggests that they might have been compiled in order to discredit his views in the Second Council of Constantinople in 553). Theodore was a pupil of Diodore, another major christologist of Antioch (for his views, see Kelly, *Early Christian Doctrines*, 302–3); for Theodore and his opponent, the Alexandrian Cyril, see 303–9.

35. As explained by Placher, *History of Theology*, 81. That this kind of interpretation seems to be correct is validated by Theodore's own comment: "Let us apply our minds to the distinction of natures; He who assumed [the human nature] is God and only-begotten Son, but the form of a slave, he who was assumed, is man." Theodore of Mopsuestia, *Catechetical Homilies* 8.13, cited in Kelly, *Early Christian Doctrines*, 305 (even this writing of Theodore is not available in English in standard patristic series).

36. Kelly, *Early Christian Doctrines*, 305.

stress on two natures leads to a doctrine of "two sons": Christ seemed to be not a single person but two persons, one human and one divine.[37] One strand of the Antiochian school did in fact emphasize the two natures so much that it affirmed a view that seemed to separate the humanity and the divinity from each other, making them more or less separate entities. This view is known as Nestorianism.

Nestorianism: Separation of Natures?

The label Nestorianism is questionable because we do not know for sure whether Nestorius, patriarch of Constantinople in the first part of the fifth century, actually taught this doctrine. It is possible, however, to lay aside the question of the origin of this view and look merely at the challenge this view presented to orthodoxy. The controversy surrounding Nestorianism arose over the use of the term *theotokos* ("God-bearing") in regard to Mary. Was Mary, the mother of Jesus, the mother of God? Nestorius, as a spokesman for a larger group, stated that *theotokos* is appropriate insofar as it is complemented by the term *anthrōpotokos* ("human-bearing"). However, Nestorius's own preference was *Christotokos* ("Christ-bearing").[38]

What was at stake in these technical terminological distinctions? What was the concern of Nestorius and his opponents? Nestorius maintained that it is impossible to believe that God would have a mother; no woman can give birth to God. Instead, what Mary bore was not God but humanity, a sort of instrument of divinity. Nestorius feared that if the term *theotokos* were applied to Mary without qualifications, it would lead to either Arianism, according to which Jesus was not equal to God, or Apollinarianism, which taught that Jesus's human nature was not real. In the East, however, the term *theotokos* was widely used by Alexandrians. It was often coupled with another ancient concept, *communicatio idiomatum* ("communication of attributes"), which played a significant role in various doctrinal contexts throughout history. With regard to Jesus's two natures, the expression means that what pertains to one nature also pertains to the other. In other words, because we can say that Mary bore the human baby Jesus, we can also at the same time say that Mary bore the divine person Christ.

What, then, made Nestorius's doctrine unorthodox? Here we come to the difficulty of establishing Nestorius's view exactly. Nestorius's opponents,

---

37. Indeed, Theodore's teacher Diodore seems to have taught that the separation between the two natures amounted to "two sons" (Kelly, *Early Christian Doctrines*, 303), an idea rejected by his pupil (305).

38. For a detailed discussion, see Kelly, *Early Christian Doctrines*, 310–17.

especially Eastern theologian Cyril of Alexandria, labeled Nestorius's view heretical, suggesting that obviously Nestorius believed that Jesus had two natures joined in a purely moral union but not in a real way (as *communicatio idiomatum* suggests). Cyril's interpretation of Nestorius's view was called Nestorianism: Christ was actually two distinct persons, one divine and the other human.[39] Nestorius repudiated this interpretation of his view, but this interpretation continued until it was rejected at the Council of Ephesus in 431.

Having rejected the view attributed to Nestorius as extreme, theologians refined the doctrine of Jesus's humanity and divinity with the help of the concept of *communicatio idiomatum*. If Jesus was fully human and fully divine, then what was true of his humanity was also true of his divinity and vice versa. This principle was also applied to Mary: Jesus Christ is God; Mary gave birth to Jesus; therefore, Mary is the mother of God. Soon this view became a test of orthodoxy. But it is easy to see that when pressed, this orthodox view gives rise to another problem: Jesus suffered on the cross; Jesus is God; therefore, God suffered on the cross.

Another Alexandrian One-Nature Heresy: Eutychianism

The controversy about issues raised by Nestorianism as well as Apollinarianism continued to concern theological orthodoxy, to which the Council of Ephesus (431) only offered tentative and elusive solutions.[40] As mentioned, they also helped bring about another Alexandrian-born heresy, one known as Eutychianism. The obscure and undeveloped robust monophysitism of Eutyches oddly insisted that while Christ had two natures before the incarnation, there was only one after it.[41]

But what kind of "one nature" might Christ have had after incarnation? Was it another version of docetism? Or was Christ's humanity swallowed up by his divinity? Whatever the case, finally Eutychianism was rejected as a form of one-nature Christology. That and other formative decisions were made at the Council of Chalcedon in 451.

39. For details of Cyril's attack, see ibid., 317–23.

40. For the checkered history around the Council of Ephesus, standard church history textbooks can be consulted; for theological developments and implications, see ibid., 323–30; more briefly, Placher, *Historical Theology*, 82–83.

41. The views of this elderly monk and archimandrite, first rejected at the 448 Standing Synod of Constantinople, were ratified at another, the Second Council of Ephesus (the so-called Robber Synod) in 449, with its rebuttal of the two natures of Christ, but were soon rebutted at Chalcedon a couple of years later. For details of Eutychianism, see Kelly, *Early Christian Doctrines*, 33–34.

The Chalcedonian "Solution": Its Meaning Then and Now

The "Definitions" and Claims of Chalcedon

Because of its supreme importance both in terms of the critical (although not ultimate) resolution of questions for the first four hundred years of christological (and trinitarian) debates and its lasting significance for the rest of theology's history, including contemporary times, let us take a closer look at the achievements and challenges of Chalcedon. Following this will be a contemporary, "global" assessment of its meaning and the need for continuing revisionary work.

The Council of Chalcedon (451) attempted to solve the christological debates in a way that could be embraced by both Alexandrians and Antiochenes. Furthermore, at Chalcedon and in the preparation of its statements, we also have to note the importance of Rome, the rapidly growing center of Latin Christianity, whose christological contributions so far had been meager (except for Tertullian).[42]

The council never reached its noble goal, but it was able to combat the major deviating views.[43] The council reaffirmed the Nicene-Constantinopolitan Creed and rejected Nestorianism and Eutychianism. The text says:

> We, then, following the holy Fathers, all with one consent, teach men to confess one and the same Son, our Lord Jesus Christ, the same perfect in Godhood and also perfect in manhood; truly God and truly man, of a reasonable [rational] soul and body; consubstantial [co-essential] with the Father according to the Godhood, and consubstantial with us according to the Manhood; in all things like unto us, without sin; begotten before all ages of the Father according to the Godhood, and in these latter days, for us and for our salvation, born of the Virgin Mary, the Mother of God, according to the Manhood; one and the same Christ, Son, Lord, Only-begotten, to be acknowledged in two natures, inconfusedly, unchangeably, indivisibly, inseparably; the distinction of natures being by no means taken away by the union, but rather the property of each nature being preserved, and concurring in one Person and one Subsistence, not parted or divided into two persons, but one and the same Son, and only begotten,

42. Indeed, views of the Christian West, particularly those of Tertullian, Hilary of Poitiers, and Augustine (and therefore also the legacy of Antiochian Christology) are visible in the Chalcedonian formulation. Particularly important is Pope Leo's *Tome*. See for details Kelly, *Early Christian Doctrines*, 334–38.

43. Complicating factors between the two christological schools had to do not only with political and authority issues (including the rise of Rome to prominence in the West) but also with language: Greek speakers hardly were familiar with Latin and with writings in that language, and vice versa. Just consider St. Augustine: despite his unparalleled learning, his acquaintance with Greek theology was embarrassingly scattered.

God the Word, the Lord Jesus Christ, as the prophets from the beginning [have declared] concerning him, and the Lord Jesus Christ himself has taught us, and the Creed of the holy Fathers has handed down to us.[44]

The main concern of Chalcedon was to steer a middle course between the dangers of Nestorianism, which separated the two natures—thus the use of the words "indivisibly" and "inseparably"—and Apollinarianism (and Eutychianism), which eliminated the distinction between the two natures—thus the use of the words "inconfusedly" and "unchangeably." Although the council was unable to state definitely how the union of the two natures occurred, it was able to say how this union cannot be expressed. The controlling principle of Chalcedon holds that provided that Jesus Christ was both truly divine and truly human, the precise manner in which this is articulated or explored is not of fundamental importance. Maurice Wiles neatly summarizes the aim and achievement of Chalcedon:

> On the one hand was the conviction that a saviour must be fully divine; on the other hand was the conviction that what is not assumed is not healed. Or, to put the matter in other words, the source of salvation must be God; the locus of salvation must be humanity. It is quite clear that these two principles often pulled in opposite directions. The Council of Chalcedon was the church's attempt to resolve, or perhaps rather to agree to live with, that tension. Indeed, to accept both principles as strongly as did the early church is already to accept the Chalcedonian faith.[45]

One could perhaps say that, on the one hand, Chalcedon functioned as a signpost pointing in the right direction, and on the other hand, it was a fence separating orthodoxy and heresy.[46]

Chalcedon's Meaning and Liabilities for a Contemporary Pluralistic World

Although Chalcedon represents the ecumenical consensus (as much as one can speak of consensus with regard to this kind of complicated statement),[47]

44. Schaff, *Creeds of Christendom*, 2:62–63. For a short, important discussion of Chalcedon's theology, see Kelly, *Early Christian Doctrines*, 338–43.

45. Quoted in McGrath, *Christian Theology*, 284.

46. For these expressions, I am indebted to my Fuller colleague Professor Emeritus Colin Brown.

47. Most fittingly, the famed historian of theology Jaroslav Pelikan calls Chalcedon "an agreement to disagree," in *The Emergence of the Catholic Tradition (100–600)*, vol. 1 of *The Christian Tradition: A History of the Development of Doctrine* (Chicago: University of Chicago Press, 1971), 266.

it has also come under devastating critique in the contemporary global and pluralistic world. What are the reasons for that? Corollary questions include the following: Should we stick with its formulations in order to be "orthodox"? What would the development of Chalcedon entail? and so forth. Although it does not belong to the task of an introductory textbook to delve into the details of these questions, let alone attempt a constructive proposal, a brief orientation is in order.[48] The many complaints and criticisms against what is often called the two-nature, "incarnational" Christology of Chalcedon can be grouped under the following five categories.

First, many wonder whether Chalcedonian Christology betrays a political bias, namely, deriving its ethos from the church's alliance with the powers-that-be of the Constantinian Empire.[49] Feminist Rosemary Radford Ruether, among others, has articulated the charge that the "orthodox Christology" of the first Christian centuries helped the marginal religious sect evolve "into the new imperial religion of a Christian Roman Empire."[50] That charge, however, has been successfully combated by the historical observation that it was the non-Chalcedonian Arian party that was more prone to looking for earthly power sympathies and agendas.[51] No more convincing is the charge that the Chalcedonian *Logos* Christology led to the "patriarchalization of Christology" that in turn led to the hierarchical view in which "just as the *Logos* of God governs the cosmos, so the Christian Roman Emperor, together with the Christian Church, governs the political universe."[52] This statement, so it seems, is naive and unnuanced; it also ignores, among other things, the long and tedious process of the development of Christian doctrine. These politically driven power-play charges also neglect the fact that even though the Christian church has been used by the empire for earthly power plays and the church has not always resisted that desire on the basis of the gospel, that abuse can hardly be based on doctrinal, biblical, or theological arguments.

Second, challenges to be taken more seriously focus on the limitations and potential liabilities of the two-nature Christology. It has been rightly asked

48. For a detailed discussion and a constructive proposal, see Kärkkäinen, *Christ and Reconciliation: A Constructive Christian Theology for the Pluralistic World* (Grand Rapids: Eerdmans, 2013), chap. 5.

49. So, e.g., J. Denny Weaver, *The Nonviolent Atonement* (Grand Rapids: Eerdmans, 2001), 86–91 especially.

50. Rosemary Radford Ruether, *Sexism and God-Talk: Toward a Feminist Theology* (Boston: Beacon, 1983), 122.

51. See the important essays by George Huntston Williams, "Christology and Church-State Relations in the Fourth Century," *Church History* 20, no. 3 (1951): 3–33; and *Church History* 20, no. 4 (1951): 3–26.

52. Ruether, *Sexism and God-Talk*, 125.

what the meaning of the concept of "nature" is when applied to Jesus the Christ. How is that originally *substantial* concept related to relationality and communion, features at the heart of trinitarian theology? Or, how compatible with each other are the uses of the term *nature* in relation to humanity, which is created, and divinity, which is not? And so forth.

Third, many wonder whether the two-nature Christology by default tends to shift focus from the "lowliness" of Jesus, his suffering and anguish, to his divinity, exaltation, and triumph.[53] As long as the human nature assumed by the eternal *Logos* is conceived as a nonpersonal human nature, it is difficult to think of a particular human person. It seems that this kind of "assumed" human nature may not look much different from "the human garment of the eternal Son."[54] In other words, it is challenging to see any kind of identity between that type of generic human nature and ours. A corollary question has to do with the sinlessness of Jesus's human nature: can it still be genuine?

Fourth, a significant weakness of the Chalcedonian Christology is the lack of focus on the whole history of Jesus the Christ. As mentioned, the creeds simply omit almost all references to Jesus's earthly life and ministry—the main focus of the Gospel writers' narratives. As Moltmann chidingly points out, in the creeds "there is either nothing at all, or really no more than a comma, between 'and was made man, he suffered' or 'born' and 'suffered.'"[55]

Finally, liberation theologians of various sorts have harshly critiqued these classic christological formulations for the fact that they have "investigated the meaning of Jesus' relation to God and the divine and human natures in his person, but failed to relate these christological issues to the liberation of the slave and the poor in the society."[56] According to leading African American theologian James Cone, the generic categories of "divinity" and "humanity" lack ethical content and can easily lead to practices in which religion supports the hegemony of the empire, as happened with Constantinian Christendom.[57] Many other liberationists have echoed this charge.[58]

Other criticisms of Chalcedon could be added, including the affinity of some of its statements with mythologies of deities visiting this world (as in many Hindu mythologies of *avataras*, embodiments of Vishnu and other

53. E.g., Jürgen Moltmann, *The Way of Jesus Christ: Christology in Messianic Dimensions*, trans. Margaret Kohl (Minneapolis: Fortress, 1993), 52.

54. Ibid., 51.

55. Ibid., 150.

56. James H. Cone, *God of the Oppressed*, rev. ed. (Maryknoll, NY: Orbis, 1997), 114.

57. Ibid., 117.

58. See, e.g., Kelly Brown Douglas, *The Black Christ* (Maryknoll, NY: Orbis, 1994), 111–13.

gods). Let us briefly add a few comments to help put Chalcedon and its critiques in perspective.

A majority of theologians think that the acknowledgment of these weaknesses and lacuna does not warrant leaving behind the Chalcedonian model of explanation. Rather, the task of contemporary theology is to correct, expand, and reorient Christology, building critically on the basis of tradition and also using the Chalcedonian formula as the minimum—and relative, as any human device—criterion. Many of the problems mentioned above go back to the use of the terms *person* and *nature* in an abstract sense. However, they are to be defined and regulated ecclesiastically and theologically. These words are used specifically and can only be understood in that particular sense and context. They are not intended to mean that this is everything the Christian church says of Christ; thus the need for continuing constructive theology. Nor is it the case that everyone means—or even originally meant—the same thing with these terms. Note what Dietrich Bonhoeffer says: "The Chalcedonian Definition is an objective, but living, statement which bursts through all thought-forms."[59]

Insightfully, Cambridge University theologian Sarah Coakley prefers to speak of Chalcedon in terms of a *horizon* rather than a *definition*, as is customary; note that the etymology of the Greek term for definition is *horos*, from which we get *horizon*.[60] The other related meanings of *horos* are boundary, limit, standard, pattern, and rule. The last one particularly reminds us of the way early Christianity understood creedal statements—they were "rules of faith" (*regula fidei*). The term "rule" means something like guidance and boundaries that help the community of faith to rule out heretical views and point to the shared consensus, even when everything—or often many things—in the rule are not exactly defined.[61]

This means that the genre of the Chalcedonian definition is not a detached, "objective," systematic explanation of the details of how to understand "nature" or "union" or similar key terms. Rather, as a rule of faith, it is a "grid" through which reflections on Christ's person must pass. As such, it only says so much, and even of those things it considers important to delineate, it does not say everything. Indeed, it leaves open a host of issues, including

59. Dietrich Bonhoeffer, *Christ the Center*, trans. John Bowden (New York: Harper & Row, 1960), 92; I am indebted to Donald G. Bloesch, *Jesus Christ: Savior & Lord* (Downers Grove, IL: InterVarsity, 1997), 70.

60. Sarah Coakley, "What Does Chalcedon Solve and What Does It Not? Some Reflections on the Status and Meaning of the Chalcedonian 'Definition,'" in *The Incarnation: An Interdisciplinary Symposium on the Incarnation of the Son of God*, ed. Stephen T. Davis et al. (Oxford: Oxford University Press, 2004), 160.

61. The term "symbol" for the early creeds served the same function (and cannot be read in the thin sense of the word's contemporary usage).

the most obvious one: what is it that "human" and "divine" nature consist of?[62] Behind Chalcedon, similarly to all rules of faith in early Christianity, is the soteriological intent. Having confessed belief in the God-man, Jesus the Savior, Christians naturally wanted to say as much as they could about the person and "nature" of the Savior. Coakley summarizes it well:

> It does not . . . intend to provide a full systematic account of Christology, and even less a complete and precise metaphysics of Christ's makeup. Rather, it sets a "boundary" on what can, and cannot, be said, by first ruling out three aberrant interpretations of Christ (Apollinarism, Euty-chianism, and extreme Nestorianism), second, providing an abstract rule of language (*physis* and *hypostasis*) for distinguishing duality and unity in Christ, and, third, presenting a "riddle" of negatives by means of which a greater (though undefined) reality may be intimated. At the same time, it recapitulates and assumes . . . the acts of salvation detailed in Nicaea and Constantinople.[63]

Afterword to Chalcedon: Some Global Implications

An important afterword to the discussion of Chalcedonian debates has to do with implications for global Christianity. Since patristic times, there have been churches that (somewhat inaccurately) are called non-Chalcedonian. This means that while they have endorsed classical Christian beliefs about Jesus Christ, they have defined them differently from Chalcedon. The above-mentioned two "heresies"—Nestorianism and monophysitism—serve as the most important examples. Christianity in Asia, particularly in India and China, is intimately involved with these "heresies." As is well known, the two non-Chalcedonian traditions continued their influence in China and India to the point that they represent the "normal" theologies there.

Christianity was introduced to China by the Nestorians in the first half of the seventh century during the rule of the powerful Tai Tsung of the Tang Dynasty. "Two-nature" Christology was preached in the most influential country of that time[64] until the mid-ninth century, when an imperial edict virtually banned Christianity (and Buddhism).[65] The Nestorian two-nature Christology was greatly interested in the human nature of Christ, allegedly

62. See further Coakley, "What Does Chalcedon Solve," 161–63.
63. Ibid., 161.
64. Of course, the Arab Empire was the other world power at the time.
65. Kenneth Scott Latourette, *A History of Christianity*, vol. 1, *Beginnings to 1500*, rev. ed. (New York: Harper & Row, 1975), 324–25. While a number of Christian communities in central and east Asia fell under the power of the Mongols and thus Islam, the Christian church slowly established itself in many places in central Asia and India and then returned to China—again

because "it had long been known for its care for the poor and hungry" and therefore saw it fitting to "emphasize Christ's humanity, for only a completely human Christ could be an ethical and moral example."[66] In the thirteenth century, the Nestorians had an archbishop in Peking (then the Mongol capital), and early in the fourteenth century the Nestorian patriarch is reported to have had twenty-five metropolitans in China, India, Turkestan, Kashgar, and elsewhere.[67] This is all to say that the Nestorian interpretation of Christ has been immensely influential in the history of the largest continent of the world.

To India, Christianity came in the form of monophysite Christology. An instrumental role in the later consolidation of monophysitism was played by West Syrian Jacobite churches in the eighth and ninth centuries. While their earliest strongholds were in Africa (Egypt and Ethiopia), monophysites soon gained influence beyond Syria in Asian regions such as in the powerful church of Armenia, and even in Persia, as the influence of Nestorianism began to fall off in Persian Asia.[68] Monophysitism also found its way to India in the seventeenth century in the form of the (Jacobite) Syrian Orthodox Church.

These two examples suffice to make the point that in our pluralistic global world, doctrinal issues appear in ever new and complex contexts. It is given to the current global church to negotiate these diverging interpretations of Christ, both of which have been labeled heretical by the mainline tradition.

Subsequent Developments

Post-Chalcedonian Issues

Although it would be naive and uninformed to claim that nothing much happened after Chalcedon (that is, after the fifth century) until the emergence of modernity in the aftermath of the Protestant Reformation, it may be justified for an introductory text to move from the end of the patristic era, in which orthodoxy was established (through its wrestling with its challenges), up to the radical revision attempts beginning from the time of modernity or the Enlightenment. With some exaggeration it can be said that after the end of the seventh century, very few, if any, formative christological innovations or debates took place—with the exception of soteriology, the doctrine of

with the Nestorians—in the eleventh century. Samuel Hugh Moffet, *A History of Christianity in Asia*, vol. 1, *Beginnings to 1500* (San Francisco: HarperSanFrancisco, 1992), 401–2.

66. Moffet, *History of Christianity in Asia*, 1:171.

67. Latourette, *History of Christianity*, 1:591.

68. For the spread of monophysitism in Persia, see ibid., 1:243–47.

salvation. That is, from the beginning of the second millennium, innovative "theories of atonement" began to emerge in order to challenge, enrich, and reshape the received first millennium's "recapitulation" and "ransom" views. These are not covered in this book, however.

This means that here at the end of this early history section we can merely register some noteworthy debates and developments after Chalcedon without going into detail. Recall that behind all of them, including developments through the Reformation, Chalcedon stood as the critical standard and milestone.

As the discussion above on global implications revealed, many Eastern theologians, while paying lip service to the formulation of Chalcedon, with its focus on two natures, did not want to give up their preference for one-nature Christology.[69] In the sixth century a movement of monophysite churches arose from the Eastern camp as a dissenting voice to Chalcedon. This was but a radicalization and continuation of the Alexandrian intuitions among the Christian churches of the eastern Mediterranean world: Coptic, Armenian, and Syrian churches. Even though dissenters, they are included in the Orthodox family.

A related problem arose from the debate concerning the natures of Christ: the question of the will(s) of Christ. Macarius of Antioch firmly declared that he would never say Christ had "two natural [independent] wills" even if he "were to be torn limb from limb and cast into the sea."[70] Monothelitism (from two Greek terms meaning "one will"), the belief that Christ had only one will rather than two, soon encountered serious opposition. First, it seemed to contradict the Bible, for in Gethsemane Christ prayed, "Not my will but thine be done," obviously implying that Christ made a distinction between his two wills. Furthermore, monothelitism seemed to go against the doctrine of salvation, as Gregory of Nazianzus noted in his famous axiom, "That which has not been assumed cannot be healed."[71] If Christ did not have a real human will, then the human will, which obviously is the root of all sin and rebellion against God, has not been saved. "If he did not assume a human will, that in us which suffered first has not been healed."[72] As a consequence, in 681, the

---

69. Not even the Second Council of Chalcedon (under the auspices of the Emperor Julian) could win over the monophysites—though it also condemned Antioch's greatest christologist, Theodore of Mopsuestia, for too radical a focus on two natures! See further Pelikan, *Emergence of the Catholic Tradition*, 277.

70. Quoted in Jaroslav Pelikan, *The Spirit of Eastern Christendom (600–1700)*, vol. 2 of *The Christian Tradition: A History of the Development of Doctrine* (Chicago: University of Chicago Press, 1974), 70.

71. Gregory Nazianzen, *Letter to Cledonius the Priest against Apollinarius*, in NPNF[2] 7:440.

72. Ibid.

Third Council of Constantinople declared that Christ had two wills. Nevertheless, monophysites never agreed with that declaration.[73]

A related debate, usually named the iconoclastic controversy, divided minds particularly in the Christian East. It had to do with reverence toward images of Christ and the saints. Its christological point of departure was simply this: provided that Christ is (both human and) divine, by worshiping Christ's image one may be in a danger of making of an image of God, strictly forbidden in the Bible. Leading Eastern theologian St. John of Damascus, among others, had to offer careful and nuanced guidance in this delicate matter.[74]

Christologies at the Reformation

Since the Protestant Reformers were interested in issues other than Christology, such as authority and Scripture, the role of the papacy, and the doctrine of salvation, and since they made every effort to stand on the foundation of classic creeds and confessions,[75] they were careful not to innovate. They engaged christological topics only at points that they were intimately related with other topics, such as the sacraments. In reflections on the incarnation, they revived the ancient debate, often referred to under the catchword *communicatio idiomatum*. As discussed, that concept arose with the rise of Nestorianism and has since been debated.[76]

Between Lutherans and the Reformed a difference of orientation emerged. Generally speaking, Lutherans strongly affirmed the union of the two natures. The technical expression is *finix capax infiniti*: the finite (human nature of Jesus) is able to bear the infinite (divine nature). While not confused with each other (which would entail an Apollinaristic type of monophysitism), the two natures are integrally united. The Reformed party's slogan *finitum non capax infiniti* keeps the two natures more distinct without of course separating them (because that would mean Nestorianism).[77]

In this light it is understandable that Luther also applied his logic to the question of Christ's suffering and death on the cross; as is well known, his "theology of the cross" (as opposed to "theology of glory") is a leading theme

---

73. For an accessible account, see Placher, *History of Christian Theology*, 91–92.

74. See further Schwarz, *Christology*, 159–60; Placher, *History of Christian Theology*, 91–94.

75. Consider that the *Book of Concord*, the collection of Lutheran confessions, opens with three classical creeds: the Apostles', Nicaea-Constantinople, and Athanasius. Lutherans' most important single confession, *The Augsburg Confession*, paragraph 2, carefully restates creedal statements on Christology.

76. For a brief consideration, see further Placher, *History of Christian Theology*, 83–84, and for a more extensive discussion, Pelikan, *Emergence of the Catholic Tradition*, 249–51, 270–74.

77. For a useful discussion, see Bloesch, *Jesus Christ*, 62.

in all of his thinking.[78] In some real sense, the Lutheran Reformer argued that God suffered and died on the cross. If Christ was both human and divine, the person who died on the cross was both the human Jesus and the divine God. In Luther's words, "Since the divinity and humanity are one person in Christ, the Scriptures ascribe to the deity, because of this personal union, all that happens to the humanity, and vice versa. . . . It is correct to talk about God's death."[79] This view has sometimes been called *theopassianism*, meaning that God suffered in a genuine way. (This is not quite the same as *patripassianism*, which means that God as the Father suffered, a form of modalism.) The Reformed Calvin and Zwingli understandably disagreed. Zwingli insisted that "strictly speaking, the suffering appertains only to the humanity."[80] Even Calvin, who was more careful here, had great reservations about the application of the *communicatio idiomatum* formula: "Surely God does not have blood, does not suffer, cannot be touched with human hands."[81] Lutherans and the Reformed could not agree on this issue. Yet neither side was labeled heretical, even though Lutherans accused the Reformed of Nestorian tendencies while the Reformed accused Lutherans of monophysitism.

A corollary dividing issue among Reformed and Lutheran Reformers emerged with regard to how best to understand the presence of Christ at the Eucharist. The most distinctive view was presented by Zwingli, to whom the ascended Christ in heaven could only be present at the Lord's table spiritually. Luther, following more strictly the principle of *communicatio idiomatum*, took Christ's presence even on earth more literally. Consider the following passage from his *This Is My Body*, his explanation of the theology of the Lord's Supper (building on the analogy of how to understand "the Hand of God"): "the right hand of God is not a specific place in which a body must or may be, such as on a golden throne, but is the almighty power of God, which at one and at the same time can be nowhere and yet must be everywhere."[82] In the hands of Lutheran Scholasticism, the post-Reformation highly technical presentation of doctrine, this view was developed into the principle of Christ's "ubiquity"; that is, because all the divine attributes can be attributed

78. For a detailed introduction, see chap. 4 in Kärkkäinen, *One with God: Salvation as Deification and Justification* (Collegeville, MN: Liturgical Press, 2004).

79. Quoted in "The Formula of Concord," article 8, in *The Book of Concord*, ed. Theodore G. Tappert (Philadelphia: Fortress, 1959), 599.

80. Ulrich Zwingli, *On the Lord's Supper*, Library of Christian Classics 24 (Philadelphia: Westminster, 1953), 213.

81. John Calvin, *Institutes of the Christian Religion*, ed. John T. McNeill, trans F. L. Battles (Philadelphia: Westminster, 1960), 2.14.2.

82. Luther, *This Is My Body* (1527), in *Luther's Works*, vol. 37, *Word and Sacrament III* (Philadelphia: Augsburg Fortress, 1961), 57.

to Christ's human nature as well, it can be also omnipresent. In other words, Christ's "bodily" presence can be had in every eucharistic meal.[83]

There were differing orientations not only between various camps of Reformation churches but also between the representatives of a single tradition. A good example is the seventeenth-century debate among Lutheran theologians about Christ's act of emptying himself in the incarnation (Phil. 2:7 talks about Christ emptying himself [Greek *kenōsis*]). All Lutheran theologians agreed that the Gospels make no reference to Christ making use of all his divine attributes on earth, but they differed on how to explain this. Two camps emerged. One argued that Christ used his divine powers in secret, the other that he abstained from using them altogether (this was called kenotic Christology, which later developed in many directions).[84] Both parties believed that Christ possessed divine attributes; the question concerned their use.

Although these debates about important nuances in christological doctrine at the time of the Reformation and earlier are noteworthy, they can still be considered in-house debates within the wider Christian consensus about Christ. That consensus itself came under devastating critique, however, after the dawn of modernity, as the Enlightenment focus on reason began its penetrating critique and its quest for the "real" Jesus. To that topic we turn next.

83. For details, see Schwarz, *Christology*, 170–75 (including Calvin's views on this issue).
84. For details, see Kärkkäinen, *Christ and Reconciliation*, 167–68.

4

Modern Christologies

The Quests of (the Historical) Jesus

Enlightenment: The Age of Independent Reason

What Are the Enlightenment and Modernity?

The Reformation era not only helped renew religion—both in its Protestant and Roman Catholic forms[1]—but it also helped initiate a reform in intellectual, cultural, and societal spheres. With the invention of the printing press, which helped disseminate writings such as Luther's bestselling catechisms into the hands of the ordinary people (at least those who were able to read), the turn to individualism and other humanistic values began to emerge and found its zenith in the Enlightenment and subsequent modernity.[2]

1. Rather than speaking of the Protestant Reformation and the Counter-Reformation, as was customary in the past in Protestant communities, a more proper set of terms is simply Protestant and Catholic Reformations, respectively.
2. For other related factors contributing to the rise of the Enlightenment, including the religious wars of the sixteenth century, see the brief discussion in William C. Placher, *A History of Christian Theology: An Introduction* (Philadelphia: Westminster, 1983), 236–37. To be more precise, there are various expressions of the "Enlightenment," based in France, Germany, and England, among which we find competing and conflicting visions of what "modernity" means. For a shorter discussion, see James Schmidt, "What Enlightenment Project?," *Political Theory* 28,

73

Leading German modern philosopher Immanuel Kant expressed the mentality of the Enlightenment (from the German *Aufklärung*, meaning literally
"clearing up") with these oft-cited words:[3]

> *Aufklärung* is our release from our self-imposed tutelage—that is, a state
> of inability to make use of our own understanding without direction from
> someone else. This tutelage is self-imposed when its cause lies not in our
> own reason, but in a lack of courage to use it without direction from some-
> one else. . . . "Have courage to use your own reason!"—that is the motto of
> *Aufklärung*.[4]

Reason rather than tradition or belief became the main locus of authority and point of departure for thinking in these various modern movements
beginning from the eighteenth century.[5] However, to call the Enlightenment
merely the "Age of Reason" is not descriptive enough. Many earlier periods
could similarly be called eras of reason. Just think of the High Middle Ages,
with masters such as Anselm of Canterbury or Thomas Aquinas. What makes
the Enlightenment unique is the *independence* of the use of reason. Reason
independent from church authorities, divine revelation, and other people's
tutelage is the essence of the Enlightenment.

Enlightenment thinkers had a specific conception of rationality and knowledge. They believed that science had developed valid and ever-cumulative
methods of acquiring knowledge about the world and human beings. By
replacing what they took as ancient superstitions, traditional religious convictions, and authorities, whether secular or ecclesiastical, the new methods
of science promised to reveal the mysteries of the world and to reduce the
conditions of ignorance, poverty, and perhaps even wars. Finally science
had the freedom it needed to pursue its own questions. That which could
be proven by reason was taken as valid knowledge; faith-based opinions,
ancient or contemporary, were considered mere illusions to be "cleared"
by modernity.[6]

---

no. 6 (2000): 734–57. A more thorough treatment is Louis K. Dupré, *The Enlightenment and
the Intellectual Foundations of Modern Culture* (New Haven: Yale University Press, 2004).
    3. While Kant was a leading Enlightenment thinker in Germany, in France figures such as
the philosopher René Descartes and the writer-intellectual Voltaire (François-Marie Arouet),
and in England John Locke, helped pave the way for modernity.
    4. Cited in Alister E. McGrath, *The Making of Modern German Christology, 1750–1990*,
2nd ed. (Grand Rapids: Zondervan, 1994), 14.
    5. Some analysts derive the beginning of the Enlightenment from the mid-seventeenth cen-
tury's ending of religious wars.
    6. For a succinct, nontechnical discussion, see Placher, *History of Christian Theology*,
238–42.

Critique of Traditional Christologies

The concept and role of religion came under critical scrutiny and radical revision. Instead of "revealed" religion (based on the divinely inspired Scriptures, whether the Bible or, say, the Qur'an), "natural" or "rational" religion came to the fore. Just consider the titles of works of two British thinkers: John Locke, *Reasonableness of Christianity* (1695), and John Toland, *Christianity Not Mysterious* (1669), with the telling subtitle *A Treatise Shewing, That There Is Nothing in the Gospel Contrary to Reason, Nor above It: And That No Christian Doctrine Can Be Properly Called a Mystery*.[7]

Protestant theology was more open to the influence of Enlightenment thinking than was Catholic theology. This is understandable in light of the fact that Protestantism involved a desire to get rid of collective decision making in favor of individual freedom to decode Scripture for oneself. Protestantism has always been less institutionally governed and more open to individual initiatives, and it has produced many varied denominational and ecclesiastical forms.

Biblical criticism was a natural result of this new openness to the independent use of human reason. Whereas in the past the biblical text had been taken as a trustworthy historical account, now it faced mounting doubts and denials. The Bible had to be studied as a historical document according to the same methods and principles applied to the study of any other historical work. It was not left to the Holy Spirit but to the human spirit and human reason to judge whether the text was convincing.

The Enlightenment found no place for the miracle stories of the evangelists or those in the rest of the New Testament.[8] Although David Hume's *Essay on Miracles* (1748) did not necessarily do away with all notions of the miraculous, it set such strict rational criteria for deciding their authenticity that the traditional concept was virtually dismissed. Great French thinker Denis Diderot went so far as to claim that "if all Paris were to assure me that a dead man had come to life again, I should not believe a word of it."[9] Similar treatment was given to traditional doctrines such as original sin and the fall, the Trinity, and so forth. Eventually, a whole-scale reevaluation of all basic Christian doctrines, particularly the Nicene-Chalcedonian christological-trinitarian tradition, was deemed necessary.

7. For details concerning the doctrine of revelation and authority in Christian theology, see chap. 1 in Kärkkäinen, *Trinity and Revelation: A Constructive Christian Theology for the Pluralistic World*, vol. 2 (Grand Rapids: Eerdmans, 2014).

8. This section is heavily indebted to the excellent survey in McGrath, *Making of Modern German Christology*, 23–28.

9. *Diderot and the Encyclopaedists*, ed. John Morley (London: Chapman and Hall, 1878), 1:54.

No wonder a full-scale reconsideration of the meaning of Jesus of Nazareth and Christology emerged—an endeavor called the "quest of the historical Jesus." Whereas during the first seven centuries all basic christological
doctrines were established and many of them put in a more or less binding
creedal form, beginning from the end of the seventeenth century, they all came
to be either rejected or revised.[10]

The Original Quest of the Historical Jesus: "Jesus of History" or "Christ of Faith"

As usually happens with defining theological terms, the phrase "quest of the
historical Jesus" was coined in hindsight, by Albert Schweitzer, the great New
Testament scholar, in his 1906 book *The Quest of the Historical Jesus: A
Critical Study of Its Progress from Reimarus to Wrede*.[11] The underlying idea
of the quest was to discover the truth about Jesus as he really was, free from the
faith interpretations of the church and theology. Those involved in the quest
anticipated that scientific research into the origins of Jesus would show that
the Jesus of history was different from the Christ of Scripture, the creeds, and
Christian piety. Famously, this agenda was expressed in terms of a distinction
(if not a separation) between the "Jesus of history" (the focus of the quest) and
the "Christ of faith" (the center of traditional Christology). As Colin Brown
puts it succinctly, whereas in pre-Enlightenment theology there was a "quest
for the theological Jesus," now it became the quest of the historical Jesus.[12]

The period covered in Schweitzer's book is commonly called the original
quest of the historical Jesus; it culminated and terminated with Schweitzer's
own critique and constructive proposal at the turn of the twentieth century.
In the 1950s a new quest arose, pioneered by Ernst Käsemann, which was
followed by a third quest that began in the 1980s. Currently we already speak
of the fourth (or even subsequent) quests.

10. It is of course not the case that the modern period marked absolutely the beginning of
skepticism concerning traditionally held beliefs about Christ—there were, e.g., the Spanish
heretic, polymath M. Servetus; Socinians (led by Faustus Socinus); Unitarians; and other non-
trinitarians who were involved in the "Quests before the Quest," as Colin Brown puts it ("Quest
of the Historical Jesus," in *DJG* [2013], 720–24). Those skeptical attempts, however, remained
fairly marginal in relation to orthodoxy.

11. The first English edition of A. Schweitzer's *The Quest of the Historical Jesus* is from
1910 (trans. William Montgomery, published in the UK by A. & C. Black), available at www
.earlychristianwritings.com/schweitzer/.

12. Brown, "Quest of the Historical Jesus," 719. His essay (718–56) is an excellent, succinct,
and well-documented survey of all things quest. My exposition is indebted to it beyond the
number of references.

At the beginning of his *Quest of the Historical Jesus*, Schweitzer speaks about the supreme importance of the new ways of investigating Christology initiated by Hermann S. Reimarus, German scholar of oriental languages: "Before Reimarus, no one had attempted to form a historical conception of the life of Jesus. . . . Thus there had been nothing to prepare the world for a work of such power as that of Reimarus."[13] Although the ideas of Reimarus—a devout churchman rather than a "secular" scholar—about Christ are hardly original among similarly minded contemporary scholars,[14] his massive *Apology or Treatise in Defense of the Reasonable Worship of God* in 1778, particularly the last part titled "The Aims (or Goal) of Jesus and His Disciples," was nothing less than a scandalous attack on traditional christological beliefs.[15]

Reimarus's main argument was that there is a radical difference between the intentions of Jesus of Nazareth himself and those of his disciples and apostles. His goal was to get beyond the New Testament theological accounts back to the "real" historical Jesus, naked and free from later layers of interpretation: "If . . . we desire to gain a historical understanding of Jesus' teaching, we must leave behind what we learned in our catechism regarding the metaphysical Divine Sonship, the Trinity, and similar dogmatic conceptions, and go out into a wholly Jewish world of thought."[16] While not denying the attribution of the Gospels and the rest of the New Testament titles and designations such as "Son of God" and "Messiah," Reimarus opined that they did not imply any notion of divinity. Indeed, Reimarus took the Son of Man designation as the favorite one of Jesus (agreeing with the traditional understanding in which that title denotes humanity, a view now discredited, as discussed above).

At first both Jesus and the disciples considered Jesus a political Messiah; only after their disappointment due to the death of their leader did the new vision of a "spiritual redeemer" emerge. Reimarus believed that it was in the interest of the disciples to make changes to the Gospel stories to accommodate their beliefs about what appeared to be the historical case. Indeed, Reimarus became convinced that the disciples in that sense turned out to be deceivers when they attributed miracles, even resurrection and ascension, to that man from Nazareth. In sum, "the Christian faith, the new system developed by the disciples, is largely a literary device and void of historical undergirding."

---

13. Schweitzer, *Quest of the Historical Jesus*, 13.

14. For likeminded English deists and others, see Hans Schwarz, *Christology* (Grand Rapids: Eerdmans, 1998), 8–9.

15. In *Fragments from Reimarus*, trans. and ed. Charles Voysey, vol. 1 (London and Edinburgh: Williams and Norgate, 1879), chap. 2, available at http://babel.hathitrust.org/cgi/pt?id=mdp.39015003351916;view=1up;seq=5.

16. Reimarus's view, summarized by Schweitzer, *Quest of the Historical Jesus*, 17.

Doctrines such as the Trinity, sacraments, and two-nature Christology do not stem from Jesus but his followers.[17]

Reimarus's companion Gotthold E. Lessing, who helped publish posthumously Reimarus's tractate on Christology—himself a noted playwright and librarian at Wolfenbüttel (whose name gave rise to the common nomenclature Wolfenbüttel Fragments in reference to Reimarus's *Apology*)—is another pioneer of the original quest. While obviously supporting his colleague's ideas—why else would he have helped publish them?—Lessing's own concerns about Christology were somewhat differently oriented. In the programmatic short essay "On the Proof of the Spirit and of the Power," he makes the famous claim that the "*accidental truths of history can never become the proof of necessary truths of reason.*"[18] This is meant to say that even if we could believe that, say, Christ rose from the dead, that in itself hardly establishes the "Christ of faith" of Christian tradition. Indeed, although Lessing himself did not "for one moment deny that in Christ prophecies were fulfilled . . . [and] that Christ performed miracles," since those happenings are based on reports of contemporaries (to the New Testament) rather than experiences of today, they have no binding authority to make the modern person hold to Jesus's teaching and Christian doctrines.[19] This is the "ugly broad ditch" between faith and history.[20] Herein one can easily see the difference between Reimarus and Lessing. Whereas for the former the question of historicity (the factual nature of the events reported in the Gospels) was the main concern, for the latter the issues of reason and rationality stood at the center.[21]

Alister McGrath employs a useful pedagogical device to illustrate the problems of Lessing as expressed in Lessing's essay (and in his tiny tractate "The Religion of Christ," 1780[22]). Three interrelated aspects of the "ugly broad ditch" between faith and history/reason can be discerned. First, "a *chronological* ditch, which separates the past from the present": the current reader of the New Testament Gospels is at the mercy of original eyewitnesses and in that sense under others' authority rather than guided by one's own reasonable judgment. Second, "a *metaphysical* ditch, which separates accidental historical truths from universal and necessary rational truths": even if, for the sake of argument, a dead man might have risen (as Lessing believed had happened

---

17. Schwarz, *Christology*, 9–14, citation from 13.
18. Gotthold E. Lessing, "On the Proof of the Spirit and of the Power," in *Lessing's Theological Writings*, trans. Henry Chadwick (London: Adam & Charles Black, 1956), 53 (emphasis original), available at http://faculty.tcu.edu/grant/hhit/Lessing.pdf.
19. Ibid.
20. Ibid., 55.
21. For useful comments, see Schwarz, *Christology*, 14–15.
22. In *Lessing's Theological Writings*, 106.

in Jesus's case), that would hardly constitute a universal law of resurrection. Third, "an *existential* ditch, which separates modern human existence from the religious message of the past": if—again, for the sake of argument—we assume that not only are the Gospel reports reliable and that Christ's resurrection guarantees a general confidence in the resurrection of others, what is its relevance to the modern person here and now?[23] These are, as one can easily see, really the questions of modernity. They also stand at the center of twentieth- and twenty-first-century skepticism about the meaningfulness and relevance of Christian belief in Jesus Christ.

Liberal and Critical Investigations into the "Life of Jesus"

In the aftermath of Lessing and Reimarus, two types of literature abounded, each of which tried to approach the life of Jesus from a distinctive perspective: the rationalist lives of Jesus and the more conservative lives of Jesus. The rationalist lives of Jesus sought to provide natural explanations for unusual events and thus to continue the Enlightenment agenda of advancing independent human reason as the guide to religion. These rationalist lives of Jesus attempted to offer a reasonable explanation of Jesus's person and actions. H. E. G. Paulus, in his *Life of Jesus as the Basis for a Pure History of Early Christianity* (1828), argued that what was truly miraculous about Jesus was his holy disposition. Individual miracle stories were capable of rational explanation. Jesus did not walk on water but was standing on the shore. The five thousand were fed by those who had brought extra provisions, and so on.[24] In contrast to rational critics, those with more conservative leanings, who were afraid of the collapse of the entire foundation of Christian faith, attempted to produce traditional harmonizations of the Gospels as evidence of the historical reliability of the Bible. These more conservative students of Christology also produced a number of meditative and spiritual lives of Jesus. J. J. Hess's popular three-volume *History of the Three Last Years of the Life of Jesus*, finished in 1772, highlighted the significance of Jesus's suffering for Christian piety, while F. V. Reinhard's *Essay on the Plan Developed by the Founder of Christianity for the Benefit of Humanity* (1781) focused on the ethical contribution of Jesus's teaching.[25]

Although the formative critical voice in the investigation into the life of Jesus was D. F. Strauss, who "forced the question of either a purely historical or a purely

---

23. McGrath, *Making of Modern German Christology*, 28–33, citation on 29.
24. See Brown, "Quest of the Historical Jesus," 726.
25. For details, see Colin Brown, "Historical Jesus, Quest of," in *DJG* (1992), 327.

supernatural Jesus,"[26] the first one to lecture on and write a full-scale monograph, *The Life of Jesus* (1820), was the "father of modern Protestant theology" and leading liberal of the nineteenth century, Friedrich E. D. Schleiermacher.

Differently from scholarship contemporary to us today, Schleiermacher took John's Gospel as a historical outline into which could be inserted materials from the other Gospels. Furthermore, his take on the meaning of Jesus's life was thoroughly filtered through human "religious experience." Whereas Kant, the above-mentioned first Enlightenment thinker, had located religion in the ethical realm—having not found any basis for rational religious beliefs in his *Critique of Pure Reason* (1781), but only in *Critique of Practical Reason* (1788)—and most other Enlightenment advocates had insisted on the rational nature of religion, Schleiermacher located religion in human experience and "feelings." The German term translated "feeling" (*das Gefühl*), however, is much broader than the English term. It denotes a primal, non-rational awareness of religious intuitions beneath and beyond all human experiences of the world, or as Schleiermacher puts it more technically: religion has to do with "the immediate consciousness of the universal being of all finite things in and through the infinite, of all temporary things in and through the eternal."[27] This Schleiermacher named the "feeling of absolute dependence" (or, strangely, "piety").[28] He then reinterpreted all traditional doctrines, including Christology, in light of this template. To give an example regarding the doctrine of Scripture and revelation: whereas for traditional theology, the Bible was divinely inspired authority, true and inerrant in its propositions, and for Enlightenment "liberals" it was an erroneous collection of humanly authored stories to be investigated with the help of critical methods, Schleiermacher chose a third way. For him, Scripture (any scripture for that matter, whether Muslim or Hindu) was a valuable collection of sharing of authentic human experiences of the dependence on the ultimate (which Christianity, along with other theistic faiths, names "God"). In Jesus the feeling of absolute dependence, religious "self-consciousness," had reached its zenith. Not a literal understanding of incarnation or the Chalcedonian two-nature Christology, then, but the presence of this profound awareness of God was crucial to understanding who Jesus was; talk of Jesus's "divinity" meant his possession

26. Brown, "Quest of the Historical Jesus," 726.

27. Friedrich Schleiermacher, *On Religion: Addresses in Response to Its Cultural Critics*, trans. Terrence N. Tice (Richmond: John Knox, 1969), 36, cited in Stanley J. Grenz and Roger E. Olson, *Twentieth-Century Theology: God and the World in a Transitional Age* (Downers Grove, IL: InterVarsity, 1992), 44; for an accessible account of Schleiermacher's theological outlook, including Christology, see 39–51.

28. For his own classic exposition, see Friedrich Schleiermacher, *The Christian Faith*, ed. H. R. Mackintosh and J. S. Stewart, 2nd ed. (London: T&T Clark, 1999), §4 (pp. 12–18) particularly.

of the highest degree of God-consciousness.[29] Jesus's redemptive role, hence, is to help us realize and cultivate this God-consciousness.

Having read Schleiermacher's *The Life of Jesus*, D. F. Strauss subjected it to sharp criticism in his late work, the posthumously published *The Christ of Faith and the Jesus of History* (1865). Strauss was suspicious of the fact that with all his liberalism Schleiermacher still held to some "supernaturalist" views. Apart from Schleiermacher's critique, Strauss was not content with the quest pioneers' total rejection of "mythical" elements in the Gospels, particularly miracles. Although Strauss of course did not believe the miracle stories were historically true, neither did he regard the disciples who shared these narratives as fraudulent. Rather, the mythical way of telling stories was a legitimate device in ancient cultures; it helped the followers of Jesus to share about their profound experiences. Strauss thought that whether the resurrection happened was not important; what was important was that belief in the resurrection communicated an expression of the cultural consciousness of a primitive people. Furthermore, Strauss both critiqued and reappropriated the teachings of his famed philosopher-teacher G. W. F. Hegel. In his analysis of religion, Hegel had come to the conclusion that incarnation, the idea of divine-human union, was a necessary idea and could be justified rationally.[30] Strauss concurred with his teacher but asked himself the obvious question: must the idea of incarnation necessarily be realized in one specific individual? Why not the entire human race or a group of human beings? In other words, incarnation for Strauss is not limited to one particular person such as Jesus of Nazareth. Rather, incarnation means the presence of God(-consciousness) in humanity in general. Jesus may just be a special, "concentrated" expression of that presence.

Strauss's main contribution to the research into the life of Jesus is his two-volume *The Life of Jesus Critically Examined* (1835–36). With all his criticism, Strauss accepted a basic historical framework for the life of Jesus as depicted in the Gospels: childhood in Nazareth, baptism by John the Baptist, public ministry of teaching, clash with the religious leaders, and finally death on the cross. (He maintained that this outline derived from the creative imagination of the early church in its desire to interpret Jesus's life as a fulfillment of Old

29. As Schleiermacher, in the epithet to §94 (p. 385) in *Christian Faith*, puts it in his awkward manner: "The Redeemer, then, is like all men in virtue of the identity of human nature, but distinguished from them all by the constant potency of His God-consciousness, which was a veritable existence of God in Him."

30. Hegel's reasoning was based on his unique (and complicated) idea of the coming to self-consciousness of the (Absolute) "Spirit" as explanation of the happenings of history. The culmination of that process was to be the coming together of the spiritual and physical (historical). For a primer, see McGrath, *Making of Modern German Christology*, 50–55.

Testament prophecy.) Be that as it may, the historical basis in itself was not the key for Strauss, because Christian proclamation has little to do with history; what matters is the philosophical interpretation of Jesus's meaning. In this, of course, he deviated radically from the early church, which, according to Strauss's explanation, grounded its belief in theological interpretation (while at the same time believing that what was proclaimed was also historically valid). This "mythical" theological interpretation of the early church finally turned the historical Jesus into a divine figure. Toward the end of his life, Strauss published yet another book, *The Old and New Faith* (1872), which conveys that Jesus has no special relevance for Christianity; what matters is a purely humanistic ethic. This work soon brought Strauss's influence to an end.[31]

The "This-Worldly" Jesus of Classical Liberalism

Although Albrecht Ritschl is routinely linked together with Schleiermacher, there is also an important difference: whereas for the latter religious experience was the key, for the former the ethical and moral implications of Christology stood at the center. In that sense, Ritschl was closer to the rationalism and ethical orientation of Kant. As a result, the pragmatic meaning of religion was most important to Ritschl and his school. That said, Ritschl also shared much of Schleiermacher's "turn to experience" mentality, as for him also the key to understanding Jesus's significance was that "Jesus was conscious of a new and hitherto unknown relation to God," that is, the highest God-consciousness. And this was what Jesus shared with his disciples, as "his aim was to bring his disciples to the same attitude toward the world as his own . . . [and that] he might enlist them into the world-wide mission of the Kingdom of God."[32] But the notion of the "kingdom" of God is not the transcendent, otherworldly reign of God expected to transform the world at the eschaton, but rather a this-worldly common sharing of values and love among human beings. Furthermore, Jesus's divinity is far from the traditional Chalcedonian doctrine and has to do, as mentioned above, with the highest level of God-consciousness. His death on the cross is not substitutionary in the traditional sense but rather "the highest proof of faithfulness to His vocation."[33]

31. For a lucid exposition, see McGrath, *Making of Modern German Christology*, 58–63.
32. A. B. Ritschl, *The Christian Doctrine of Justification and Reconciliation: The Positive Development of the Doctrine*, trans. H. R. Mackintosh and A. B. Macaulay (Edinburgh: T&T Clark, 1900), 3:386, available at https://archive.org/stream/christiandoctri00edgoog#page/n8 /mode/2up. See further Schwarz, *Christology*, 26–28.
33. Ritschl, *Christian Doctrine of Justification and Reconciliation*, 3:447, cited in Schwarz, *Christology*, 27.

In his massive three-volume *The Christian Doctrine of Justification and Reconciliation* (1870–74), particularly in the last volume, Ritschl sets out clearly this ethical-moral orientation of not only the doctrine of salvation but all of Christology as well. Based on Jesus's desire to share his God-consciousness with his followers, the "missionary" power of the Christian message can be found in "the faith of the Christian community . . . the representations of the original consciousness of the community."[34] It is an ethical vocation.[35] This means that "axiomatic for Ritschl is that there is no direct or immediate relationship between the believer and God, in that the presence of God or Jesus Christ is always mediated through the community of faith."[36]

Another leading liberal at the turn of the twentieth century, Adolf von Harnack, a church historian from the University of Berlin, set himself a noble task with the publication of the pamphlet *What Is Christianity?* (1902).[37] In this work he responds to the basic, simple question of what Christianity was originally, that is, in the mind of Jesus, apart from later theological developments. Harnack came to the conclusion that there were three basic principles in Jesus's teaching: the (ethical) kingdom of God, the Fatherhood of God, and the infinite value of the human soul.[38] In Harnack's view Jesus's preaching was concerned exclusively with the individual and summoned a call to repentance. All Christian dogmas, especially trinitarian and christological doctrines, were later hellenizations of the simple gospel of Christ. In this sense Harnack talks about the "deterioration of dogma"; he regarded the development of dogma as a sort of chronic illness. The notion of dogma owed nothing to Jesus but was a result of the transition of the gospel from a Jewish to a Hellenistic milieu.

The most famous statement of Harnack, often quoted and often misinterpreted, is, "The Gospel, as Jesus proclaimed it, has to do with the Father only and not with the Son, . . . [though Jesus] was its personal realization and its strength, and this he is felt to be still."[39] This does not mean that Jesus was not conscious of his calling but rather that the entire thrust of Jesus's message and life was to serve the kingdom of his Father. Central to Harnack's project

---

34. Ritschl, *Christian Doctrine of Justification and Reconciliation*, 3:3; I am indebted to McGrath, *Making of Modern German Christology*, 84.

35. Ritschl, *Christian Doctrine of Justification and Reconciliation*, 3:446.

36. McGrath, *Making of Modern German Christology*, 84; see 82–87 for a useful exposition of Ritschl's Christology.

37. With the subtitle *Lectures Delivered in the University of Berlin during the Winter Term 1899–1900*, trans. Thomas Bailey Saunders, available at https://archive.org/details/whatischristian 01saungoog.

38. Adolf von Harnack, *What Is Christianity?*, trans. Thomas Bailey Sanders, 2nd rev. ed. (London: Williams and Norgate; New York: G. P. Putnam's Sons, 1902, 1957), 55.

39. Ibid., 154 (emphasis in original removed).

was the rejection of classical Christologies and the rejection of the claim that exegetes can reach the historical Jesus, the image of the ethical kingdom. In line with liberalism, he dismissed apocalyptic elements in the Gospels and saw doctrines as secondary, for the gospel is nothing other than Jesus Christ himself. The gospel is not a doctrine about Jesus but is the person of Jesus.

Classical liberalism brought the quest to its logical end. Those involved in a naturalistic inquiry into the life and psychology of Jesus of Nazareth were naive in that they hoped to go behind the interpretations of Jesus's followers. Several scholars, mainly in the area of New Testament studies, trained in the spirit of liberalism, however, soon began to doubt the possibility of what liberalism attempted and raised a series of questions that the movement could not address. To this topic we turn next.

The Collapse of the Original Quest and Liberal "Jesusology"

Soon after the heydays of Ritschl's and Harnack's liberal proposals, severe doubts began to emerge about the propriety of the methodology and aim of the original quest. The aim of classical liberalism to construct an authentic, psychological life of Jesus as an ethical teacher and a model of righteousness came to an end with the rise of various types of criticism. The decisive beginning of the growing skepticism was marked by Albrecht Ritschl's son-in-law, Johannes Weiss, in his work *Jesus' Proclamation of the Kingdom of God*, published in 1892. The basic thesis of Weiss was that, as unappealing as the idea of apocalypticism and the coming end of the world was to modern readers of the Bible, there was no denying the thoroughly eschatological nature of Jesus's preaching. Late Jewish apocalypticism and the expectation of the imminent end of the world and the coming of the Messiah and the kingdom of God are radically otherworldly; for Weiss the kingdom of God as proclaimed by Jesus was a "radically superworldly entity which stands in diametric opposition to this world."[40] The this-worldly liberal portrait of Jesus was but a "Kantian ideal,"[41] a hangover from the first generation of the quest. If eschatology is removed from his preaching, Jesus is turned into a liberal teacher who has little to do with the "real" Jesus of Nazareth.[42]

Albert Schweitzer took up the basic theses of Weiss and brought them to their logical conclusion. For Schweitzer, similarly, liberalism's portrait of Jesus

40. Johannes Weiss, *Jesus' Proclamation of the Kingdom of God*, trans. R. Hyde and D. Holland (1892; repr., Minneapolis: Fortress, 1971), 114.

41. Ibid., 133.

42. For details, see McGrath, *Making of Modern German Christology*, 102–4.

was a false modernization in its neglect of the apocalyptic and eschatological.[43] Jesus did not send the Twelve to teach the people about ethical life but to warn them of the coming end and judgment; indeed, the disciples were not expected to come back from their mission trip until the end. When the end did not come, Jesus decided to offer his own life as a sacrifice, in order to prompt the coming of the kingdom. Out of these accounts emerged a portrait of Jesus as a remote and strange figure. Rather than a polished liberal teacher of ethics, "He comes to us as one unknown."[44] Jesus expected to be the Son of Man, the Messiah coming on the clouds as a judge; he truly believed that this was to be his vocation. Similarly to the early disciples, the modern followers of Jesus, rather than taking only his ethical lessons and carving out the rest, should rather forsake everything for the sake of the kingdom, whose value is infinite. Schweitzer himself did that: though a noted medical doctor, musical expert (on J. S. Bach), and cultural figure, he left for Africa to do medical missions!

Is Schweitzer's, then, a call to traditional belief? Not at all. Ironically—and similarly to Weiss—he did not believe that Jesus's eschatological message is historically true. No eschaton will happen, soon or later. Jesus was badly wrong. The end did not come! He was mistaken in his hopes. These are the oft-cited words of Schweitzer, speaking of the One who follows John the Baptist:

> Soon after that comes Jesus, and in the knowledge that He is the coming Son of Man lays hold of the wheel of the world to set it moving on that last revolution which is to bring all ordinary history to a close. It refuses to turn, and He throws Himself upon it. Then it does turn; and crushes Him. Instead of bringing in the eschatological conditions, He has destroyed them. The wheel rolls onward, and the mangled body of the one immeasurably great Man, who was strong enough to think of Himself as the spiritual ruler of mankind and to bend history to His purpose, is hanging upon it still. That is His victory and His reign.[45]

What then is the significance and value of the life of Jesus for us? Unrelated to historical events or factuality, it has to do solely with the "mighty spiritual force [which] streams forth from Him and flows through our time also . . . [and] can only be understood by contact with His spirit which is still at work in the world."[46] Schweitzer responded that the value of Jesus comes through knowing him in a mystical encounter, "in spirit": Jesus still "comes" to us as we follow

43. Before *The Quest of the Historical Jesus*, Schweitzer had joined the long row of life of Jesus students with his less renowned work *The Mystery of the Kingdom of God: The Secret of Jesus' Messiahship and Passion* (1901); for an introduction, see Schwarz, *Christology*, 30–31.

44. Schweitzer, *Quest of the Historical Jesus*, 403.

45. Ibid., 370–71.

46. Ibid., 399, 401, respectively.

him in discipleship. Through this encounter we gain inspiration to live authentic lives and to put into practice the noble teachings and life-example of Jesus.

Weiss and Schweitzer were of course not the only ones who facilitated the collapse of the original quest and subsequent liberal Christology. McGrath—again, employing a highly useful pedagogical device—presents the actors of the collapse under four groups. Let it suffice to list them here with brief descriptions; interested readers can easily find details elsewhere:

1. The *apocalyptic* critique of Weiss and Schweitzer, analyzed above.
2. The *skeptical* critique, which doubted seriously whether in the first place any solid historical information about Jesus was available. Particularly important here was Gospel of Mark student William Wrede, who showed that even this shortest Gospel—previously considered a less-theological account of Jesus's life and ministry—is a theological rather than neutral biographical narrative.
3. The *dogmatic* critique, associated with Martin Kähler, to whom, even if it were available, historical information was of little value. What the church needs is not the "historical Jesus" but the "Christ of faith" (so much ridiculed by the quest). Consider the somewhat ironic title of his monograph, *The So-Called Historical Jesus and the Historic, Biblical Christ* (1892).
4. The *historicist* (of the history of religion) critique, which considered Jesus's meaning and significance merely in the context and light of the contemporary (to Jesus) religio-cultural matrix.[47]

The Diverse "Quest(s)" of Jesus in the Twentieth Century

The "New Quest" of the Mid-Twentieth Century

In the 1950s the new quest of the historical Jesus was taken up by Ernst Käsemann, a student of Rudolf Bultmann who wanted to revise the agenda of the original quest. Käsemann believed that writing a biography of Jesus, as the original quest had hoped to do, was not possible, nor could he agree with Bultmann and others that the historical details of Jesus's earthly life were secondary to faith in Christ. Nevertheless, Käsemann believed that the main content of Jesus's public life could be reconstructed; available sources give a clear enough picture of Jesus's life and teaching.

47. McGrath, *Making of Modern German Christology*, chap. 5; for a brief description, see 101–2.

In order to discern the agenda of this "new quest," as it is also called sometimes, a brief look at the Christology of Rudolf Bultmann is necessary. It was
mainly his own students who started the second quest and in doing so critiqued
their teacher in more than one way. What makes the figure and thinking of
Rudolf Bultmann so fascinating is that he drew from many different sources,
including neo-orthodoxy, existentialism (particularly Martin Heidegger), and
liberalism, even though he saw himself as a critic of that movement. A contemporary of Karl Barth, Bultmann was both indebted to and critical of his ideas.

Bultmann had to deal with the aftermath of the collapse of the liberal
quest of the historical Jesus, but he did so in light of a rapidly developing
New Testament methodology. One of his most contested methodological
choices is the strict application of the double dissimilarity principle; that is,
only those features of Jesus's teaching that are unlike both Jewish background
and evolving Christian characteristics are considered authentic. Bultmann
was one of the main architects of a new approach to Gospel study, namely,
form criticism. Doing form criticism, he also wanted to analyze in detail
the traditions that lay behind the Gospels as they were shaped by Christian
communities. In this perspective, the *Sitz im Leben*, life situation, of the early
church, rather than the historical life of Jesus, becomes the main hermeneutical cue. Understandably, then, many sayings attributed to Jesus were seen as
the theological interpretations of his followers. Furthermore, Bultmann also
continued the history of religions interpretation, according to which leading
ideas of the New Testament, including the titles of Jesus, go back to ancient,
non-Jewish sources of ancient cultures.[48]

In sum, rather than the history of Jesus, it is the *kerygma*, the proclamation, that is central to faith. The resurrection of Jesus, rather than a historical
event, belongs to the faith and proclamation of the church, which found in it
a new hope and inspiration. For that kind of purpose, the understanding of
the category of myth as developed by Strauss is useful: rather than dismissing
(or making a judgment on the use of) the myth, it has to be identified and
demythologized in order to make sense for the modern reader of the New
Testament. Bultmann's concept of *Entmythologisierung* ("demythologiza-
tion") may be his single best-known contribution. In that sense, the concept
of myth was not negative for Bultmann—as it is for most people. Most people
think that because there is a conflict between history and myth, myth expresses
something negative, something that did not happen. But myth is Bultmann's

48. For Wilhelm Bousset's Christology as the forerunner, as expressed in his widely acclaimed
Kyrios Christos (1913), to whose English translation (1970) Rudolf Bultmann wrote the preface,
see Brown, "Quest of the Historical Jesus," 731.

device for speaking of events that cannot be dealt with in the confines of the language of history and scientific observation. Yet Bultmann seemed not to be bothered by the implication of cultural supremacy: that he considered the beliefs of the primitive people to be mythical, in contrast to enlightened modern people, smacks of elitism.[49]

As mentioned above, many of Bultmann's students became critical of him. Käsemann was far more optimistic about the possibility of gaining a basic outline of Jesus's public ministry. While not necessarily disavowing the strictures of the double dissimilarity principle, he also believed that the Gospels contain both history and *kerygma*, not only the latter. In other words, although the Jesus of history and the Christ of faith cannot be equated, they are linked, and the latter is already present in the former. In Käsemann's understanding, there is a dynamic continuity (again, against Bultmann) between the preaching *of* Jesus and preaching *about* Jesus (by his followers). Moreover, the preaching about Jesus is the only source for the history of Jesus.

Käsemann's colleague Gerhard Ebeling similarly contended that if it were shown that Christology had no basis in the historical Jesus but rather was a misinterpretation of Jesus, the entire idea of Christology would be ruined. In other words, to confess Christ, we have to know something about the Jesus of history. Somewhat similarly, another famed student of Bultmann, Günther Bornkamm, argued in *Jesus of Nazareth* (1956), "Quite clearly what the Gospels report concerning the message, the deeds and the history of Jesus is still distinguished by an authenticity, a freshness, and a distinctiveness not in any way effaced by the Church's Easter faith. These features point us directly to the earthly figure of Jesus."[50]

The double dissimilarity principle was understandably rejected by more traditional scholars, who were also influenced by the towering figure of Bultmann but who at the same time held quite radically different views. More prominent among those are the Germans: Joachim Jeremias argued that although "it might not be possible to recover Jesus' actual words, it was possible to hear his *ipsissima vox*, the voice of Jesus with its distinctive manner of speaking."[51] Another important figure was Oscar Cullman, whose *The Christology of the New Testament* (1957) constructed a functional Christology based on the titles of Jesus.[52]

49. See further J. D. G. Dunn, "Myth," in *DJG* (1992), 567–68.

50. G. Bornkamm, *Jesus of Nazareth*, trans. I. McLuskey, F. McLuskey, and J. M. Robinson (New York: Harper, 1960), 24, cited in Brown, "Quest of the Historical Jesus," 733; see 733–34 for details of the "new quest"; a useful, accessible account is Schwarz, *Christology*, 48–51.

51. As described by Brown, "Quest of the Historical Jesus," 734.

52. Along with the German scholarship, British and American scholars of course also labored in the field, representing, generally speaking, more traditional views than leading German theologians. For a survey, see Brown, "Quest of the Historical Jesus," 735–38.

Not surprisingly, Bultmann responded with harsh criticism against these and other former students of his in the loosely connected "new quest" movement. By the beginning of the 1960s, that initiative had basically been dissolved—and soon new quests emerged, very different from the former two. At the same time, both globalization and extreme diversity began to characterize these quests, which still continue.

The "Third Quest" and Beyond

Yet to be seen is the future of the third quest and whether it has a common agenda other than the conviction that more can be known about Jesus than was discovered or admitted in the earlier quests. Even though it is not easy to present common "results" of this latest phase of the quest, it can be said that most participants share the conviction that Jesus was neither the Jesus of liberal Protestantism nor of the new quest. Rather, he was a historical figure whose life and actions were rooted in first-century Judaism with its particular religious, social, economic, and political conditions.

Three main varieties of the third quest have been distinguished: the radical, the conservative, and the "new perspective."[53] The most radical approach to the study of Jesus is exemplified by the Jesus Seminar in the United States, founded by the late Robert W. Funk and John Dominic Crossan. It seeks to examine the layers of tradition in both the New Testament and extracanonical accounts of Jesus's words in order to find a valid base for determining who Jesus really was. The Jesus Seminar has become famous for its series of red-letter editions of Jesus's words, such as *The Parables of Jesus*, published in 1988. Utilizing various colors, this particular scholarly consensus communicates its opinion concerning which words of Jesus most likely came from Jesus himself (red). Contesting the ecclesiastical canonical principle, the Jesus Seminar also treats the apocryphal *Gospel of Thomas* as the "fifth Gospel."

Related to the Jesus Seminar is successful popularizer of academic Christology Marcus J. Borg, whose main claim is the non-eschatological Jesus. He contests the authenticity of the "Son of Man" sayings (which refer to eschatological coming) and, in line with the old liberalism, considers the kingdom of God as a this-worldly entity.[54] Borg's proposal has understandably met

53. Suggested by Brown, "Historical Jesus, Quest of," 337–40. A more up-to-date exposition is his "Quest of the Historical Jesus," 738–48, which is followed here.

54. For a strong argument for a non-eschatological understanding, see Marcus J. Borg, *Jesus in Contemporary Scholarship* (Valley Forge, PA: Trinity Press International, 1994), 47–68. For his "new vision" of Christianity, see, among others, *Jesus, A New Vision: Spirit, Culture, and the Life of Discipleship* (San Francisco: Harper & Row, 1987).

with harsh opposition. A nuanced defense of the traditional position is Ben Witherington III's case for "an eschatological but not apocalyptic Jesus."[55] In other words, Witherington dismisses Borg's non-eschatological interpretation as incompatible with too many Gospel passages referring to the eschaton; at the same time, he wants to save Jesus from linkage with extreme apocalypticism of the intertestamental period that focuses almost exclusively on otherworldly expectation at the expense of this-life concerns.[56]

The conservative tradition is represented by the British scholar C. F. D. Moule and his *Origin of Christology*.[57] Moule is critical of the idea of an evolutionary process, after the history of religions school, which connects belief in Christ as a divine figure with conceptions from the surrounding mythical and mystery religions. Instead, Moule believes that the development process through which the Jesus of history became the confessed Christ of faith goes back to Jesus himself and that the process was legitimate. In this regard Moule shows evidence that the titles "Son of Man," "Son of God," "Christ," and "Lord" relate to the historical Jesus and are not foreign to him. In other words, these New Testament titles are not later interpretations of Jesus but are firmly rooted in Jesus's own life and words. The same principle applies to the Pauline developments of Christology.

The leading figure in the "new perspective" (or the "third quest" proper, so to speak) is the British scholar N. T. Wright. His massive six-volume series titled Christian Origins and the Question of God has so far released four monographs focused on Christology and the Gospels: *The New Testament and the People of God* (1992), *Jesus and the Victory of God* (1996), *The Resurrection of the Son of God* (2003), and *Paul and the Faithfulness of God* (2013). Turning around Bultmann's double dissimilarity principle, Wright applies the double similarity principle, where relevant. His overall framework for considering the coming of Jesus is the Old Testament theme of exile and restoration. Although people returned from the exile, the assumption among the Second Temple Jews was that the God of the people of Israel had not yet returned. The Christian contribution is the claim that in Jesus of Nazareth Israel's God has come and now a new future has dawned. Jesus's resurrection from the dead is the announcement of that divine program.

Another highly acclaimed, formative figure of the third quest is J. D. G. Dunn, also from the British Isles. In his mature scholarship he has investigated widely the importance of remembrance of Jesus, as seen from the

---

55. As paraphrased by Schwarz, *Christology*, 64; see 64–65 for details.
56. Ben Witherington III, *The Christology of Jesus* (Minneapolis: Fortress, 1990).
57. C. F. D. Moule, *Origin of Christology* (Cambridge: Cambridge University Press, 1977).

name of his massive monograph *Jesus Remembered* (2003).[58] In complete disagreement with the original quest and Bultmann, Dunn takes the recollection of Jesus by the community and later followers as the key to the knowledge of Jesus. As he puts it, "the quest should start from the recognition that Jesus evoked faith from the outset of his mission and that this faith is the surest indication of the historical reality and effect of his mission."[59] Furthermore, in opposition to the double dissimilarity principle, the Jewishness of Jesus is highly appreciated rather than made an obstacle to historical knowledge.

A distinctive orientation of the third quest—what has been called the "new perspective"—seeks to place Jesus in the context of the religious, social, economic, and political world of Judaism. It asks, Why did Jesus instigate such opposition from the political and religious establishment of the Jews? Several Jewish scholars, including J. C. G. Montefiore, have joined the quest here. Similarly, several non-Jewish scholars, such as John K. Riches, with his work *Jesus and the Transformation of Judaism*, have tried to examine the Jewish background and conditions of the Jesus event.[60]

Of special interest to the third quest is the relationship between Jesus and politics, especially his relationship with the revolutionary movements of his time. For example, it has been suggested that Jesus sympathized with the goals of the Zealot movement, an aggressive nationalist movement, but these sympathies were downplayed by the evangelists. This proposal, however, has met with rejection by the majority of scholars.

The topic of miracles, which has been discussed since the beginning of the original quest of the historical Jesus, has been a subject of lively debate in recent decades. The most radical position has maintained that the miracle stories point to the fact that Jesus was a magician and that the Gospels deliberately tried to obscure the truth. This was the claim of the debated *Jesus the Magician: Charlatan or Son of God?* by Morton Smith (1978).[61] A more balanced and traditional view is represented by Graham H. Twelftree, whose many publications on the topic of miracles, healings, and exorcisms, including

58. J. D. G. Dunn, *Jesus Remembered* (Grand Rapids: Eerdmans, 2003); Dunn, *A New Perspective on Jesus: What the Quest for the Historical Jesus Missed* (Grand Rapids: Baker Academic, 2005).

59. J. D. G. Dunn, "Remembering Jesus: How the Quest of the Historical Jesus Lost Its Way," in *The Historical Jesus: Five Views*, ed. J. K. Beilby and P. R. Eddy (Downers Grove, IL: InterVarsity, 2009), 203, cited in Brown, "Quest of the Historical Jesus," 751.

60. John K. Riches, *Jesus and the Transformation of Judaism* (1980; repr., New York: Seabury, 1982).

61. Morton Smith, *Jesus the Magician: Charlatan or Son of God?* (Berkeley: Ulysses Press, 1998 [1978]).

Jesus the Exorcist (1993), argue for the integral relation of "signs and wonders" to Jesus's ministry and announcement of the kingdom.[62]

It is one of the ironies of history (and theological scholarship) that as soon as everyone thought the quest of the historical Jesus was a chapter in history—interesting in itself but shown to be impossible—a new wave of inquiry emerged in the 1950s. This was followed by the unprecedented enthusiasm of yet another wave, the third quest. While there are radical, irreconcilable differences between these various stages—and one almost questions the wisdom of connecting them terminologically—they share the desire of questioning much of two thousand years of ecclesiastical and theological formulations of Christology. The third quest is alive and well and is currently feeding subsequent quests (a "fourth" quest), and one hopes that those involved will begin to dialogue more widely with systematic and doctrinal theology.

---

62. G. H. Twelftree, *Jesus the Exorcist: A Contribution to the Study of the Historical Jesus* (Tübingen: Mohr Siebeck, 1993).

PART 3

CHRIST IN THE CONTEMPORARY WORLD

Diversity and Unity

The third part of this book is devoted to introducing various christological interpretations that arose during the twentieth century on the basis of the historical and biblical developments studied above. The twentieth century produced more christological interpretations than any other century in the history of Christian theology. And the continual appearance of new monographs and articles on the topic has created a situation in which no one can keep up with all the developments. For a basic survey such as this, however, a discussion of selected approaches is sufficient.

This wide network of interpretations will be divided into three subsections: the first will map out Euro-American Christologies, which still lay the foundation for much of global thinking about Christ. The next chapter will delve into the rich interpretations of Christ in the Global South among African, Latin American, and Asian theologians. The following chapter, then, will introduce "contextual" Christologies represented by various types of female theologians (feminist, womanist, *mujerista*, and others), black theologians, Hispanic or Latino/a, and Asian Americans, as well as postcolonialists and queer scholars. These interpretations challenge the more mainstream and traditional Euro-American ones.

Among the wide array of "mainstream" Euro-American christologists to be covered first, the following nine scholars have been selected with denominational and "agenda"-related diversity in mind. All the selected figures are also household names in their own fields, beginning with the late Swiss Reformed Karl Barth, often called the church father of the twentieth century. John Zizioulas of Greece with his communion theology represents the Eastern Orthodox tradition, less well known among Western Christians. The late Karl Rahner of Germany, a leading twentieth-century Roman Catholic theologian, represents the world's largest Christian tradition. Two Germans, Lutheran Wolfhart Pannenberg and Reformed Jürgen Moltmann, are self-evident choices to cover key Protestant views, as both of them have left a lasting mark on constructive theology at large and Christology in particular. Often marginalized, two younger church traditions—Baptist and Anabaptist/Mennonite traditions—are represented by the late Canadian Stanley Grenz and the American Norman Kraus. The late John Hick, the world's leading pluralist, and American process theologian John Cobb Jr. are highly renowned grand old men in their respective orientations. Regretfully, some key Christian traditions had to be omitted because of lack of space: there are no Anglicans or Pentecostals/charismatics in the list, any more than Methodists.

5

European-American Christologies

Karl Barth: Dialectical Christology

The Theology of the "Wholly Other"

No other theologian in the early part of the twentieth century reacted so vehemently and with such influence against classical liberalism as Karl Barth. Having been trained by the leading liberals of the end of the nineteenth century, including Adolf von Harnack, Barth grew completely frustrated with its program, not least because of his pastoral work. Preaching to the simple mountain folks in his homeland, Switzerland, he felt as if the Bible had been emptied of its life-changing power in the hands of modern liberals. With the rise of Nazi tendencies in Germany and his homeland, Barth also became deeply concerned about the this-worldly agenda of liberalism. He proposed a theology of the "Wholly Other" and juxtaposed it with liberalism—to which he posed this question: "What did it know and say of the *deity* of God?" And he answered the rhetorical question with these chiding critical comments:

> For this theology, to think about God meant to think in a scarcely veiled fashion about man. . . . To speak about God meant to speak in an elevated tone about . . . man—his revelations and wonders, his faith and his works. There is no question about it: here the man was made great at the cost of God—the divine God who is other than man, who sovereignly confronts him, who immovably

and sovereignly stands over against him as the Lord, Creator, and Redeemer. This God . . . was in danger of being reduced . . . to a pious notion—to a mystical expression and a symbol of a current alternating between a man and his own heights and depths.[1]

Fittingly, Barth's theology is often called "dialectical theology"—or "theology of crisis"—as it presupposes both a gulf and an incompatibility between humanity and God. Only God, in his love and freedom, may reach across the divide. This is of course diametrically opposed to liberalism's principle of continuity and the immanence of God and Christ in human experience. This program of Barth's was forcefully presented in his commentary *The Epistle to the Romans*, first published in 1919 and completely revised three years later. Reading the epistle, so formative for the Protestant Reformation, Barth found that it speaks of a holy, transcendent God and sinful, fallen humanity. Only because of Christ, the God-man, can the broken relationship and missing knowledge of God be healed.

Another descriptive nomenclature for Barth's theology is "neo-orthodoxy." On the one hand, Barth helped theology return to the orthodoxy of pre-Enlightenment times with the affirmation of divine revelation, the deity of God, the two-nature Christ, the virgin birth, the incarnation, death on the cross, the resurrection, and the ascension. He did not have any queries about the deity of Christ. And while he gladly acknowledged the humanity of Jesus Christ as well, in his "from above" approach (as discussed in the introduction) he was not interested in the historical questions. What mattered was the decision of faith.[2] On the other hand, with all his opposition to modernity's influence on theology, the Swiss scholar also remained the child of the Enlightenment. This is best illustrated in his theology of revelation: while insisting on the need for God, in his freedom and love, to reveal God's own life and purposes toward humanity (which represents the "old" paradigm), he also believed that the Bible as such is not the divine revelation but rather its witness—and as such a fallible human document (the "new," that is, *neo-*).

Christ as the Mediator

When constructing his theology of the Wholly Other, Barth also left a lasting mark on the revival of trinitarian theology—another topic dismissed by

1. Karl Barth, *The Humanity of God*, trans. Thomas Wieser and John Newton Thomas (Louisville: John Knox, 1960), 39–40; the essay is from 1956.
2. For useful comments and citations from Barth, see Hans Schwarz, *Christology* (Grand Rapids: Eerdmans, 1998), 192–93.

liberalism.[3] In his monumental *Church Dogmatics*—four parts with thirteen volumes (which remained unfinished at the time of his death in 1968)—the doctrine of the Trinity forms the preface, even before the doctrine of revelation. This alone makes Barth's Christology fairly traditional, as one can hardly have a classic trinitarian doctrine of God without Jesus as the God-man.

Not surprisingly, then, Christ is the key to God's revelation. Revelation is possible only by virtue of Christ's mediation. Thomas Aquinas and other medieval theologians had assumed with their "analogy of being" conception that knowledge of God is an innate capacity within human experience or human nature; in other words, they assumed an analogy between creation and the Creator. Barth repudiates this idea and suggests the principle of an "analogy of faith": knowledge of God and faith are possible only because God graciously gives them in Jesus Christ, who is both God and human. Barth's simple formula of revelation puts it this way: "*God* reveals Himself. He reveals Himself *through Himself*. He reveals *Himself*."[4] Roman Catholic commentator Hans Urs von Balthasar brilliantly called Christ the "hour glass" in Barth's theology: all dealings of the Triune God are filtered through Christ.[5] Similarly, Anglican commentator Alister McGrath says, "Every theological proposition in the *Church Dogmatics* may be regarded as christological, in the sense that it has its point of departure in Jesus Christ."[6] As a result, Barth did not give any credit to "revelations" outside Christ. While he was not of course naive enough to dismiss the presence of religious and perhaps even salvific insights among religions and cultures, he refused to call them "revelation." Revelation can only be had in and through Christ.

In Barth's Calvinist-Reformed tradition, Christ is called the Mediator—often expressed with the help of three mediatorial roles: prophet, king, and priest. The role of Christ as the mediator between the transcendent God and humankind comes to focus in Christ's dual role as the agent of revelation and of reconciliation. By virtue of the incarnation, God and humanity are united. In his divinity, Jesus represents God to humankind; in his humanity, Jesus represents humankind to God. By virtue of the incarnation, human beings can be made participants in the covenant to which God has obliged himself.

3. Consider that in Schleiermacher's monumental, eight-hundred-pages-plus *The Christian Faith*, the Trinity appears in the appendix and covers merely ten-plus pages!

4. Karl Barth, *Church Dogmatics*, ed. Geoffrey William Bromiley and Thomas Forsyth Torrance, trans. G. W. Bromiley (Edinburgh: T&T Clark, 1956–75; online ed. by Alexander Street Press, 1975), I/1, 296.

5. Hans Urs von Balthasar, *The Theology of Karl Barth*, trans. Edward T. Oakes, SJ (San Francisco: Ignatius Press, 1992), 197.

6. Alister E. McGrath, *The Making of Modern German Christology, 1750–1990*, 2nd ed. (Grand Rapids: Zondervan, 1994), 131.

In this covenant, God acts on behalf of humankind through and in Christ. Because of his christocentrism, Barth takes the category of the Mediator as the defining feature of Christ. He puts it succinctly:

> When Holy Scripture speaks of God it concentrates our attention and thoughts upon one single point. . . . It is the God who in the first person singular addressed the patriarchs and Moses, the prophets and later the apostles. . . . We may look closer and ask: Who and what is the God who is to be known at the point upon which Holy Scripture concentrates our attention and thoughts? . . . From first to last the Bible directs us to the name of Jesus Christ. It is in this name that we discern the divine decision in favour of the movement towards this people. . . . And in this name we may now discern the divine decision as an event in human history and therefore as the substance of all the preceding history of Israel and the hope of all the succeeding history of the Church.[7]

An Electing God and Elected Man

Another formative category in Calvinist-Reformed theology is election. Building on the legacy of St. Augustine, Calvin worked out a robust theology of divine election that has two sides to it: election (proper), the divine choice from eternity to save some, and reprobation, the damnation of others. Reformed Orthodoxy (sometimes called Reformed Scholasticism) of post-Reformation times, under the ablest successor of Calvin, Theodore of Beza, made this a technical doctrine with much sophistication. Barth both affirmed and radically revised his own tradition's teaching.

Where Barth endorsed Calvinism had to do with the mediatorial role of Christ in election. All God's dealings go through Christ: "Between God and man there stands the person of Jesus Christ, Himself God and Himself man, and so mediating between the two. . . . In Him God stands before man and man stands before God, as is the eternal will of God, and the eternal ordination of man in accordance with this will."[8] Where he sharply diverged from his own tradition was his novel idea of the Christ as both the electing God and the elected human being: Christ is "not only the Elected. He is also Himself the Elector."[9] This is the newly revised meaning of "double predestination" for Barth. This is also the ground for the election of us all.

> If God elects us too, then it is in and with this election of Jesus Christ, in and with this free act of obedience on the part of His Son. It is He who is manifestly

7. Barth, *Church Dogmatics*, II/2, 52–53.
8. Ibid., 94.
9. Ibid., 105.

the concrete and manifest form of the divine decision—the decision of Father, Son and Holy Spirit—in favour of the covenant to be established between Him and us. It is in Him that the eternal election becomes immediately and directly the promise of our own election as it is enacted in time, our calling, our summoning to faith. . . . When we ask concerning the reality of the divine election, what can we do but look at the One who performs this act of obedience, who is Himself this act of obedience, who is Himself in the first instance the Subject of this election.[10]

In other words, in contrast to the traditional Reformed position, it is not individuals who are the object of election but rather Jesus the Christ. And, differently from Calvinism, rather than two destinies, it seems as if Barth ends up—with the force of his theological logic—endorsing some kind of universalist position: now that everyone has been elected in Christ, who was put to death (having chosen "reprobation, perdition, and death"[11] on our behalf) and raised to new life, no one will be judged again. "If the teachers of predestination were right when they spoke always of a duality, of election and reprobation, of predestination to salvation or perdition, to life or death, then we may say already that in the election of Jesus Christ which is the eternal will of God, God has ascribed to man the former, election, salvation and life; and to Himself He has ascribed the latter, reprobation, perdition and death."[12] The difference between Christians and non-Christians is that whereas the former know they are elected, others do not. Although opinions about details vary among Barth experts, the face-value reading of Barth's treatment in *Church Dogmatics* seems to imply something like that.

John Zizioulas: Communion Christology

Being as Communion

John Zizioulas, bishop of Pergamon, Greece, is among the most significant Eastern Orthodox theologians of our day. Like Bishop Kallistos (born

10. Ibid., 105–6.
11. Ibid., 163.
12. Ibid., 162–63; so also 306: "The man who is isolated over against God is as such rejected by God. But to be this man can only be by the godless man's own choice. The witness of the community of God to every individual man consists in this: that this choice of the godless man is void; that he belongs eternally to Jesus Christ and therefore is not rejected, but elected by God in Jesus Christ; that the rejection which he deserves on account of his perverse choice is borne and cancelled by Jesus Christ; and that he is appointed to eternal life with God on the basis of the righteous, divine decision."

Timothy Ware of England), Zizioulas has built bridges between the East and the West and has introduced the distinctive theological heritage of Orthodoxy to the West. Zizioulas is, however, not only a faithful interpreter and teacher of his own tradition but also a self-critical constructive theologian who is not afraid to correct Eastern theology in light of ecumenical influences. Because his whole lifework has been done in the West, his ideas have been accessible to the Western guild of theologians. However, most if not all general introductions to theology ignore the contributions of Zizioulas's theology and the Eastern tradition.

Zizioulas's most distinctive idea, which permeates his theology and his view of Christ, is that of *koinōnia*, communion. The title of his main book reflects the basic orientation of his thought: *Being as Communion*. His theology in general and his Christology in particular are based on an ontology of personhood acquired from a consideration of the being of the Triune God. Zizioulas opposes any kind of individualism that is destructive to community. There is no true being without communion, relationality; nothing exists as an "individual" in itself. Even God exists in communion, as eternal communion of Father, Son, and Spirit: "The being of God could be known only through personal relationships and personal love. Being means life, and life means *communion*."[13]

Zizioulas draws an analogy between the being of God and human beings. What is most characteristic of God is his being in relation. As the Trinity, the three persons of the Godhead interrelate with one another. They have an intra-trinitarian love relationship. With this same love, the Triune God relates to human beings and the world and embraces them in divine-human *koinōnia*. Zizioulas's basic argument thus runs as follows:

> From the fact that a human being is a member of the Church, he becomes an "image of God," he exists as God Himself exists, he takes on God's "way of being." This way of being . . . is a way of *relationship* with the world, with other people and with God, an event of *communion*, and that is why it cannot be realized as the achievement of an *individual*, but only as an *ecclesial* fact.[14]

In fact, Zizioulas insists that communion is not just another way of describing being, whether individual or ecclesial, but that it belongs to the *ontology* of being. Thus, we should speak of an actual "ontology of communion." This concept, interestingly, parallels the way the Roman Catholic Church defined its

13. John Zizioulas, *Being as Communion: Studies in Personhood and the Church*, trans. John Meyendorff (Crestwood, NY: St. Vladimir's Seminary Press, 1997 [1985]), 16.
14. Ibid., 15 (emphasis added).

view of community at the Second Vatican Council (1962–65). *Lumen Gentium* (no. 9) of Vatican II, the main ecclesiological document, says that God "has, however, willed to make men holy and save them, not as individuals without any bond or link between them, but rather to make them into a people who might acknowledge him and serve him in holiness."

"Person" and "Individual"

Foundational to Zizioulas's Christology is the thesis that, on the one hand, God exists only as person in communion within trinitarian persons and that, on the other hand, Christ is the person par excellence. Christ is not merely an individual but rather a person, since his identity is constituted by a twofold relationship: his relationship as Son to the Father and his relationship as head to his body, the church. According to Zizioulas, in the personhood of Christ and his incarnation, alienating individualism was overcome. Christology is the proclamation to humankind that their individualized natures can be "assumed" into the personhood of Christ and so freed from individualism in a true personhood and communion.

From this "ontology" of communion, Zizioulas constructs the concept of "person" (note that the subtitle for his main book is *Studies in Personhood and the Church*). He makes a distinction between "biological" and "ecclesial" being: the former, which is not yet "personal" in nature, refers to a human being apart from communion with God and others, while the latter denotes a person living in *koinōnia*. As a result of the fall, the human being exists "biologically," in individualism, in a perverted existence. The human being as an individual affirms himself or herself against God and other human beings. The ultimate consequence of this is death. Sin for Zizioulas means turning away from personal communion with God and other fellow humans to communion with only the creaturely world. This kind of "individual" can never be a "person" in the true sense of the term.

The individual, however, can move from biological to ecclesial being—being in communion with God and other people—by virtue of joining the church communion through baptism and faith. In contrast to the merely biological existence in which humans exist as disconnected individuals, in the church humans are made persons, persons in communion.

This distinction between person and individual is the foundational principle underlying all of Zizioulas's theology and Christology. In Christ and in his church, the way of existence as an individual is overcome. To be a person means that one is "ecstatic" (from two Greek terms meaning "out" and "stand") with "a movement toward communion." In other words, no person is a person in his or her individuality but in referring to something outside his or her self. The movement toward communion gives true human freedom because the human being is able to transcend himself or herself. It is only in communion with others (including God) that individuals become persons and can fulfill their destiny.

Being in communion does not, however, mean downplaying the distinctive personhood of each individual. "The person cannot exist without communion; but every form of communion which denies or suppresses the person is inadmissible."[15]

Christ and the Spirit

One of the most foundational differences of orientation between the Western (Roman Catholic, Protestant, Anglican) and Eastern (Orthodox) traditions has to do with the deeply pneumatological (Spirit-oriented) emphasis of the latter. Without in any way undermining the centrality of Christ, Eastern theology is "Spirit-sensitive" in that all theological foci are influenced by the Spirit, including Christology. The doctrine of the church, ecclesiology, is a case in point. Eastern theology aims at a proper synthesis between Christology and pneumatology, rather than (as is the norm in Western Christianity) speaking of the church merely as the body of Christ. Eastern theologians remind us that, in the New Testament, Easter (the work of Christ) and Pentecost (the outpouring of the Spirit) belong together. We see the mutual relationship between the Son and the Spirit in that just as the Son came down to earth and accomplished his work through the Spirit, so also the Spirit came into the world, sent by the Son (John 15:26). The work of the Spirit is not subordinate to the work of the Son; nor is Pentecost a continuation of the incarnation but rather its sequel, its result.[16]

Zizioulas rightly notes that the New Testament shows a mutuality between Son and Spirit rather than a priority of either one. On the one hand, the Spirit is given by Christ (John 7:39); on the other hand, there is no Christ until the Spirit is at work either at his baptism (Mark) or at his birth (Matthew and Luke). Both of these views can coexist in one and the same canon. In the Eastern liturgy this mutuality of the Son and the Spirit is exemplified in the way two crucial soteriological events are kept together: baptism, which symbolizes one's identification in Christ's death and resurrection, and confirmation, the occasion for the anointing with the Spirit, happen at the same time. In contrast, in the West they are separated. In fact, in some churches confirmation takes place many years after baptism.

15. Ibid., 18.
16. Chap. 3 of Zizioulas, *Being and Communion*, is devoted to the discussion of the relationship between Christology and pneumatology and their implications for the church.

Speaking of communion, we can say that Christ becomes a historical person only in the Spirit (Matt. 1:18–20; Luke 1:35). Zizioulas is even ready to say that "Christ *exists only pneumatologically.*" In line with Eastern trinitarian sensitivity, he adds that to speak of Christ means to speak at the same time of the Father and the Holy Spirit. This same principle applies also to church communion, the main focus of Zizioulas's theology: "Thus the mystery of the Church has its birth in the entire economy of the Trinity and in a pneumatologically constituted Christology."[17]

Karl Rahner: Transcendental Christology

Anthropological-Transcendental Framework of Christology

If John Zizioulas is the leading contemporary Eastern Orthodox theologian, then the late Karl Rahner is the main figure in recent Roman Catholic theology. No other twentieth-century Catholic theologian exercised such a universal influence, not only within the confines of the largest church in the world—about one-half of all Christians belong to the Roman Catholic Church—but also ecumenically. Rahner's contribution to the Second Vatican Council (1962–65), the formative council that decisively set the Roman Catholic Church on the path of renewal and modernization, has been unsurpassed.

His theology can be called both "anthropological" and "transcendental." In order to understand his Christology, a basic grasp of these terms is essential. First of all, Rahner's approach to theology is anthropological in the sense that while he fully affirms the traditional theology of God—rather than, say, the immanentism of Protestant liberalism—he also believes that the way for human beings to know about God and receive divine grace has to pass through human experience of the world. In that sense, Rahner offers a third way between liberalism and Barth, who opposed it: to paraphrase Barth, in order for Rahner to be able to speak "loudly" of God, we need to speak of humanity but not at the expense of the deity of God. The reason this turn to humanity (as a way of speaking of God) is theologically justified and necessary has to do with incarnation. In the incarnation of Jesus the man, which represents the highest form of God's self-identification with humanity, "God has uttered himself to man victoriously and unsurpassably."[18] Rahner argues: "It is a fact of faith that when God desires to manifest himself, it is as a man

17. Ibid., 112.
18. Karl Rahner, "The Quest for Approaches Leading to an Understanding of the Mystery of the God-Man Jesus," in *Theological Investigations*, trans. David Bourke (New York: Seabury, 1975), 13:200.

that he does so,"[19] which happened when the "Word became flesh" (John 1:14). Indeed, on the basis of this divine embodiment, we not only know the Divine but also the meaning of the human:

> If we want to know what man is, or what flesh means, then we must, so to speak, choose this theological definition of the statement "And the Word became flesh," saying: flesh, man as a bodily, concrete, historical being is just what comes into being when the Logos, issuing from himself, utters himself. Man is therefore God's self-utterance, out of himself into the empty nothingness of the creature.[20]

From this anthropological, incarnation-driven theology, Rahner's key concept of "transcendental method" (and "transcendental experience") can also be grasped.[21] His basic thesis is that God reveals Godself to every person in the very experience of that person's own finite, yet open (to God and divine revelation), transcendence. In Rahner's complicated technical language: "Man is a transcendent being insofar as all of his knowledge and all of his conscious activity is grounded in a pre-apprehension of 'being' as such, in an unthematic but ever-present knowledge of the infinity of reality."[22] Transcendental experiences (whenever a human being acknowledges that human life is more than just what one sees in everyday life) reveal evidence for this openness to revelation and that the grace of God in Christ is nothing foreign to the structure of the human being but belongs to its core. Think of this as an example: one often intuits something one does not yet know for sure. Or think of the category of "transcendental" as the condition of knowledge. In Rahner's technical vocabulary, the natural transcendental nature of humanity is called *potentia oboedientalis*. For him,

> not only are humans always by nature open to God (*potentia oboedientalis*), they are also always supernaturally elevated by God in that transcendental openness so that such elevation becomes an actual experience of God in every human life. God actually communicates himself to every human person in a gracious offer of free grace, so that God's presence becomes an existential, a constitutive element, in every person's humanity.[23]

19. Karl Rahner, "The Body in the Order of Salvation," in *Theological Investigations*, trans. Margaret Kohl (New York: Crossroad, 1981), 17:74.

20. Ibid.

21. For a basic definition and discussion, see Karl Rahner, *Foundations of Christian Faith: An Introduction to the Idea of Christianity*, trans. William V. Dych (New York: Crossroad, 1982), 20–22.

22. Ibid., 33.

23. As paraphrased by Stanley J. Grenz and Roger E. Olson, *Twentieth-Century Theology: God and the World in a Transitional Age* (Downers Grove, IL: InterVarsity, 1992), 245, based on

Evolutionary Christology and Incarnation

Applied now to Christology, it can be said that transcendental Christology "asks about the a priori possibilities in man which make the coming of the message of Christ possible."[24] Not only that, but it "discovers in the human being an inner dynamism or supernatural existential, a longing and affinity for God's very self that reaches its fulfillment in Jesus Christ."[25] Think of its opposite, much more typical of traditional Christologies both in Catholic and Protestant traditions, which could be termed an "extrinsic" approach, in which "God's address to human existence in Jesus Christ comes entirely from the 'outside' and runs counter to human interests and the inner exigencies of human freedom."[26]

Now it is easy to see that anthropological (read here "inner") and transcendental belong integrally together. A deeper look at Rahner's theology of Christ's incarnation helps further clarify this. His doctrine of incarnation not only is based on this anthropological-transcendental orientation but also takes into account the current scientific evolutionary understanding.[27] This is understandable in light of the fact that according to our current knowledge, humanity is the product of a long evolutionary process. Hence, the coming of the divine in humanity cannot be totally divorced from it.

Following his anthropological-transcendental orientation, Rahner teaches that, as the image of God, the human person is "the event of a free, unmerited and forgiving, and absolute self-communication of God." This is because "God . . . has already communicated himself in his Holy Spirit always and everywhere and to every person as the innermost center of his existence."[28] Consequently, human nature is the most fitting vessel to be united with divinity. Incarnation, according to this Jesuit, can thus be understood as the "free, unmerited, unique, and absolutely supreme fulfillment of what humanity means." This view renders incarnation a mystery that "makes sense," rather than an

Rahner, *Foundations*, 116. Grenz and Olson offer a detailed discussion of Rahner's theology, including transcendental method and Christology (238–45).

24. Rahner, *Foundations*, 207. Note that section 3 of chap. 6, on Jesus Christ, is titled "Transcendental Christology."

25. Mark F. Fischer, "Karl Rahner's Transcendental Christology," presentation at Karl Rahner Consultation, Catholic Theological Society of America, Annual Convention in Miami, Florida, June 5, 2013, p. 3 (unpublished, available at http://karlrahnersociety.com/wp-content /uploads/2013/05/Transcendental-Christology-06.08.13.docx.doc).

26. Roger Haight, *Jesus, Symbol of God* (Maryknoll, NY: Orbis, 1999), 17.

27. Note that in Rahner, *Foundations*, section 1 of chap. 6 is titled "Christology within an Evolutionary View of the World."

28. Rahner, *Foundations*, 116, 139, respectively.

unintelligible, contra-rational paradox.[29] In other words, Rahner understands "creation and Incarnation as two moments and two phases of the *one* process of God's self-giving and self-expression, although it is an intrinsically differentiated process."[30] The world—to be more precise, humanity in the world—has been prepared for the coming together of the divine and human.[31]

How would this humanity-driven and world-embracing view of Christology relate to the most urgent question in our pluralist world, namely, the normativity of Christ and interfaith issues? That question bothered Rahner for decades, and he was a formative pioneer in this so-called theology of religions question.

Anonymous Christians and the Normativity of Christ

Rahner was a leading Roman Catholic theologian who witnessed a definitive turn in the relations to other religions of his own church. Indeed, he himself was a formative thinker behind the authoritative formulations of Vatican II (1962–65) on other religions. While some of Rahner's own proposals, particularly the (in)famous "anonymous Christianity," do not represent an official Catholic position, the process of its development certainly has left a mark on his church's standpoint. At Vatican II the Catholic Church formulated an "inclusive" view of other religions, which can be very briefly summarized in the following manner: while Christ is the only way of salvation, persons in other religions who have not heard the gospel may still be saved because of the universal effects of Christ's atoning work. Two conditions are set for the reception of salvific benefits, namely, that one follows sincerely the teachings of one's faith tradition and seeks to pursue ethical virtues as best as one can; these are not merits but rather indications of an incipient, "anonymous" faith that finds its fulfillment only in Christian faith. This view is also "inclusivist" in that many people among other faiths may be included in salvation. At the same time, it rejects pluralism as it holds up the normativity of Christ as the only Savior.[32]

For Rahner, religions are God-given means to seek God, even among those who may not have the opportunity to hear about Christ during their lifetime. In that qualified sense, all religious traditions potentially express truth about

---

29. Karl Rahner, "Jesus Christus, III.B.," in *Lexikon für Theologie und Kirche*, ed. Josef Höfer and Karl Rahner, 2nd ed. (Freiburg: Herder, 1957–68), 5:956; cited in Wolfhart Pannenberg, *Systematic Theology*, trans. Geoffrey W. Bromiley (Grand Rapids: Eerdmans, 1994), 2:293.

30. Rahner, *Foundations*, 197.

31. This section is based on Kärkkäinen, *Christ and Reconciliation: A Constructive Christian Theology for the Pluralistic World* (Grand Rapids: Eerdmans, 2013), 150–51.

32. For details see Kärkkäinen, *An Introduction to the Theology of Religions: Biblical, Historical & Contemporary Perspectives* (Downers Grove, IL: InterVarsity, 2003), chap. 19.

God's self-communication in Christ through the Spirit and therefore are part of the history of revelation. This does not mean, of course, that all religions present equally valid expressions of divine self-revelation: there is error in any religion. Through Christ's death and resurrection, God's gracious self-communication in the Spirit was manifested in history and among humans having been created in God's image.

Rahner argued (along with another noted late Catholic thinker, Yves Congar of France) that there is a state of being (a natural, not-yet-Christian state) in which a person can respond positively to the grace of God even before hearing the gospel. A person in this state qualifies as an "anonymous Christian" insofar as this acceptance of grace is "present in an implicit form whereby [the] person undertakes and lives the duty of each day in the quiet sincerity of patience, in devotion to his material duties and the demands made upon him by the persons under his care."[33] According to Rahner, Christ is present and efficacious in non-Christian believers (and therefore in non-Christian religions) through his Spirit. Rahner even seems to be arguing that anonymous Christians are justified by God's grace and possess the Holy Spirit.

Joseph Wong adequately summarizes Rahner's christologically driven, pneumatological theology of religions:

> Wherever persons surrender themselves to God or the ultimate reality, under whatever name, and dedicate themselves to the cause of justice, peace, fraternity, and solidarity with other people, they have implicitly accepted Christ and, to some degree, entered into this Christic existence. Just as it was through the Spirit that Christ established this new sphere of existence, in the same way, anyone who enters into this Christic existence of love and freedom is acting under the guidance of the Spirit of Christ.[34]

In line with the Catholic standpoint, rather than believing that the anonymous Christians thesis undermines the validity of the church or its mission, Rahner argued that the individual should be brought to the fullness of faith by the church as it obediently carries out its evangelistic mandate.

Having now looked (after Barth) at a formative Eastern Orthodox and a Roman Catholic theologian of Christ, we will turn next to two leading Protestant christologists: Moltmann and Pannenberg.

33. Karl Rahner, "Anonymous Christians," in *Theological Investigations* (Baltimore: Helicon, 1969), 6:394.
34. Joseph H. Wong, "Anonymous Christians: Karl Rahner's Pneuma-Christocentrism and an East-West Dialogue," *Theological Studies* 55 (1994): 630. Wong references Rahner, "Observations on the Problem of the 'Anonymous Christian,'" in *Theological Investigations* (New York: Seabury, 1976), 10:291.

Jürgen Moltmann: Messianic Christology

Jesus Christ "on the Way": A Dynamic Christology

Unlike his famed Lutheran colleague Pannenberg, Moltmann never set out to write a unified systematic theology or summa. Rather, he has produced a great number of important monographs on most all theological topics. Another noted difference has to do with method in theology: whereas Pannenberg aimed at the highest precision and strictures, Moltmann's approach is much more open-ended and creative; for him "theology was, and still is, an adventure of ideas. It is an open, inviting path."[35] Although he had already spoken much of Christology in earlier books, particularly in *The Crucified God* (ET 1972) in relation to divine suffering, and in *The Trinity and the Kingdom of God* (ET 1980) in the context of trinitarian doctrine, his magnum opus on Christology is *The Way of Jesus Christ* (ET 1987).

Since the introductory chapter already has touched on some of the key contributions of Moltmann, it suffices to summarize them here as a way of orientation. First, Moltmann's approach to Christology does not follow the traditional two-nature outline in which Jesus's divinity and humanity and thereafter their union in one person serves as the focus of investigation. Rather, as the title puts it, Moltmann's Christology follows *The Way of Jesus Christ*, that is, the "stations" on the way to his messianic future: earthly life, suffering, death on the cross, resurrection, current rule at the right hand of God, and awaited parousia (return). Second, as the subtitle of the christological book implies—*Christology in Messianic Dimensions*—the Jewish background of Christian understanding is essential to Moltmann. Importantly, he argues that the explanatory categories of the Jewish faith that provide the explanatory frameworks for New Testament Christology are the genesis and development of the hope for the Messiah and the figure of the Son of Man (especially in Dan. 7:14).[36] Third, while deeply theological, Moltmann's approach is "practical" and "therapeutic." It is not enough for him to merely elucidate intellectual fine points about Christology; the work of liberation, healing, and restoration is the ultimate goal.

Third, add to these christological features the following two underlying themes, which shape and orient all of his theology: the prominence of eschatology (as first defined in his inaugural monograph, *Theology of Hope*,

---

35. Jürgen Moltmann, *Experiences in Theology: Ways and Forms of Christian Theology*, trans. Margaret Kohl (Minneapolis: Fortress, 2000), xv.

36. For a careful theological analysis, see Jürgen Moltmann, *The Way of Jesus Christ: Christology in Messianic Dimensions*, trans. Margaret Kohl (Minneapolis: Fortress, 1993), 5–27.

ET 1964) and commitment to an integral trinitarian framework (as most fully developed in *Trinity and the Kingdom of God* but also honed in every major monograph, including the one on pneumatology, *The Spirit of Life*, ET 1992). Finally—and importantly to the pluralistic, global context of the third millennium—Moltmann is far more sensitive to contextual issues than most all Euro-American male theologians. Speaking of his own European context and its limitations, Moltmann remarks, writing in the third person: "For him this means a critical dissolution of naïve, self-centered thinking. Of course he is a European, but European theology no longer has to be Euro*centric*. Of course, he is a man, but theology no longer has to be *androcentric*. Of course he is living in the 'first world,' but the theology which he is developing does not have to reflect the ideas of the dominating nations."[37] Finally, note that, differently from most Euro-American theologians, Moltmann brings into his theological work personal experiences, particularly the horrors of the WWII soldier and POW.[38]

The Theological Significance of Jesus's Earthly Life

A constant criticism by Moltmann against traditional and even contemporary systematic theological accounts of Christ has to do with the curious omission of his earthly life. What is strangely missing, as Moltmann aptly puts it in reference to the ancient creeds, is an interest in what lies between "born of the Virgin Mary" and "suffered under Pontius Pilate." Indeed, "there is either nothing at all, or really no more than a comma, between 'and was made man, he suffered' or 'born' and 'suffered.'"[39] This is markedly different from the Gospels, in which the teachings, healings, exorcisms, pronouncements of forgiveness, table fellowship, and prophetic acts receive most of the space. Over against the creeds' lack of focus on the earthly life of Jesus, Moltmann suggests an amendment, an addition to the creed after "born of the Virgin Mary" or "and was made man":

> Baptized by John the Baptist,
> filled with the Holy Spirit:
> to preach the kingdom of God to the poor,
> to heal the sick,

37. Jürgen Moltmann, *The Trinity and the Kingdom of God: The Doctrine of God*, trans. Margaret Kohl (San Francisco: Harper & Row; London: SCM, 1981), xii (emphasis original).

38. In most every preface to his monographs, Moltmann reflects on the implications for theology of his own experiences of suffering. That is certainly the case with the christological monograph.

39. Moltmann, *Way of Jesus Christ*, 150.

> to receive those who have been cast out,
> to revive Israel for the salvation of the nations, and
> to have mercy upon all people.[40]

One of the surpluses of attending to the theological meaning of Jesus's earthly life has to do with the rediscovery of what he calls "Christopraxis," or "christological theory which is concerned with the knowledge of Christ in his meaning for us today," which leads to discipleship and following Jesus in the community and service to the world.[41] "Christopraxis," Moltmann envisions, "inevitably leads the community of Christ to the poor, the sick, to 'surplus people' and to the oppressed . . . to unimportant people, people 'of no account.'"[42] Moltmann reminds his colleagues in Europe and the United States that so far it has been left mostly to liberation Christologies and Christologies from the Global South to mind the importance of the earthly life of Jesus of Nazareth. Their main concern has been that traditional Christologies, with their focus on creedal traditions and the methodological debate between the "from below" and "from above" camps, lead to christological discussions with no or little relevance to praxis. The New Testament presents Jesus as the friend of the poor, the marginalized, children, and outcasts. Without in any way idealizing poverty, Moltmann rightly speaks of the dignity of the poor—"the hungry, the unemployed, the sick, the discouraged, and the sad and suffering . . . the subjected, oppressed and humiliated people (*ochlos*)."[43]

Yet another benefit of minding the theology of Jesus's earthly ministry is the highlighting of the importance of "Spirit-Christology," that is, the integral relation of Jesus to the Spirit and vice versa. Moltmann reminds us that "Jesus' history as the Christ does not begin with Jesus himself. It begins with the *ruach*/the Holy Spirit."[44] In that sense it can also be said that the workings of the Spirit precede those of the Son.[45] Jesus appears to be the "man of the Spirit," who performs cures of various illnesses, frees people from under demonic powers, and even resuscitates the dead. The charismatic features of Jesus's ministry occupy an important place in the Christology of this German Reformed scholar (which is not the case with most Euro-American systematicians).

40. Ibid.
41. Ibid., 41.
42. Ibid., 43.
43. Ibid., 99.
44. Ibid., 73.
45. Jürgen Moltmann, *The Spirit of Life: A Universal Affirmation*, trans. Margaret Kohl (Minneapolis: Fortress, 1992), xi, 60. On "Messianic Expectations of the Spirit" in the Old Testament, see 51–57.

The Cross of Christ and the Christian Doctrine of God

In his *Crucified God*, the second major monograph, Moltmann established his fame as a "theologian of the cross." Gleaning from Luther, Jewish scriptural scholars of the early twentieth century, and his own wartime experiences, he made the suffering and death of Jesus Christ the center of his attention. At the same time, he wanted to locate suffering and the cross in the wider context of *The Way of Jesus Christ*: "We shall attempt to achieve an understanding of the crucified Christ, first of all in the light of his life and ministry, which led to his crucifixion, and then in the light of the eschatological faith which proclaims his resurrection from the dead, and in so doing proclaims him as the Christ."[46]

Indeed, no other contemporary theologian has underscored this more than Moltmann, who boldly considers "the cross of Christ as the foundation and criticism of Christian theology."[47] In the preface to *The Crucified God* he claims that "whatever can stand before the face of the crucified Christ is true Christian theology. What cannot stand there must disappear."[48]

Jesus was put to death as a blasphemer who was believed to violate the law and tradition as well as to usurp the status of God.[49] There was also a collision with religious authorities, as he was regarded a rebel.[50] Jesus's sufferings were real. Yet even more painful was the rejection, first by his own people and then ultimately by his Father. "To suffer and to be rejected are not identical. Suffering can be celebrated and admired. It can arouse compassion. But to be rejected takes away the dignity from suffering and makes it dishonourable suffering. To suffer and be rejected signify the cross."[51] That said, it is important to understand, Moltmann reminds us, that highlighting the critical role of the cross in Christian faith and theology has nothing whatsoever to do with glorification of suffering in general or of Christ's suffering in particular. On the contrary, "the cross is the really irreligious thing in Christian faith," despite many "roses" added to the cross for mistaken religious, spiritual, and cultural reasons.[52]

46. Jürgen Moltmann, *The Crucified God: The Cross of Christ as the Foundation and Criticism of Christian Theology*, trans. Margaret Kohl (Minneapolis: Fortress, 1993), 112.

47. Subtitle of his *Crucified God*.

48. Moltmann, *Crucified God*, x; so also 65. For the significance of the cross to Christian theology's identity, see 24, and for discussion of the theology of the cross in Paul, Luther, and others, see 69–75.

49. Ibid., 128–35.

50. Ibid., 136–45.

51. Ibid., 55.

52. These misinterpretations of the cross are discussed in detail in Moltmann, *Crucified God*, chap. 2; quote on 37.

While the New Testament gives a due place to the "for us" motif in the suffering of Jesus, including for the whole world (John 3:16), there is also a wider horizon, including the "birth pangs" of the whole of creation (Rom. 8:18–23). This is what Moltmann names the "apocalyptic sufferings of Christ":

> At the centre of Christian faith is the history of Christ. At the centre of the history of Christ is his passion and his death on the cross. We have to take the word "passion" seriously in both its senses here, if we are to understand the mystery of Christ. For the history of Christ is the history of a great passion, a passionate surrender to God and his kingdom. And at the same time and for that very reason it became the history of an unprecedented suffering, a deadly agony. At the centre of Christian faith is *the passion of the passionate Christ*. The history of his life and the history of his suffering belong together. They show the active and the passive side of his passion.[53]

As much as Christ's suffering and cross relate to humanity and the world, in Moltmann's profound theology of the cross they deal ultimately with God. Indeed, for him suffering is a question about God. Hence, the cross is the key to his distinctive trinitarian doctrine. The trinitarian account begins from the cry of dereliction: "Basically, every Christian theology is consciously or unconsciously answering the question, 'Why hast thou forsaken me,' when their doctrines of salvation say 'for this reason' or 'for that reason.' In the face of Jesus' death-cry to God, theology either becomes impossible or becomes possible only as specifically Christian theology."[54] This means that the God of the dying Son Jesus Christ does not shy away from the suffering either of his Son or of the world but rather makes the suffering his own and so overcomes it in hope. All suffering becomes God's so that God may overcome it. At the cross, the Father suffers in deserting his Son.[55] The Son suffers the pain of being cut off from the life of the Father, and the Father suffers the pain of giving up his Son. By doing so, God "also accepts and adopts [suffering] in himself, making it part of his own eternal life."[56] Therefore, the cross is not only an event between God and humanity: "What happened on the cross was an event between God and God. It was a deep division in God himself, in so far as God abandoned God and contradicted himself, and at the same time a unity in God, in so far as God was at one with God and corresponded to himself."[57] Thus, the cross belongs to the inner life of God, not only occurring

53. Moltmann, *Way of Jesus Christ*, 151 (emphasis original).
54. Moltmann, *Crucified God*, 153.
55. Ibid., 243.
56. Moltmann, *Trinity and the Kingdom*, 119.
57. Moltmann, *Crucified God*, 244.

between God and estranged humanity.[58] "God's being is in suffering and the suffering is in God's being itself, because God is love."[59]

What, then, is the reason or motive for God's willingness to suffer? According to the Bible, it is love. Rather than a neutral observer of world events, God is "pathetic" in that "he suffers from the love which is the superabundance and overflowing of his being."[60] Perhaps the best parallel in human life is the self-sacrificial, persistent, and caring love of the mother. Far from this are the classical notions of God's aseity and God's inability to suffer and be vulnerable. The nature of love also requires us to take seriously the idea of the suffering of God. Suffering does not make God less God but rather a truly loving, passionate, involved person. Moltmann lays down his understanding of divine love in these words:

> A God who cannot suffer is poorer than any human being. For a God who is incapable of suffering is a being who cannot be involved. Suffering and injustice do not affect him. And because he is so completely insensitive, he cannot be affected or shaken by anything. He cannot weep, for he has no tears. But the one who cannot suffer cannot love either. So he is also a loveless being.[61]

The Resurrection of the Crucified

One of the defining features of Moltmann's theology is a wide ecumenical engagement. Through his extensive global traveling, his working with Faith and Order (of the World Council of Churches), and his interaction with liberationists in various contexts as well as Pentecostals/charismatics and Eastern Orthodox theologians, he gleans from diverse sources. From the Eastern Church he has learned the importance of the resurrection and ascension, themes routinely ignored in the Christian West. Differently from Eastern traditions, however, Moltmann also pays a lot of attention to suffering and the cross, as explained above.

He describes the theological meaning of resurrection with the help of two terms, "endorsement" and "fulfillment." The former means that the resurrection confirms the validity of Jesus's earthly life and his claims; on the other hand, it is an eschatological event that points to our resurrection (1 Cor. 15:12–23), which is the fulfillment. Correctly, Moltmann reminds us that a proper "theology of hope" can only be developed from the perspective

58. Ibid., 249.
59. Ibid., 227.
60. Moltmann, *Trinity and the Kingdom*, 23.
61. Moltmann, *Crucified God*, 222.

of resurrection.[62] These two effects of the resurrection belong together and mutually condition each other:

> If we wished to confine ourselves to the endorsement, "resurrection" would be no more than an interpretative theological category for his death; and all that would remain would be a theology of the cross. If we were to concentrate solely on the fulfillment, the Easter Christ would replace and push out the crucified Jesus. But if . . . the earthly Jesus is "the messiah on the way," and the Son of God in the process of his learning, then Easter endorses and fulfils this life history of Jesus which is open for the future. At the same time, however, resurrection, understood as an eschatological event in Jesus, is the beginning of the new creation of all things.[63]

As much as the resurrection is an eschatological event, pointing to the coming consummation, it is also deeply anchored in the historical realities of this world. In this event Christian theology sees "not the eternity of heaven, but the future of the very earth on which his cross stands." Even more, "It sees in him the future of the very humanity for which he died."[64]

The Cosmic Rule of Christ

One of the omissions of the theology of the Western church—differently from the East—has to do with the theological significance of the ascension and the current rule of Christ. For this reason, Moltmann finds the "cosmological" Christology of the patristic era, with all its flaws (for example, the problem of the two-nature view that makes the divinity of Christ impassible), more appealing than the immanentist, anthropologically oriented, reductionist "Jesusology" of classical liberalism.

Moltmann appreciates the cosmic implications of Christ's ascension. In his vision, the ascended Christ as the *Pantocrator* encompasses not only the "conquest of enmity and violence and in the spread of reconciliation and harmonious, happily lived life"[65] but also the world of nature and evolution. His chapter on ascension is titled "The Cosmic Christ," and in it he also discusses Christ as the "Ground" and "Redeemer" of evolution.[66] In his *God in Creation* (ET 1985) Moltmann constructs a profound doctrine of creation

---

62. Ibid., ix.
63. Moltmann, *Way of Jesus Christ*, 171.
64. Moltmann, *Theology of Hope: On the Ground and the Implications of a Christian Eschatology*, trans. J. W. Leitch (London: SCM, 1967), 21.
65. Moltmann, *Way of Jesus Christ*, 279.
66. Ibid., chap. 6.

in the context of current evolutionary theory. Throughout, he connects the doctrine with Christology and its cosmic ramifications.

Wolfhart Pannenberg: Universal Christology

Theology in Search of the Universal Truth

The two works that brought the late Wolfhart Pannenberg to international fame were a collection of essays that he coedited, *Revelation as History*, originally written in German in 1961, and his major christological work, published in German in 1964 (and later in English under the obscure and somewhat misleading title *Jesus, God and Man*).[67] From the beginning of his theological career, therefore, Pannenberg, whom many regard as the most influential and learned systematic theologian of the latter part of the twentieth century, dealt with foundational issues in Christology. The main focus of *Jesus, God and Man* was the defense and rigorous application of the from below methodology, as explained in the introductory chapter above. In his magnum opus, the three-volume *Systematic Theology* (ET 1991–97), he continued the main orientation of the earlier work, even though he did so in a self-critical manner and also moved beyond methodological issues to deal with the major topics of Christology. Therein, the somewhat one-sided from below methodology was balanced with the principle of the mutual conditioning of from below and from above.

As mentioned above, there is a marked difference between Pannenberg and his German counterpart Moltmann. Throughout his life, Pannenberg honed his theological method, as laid out in his massive *Theology and the Philosophy of Science*, with the goal of a coherent and rational argumentation for theology as "the science of God," in the tradition of the medieval masters.[68] For Pannenberg, theology is a public discipline rather than an exercise in piety, and he adamantly opposes the widespread privatization of faith and theology. Theology has to speak to common concerns because there is no special "religious truth." As Pannenberg untiringly insists, if something is true, it has to be true for everyone, not just for oneself.[69] To its detriment,

---

67. Wolfhart Pannenberg, Rolf Rendtorff, and Ulrich Wilkens, eds., *Revelation as History*, trans. David Granskou (New York: Macmillan, 1968); Wolfhart Pannenberg, *Jesus, God and Man*, trans. Lewis L. Wilkins and Duane A. Priebe (Philadelphia: Westminster, 1977).

68. Wolfhart Pannenberg, *Theology and the Philosophy of Science*, trans. Francis McDonagh (London: Darton, Longman & Todd, 1976).

69. Wolfhart Pannenberg, *Anthropology in Theological Perspective*, trans. Matthew J. O'Connell (Philadelphia: Westminster, 1985), 15.

modern theology has by and large left the truth question behind, but Pannenberg has not been willing to surrender the quest for one truth. Consequently, his theology focuses on reason and argumentation; theological statements—in the form of hypotheses—have to be subjected to the rigor of critical questioning. Faith is not a blind act, a leap of faith, but is grounded in public, historical knowledge. Pannenberg's idea of truth comes closest to the coherence model, in which the aim of Christian dogmatics is to show its truth with regard to its inner logic and especially in relation to the rest of human knowledge, the sciences included. In Pannenberg's own words, as stated at the beginning of his career, "The question about the truth of the Christian message has to do with whether it can still disclose to us today the unity of the reality in which we live."[70]

For Pannenberg, the task of Christology is to offer rational support for belief in the divinity of Jesus; this cannot be assumed but has to be argued on the basis of historical proofs. If we rest our faith on the *kerygma* (proclamation) alone and not on historical facts, there is a chance that our faith will be misplaced. Even though Pannenberg believes it is necessary to engage in critical-historical study of the historical foundations of the Jesus event, he also argues that we should bring openness to historical study and not limit it by dismissing miracles and other supernatural events. Historical sources talk about the miracles associated with the life of Jesus, the greatest of which is, of course, the resurrection. Critical study into the origins and historical basis of Christology, according to Pannenberg, may not decide beforehand which events are not historically possible.

Pannenberg believes that historical study alone is not capable of leading one to a final commitment of faith in the divinity of the person of Jesus Christ. At the same time, careful study is needed before one is ready to confess, for example, that Jesus's claim of resurrection is valid or at least probable. This means that faith in the divinity of Christ (humanity is not the challenge to his approach) is a result of historical study and not its presupposition.

Jesus Christ as the Eschatological "New Adam"

In the second volume of his *Systematic Theology*, Pannenberg develops Christology in three parts, parallel to how Christology has most often been done in systematic treatments: he considers first Jesus's relationship to humanity (chap. 9), then the support for the claim of his divinity (chap. 10), and

70. Wolfhart Pannenberg, "What Is Truth?," in *Basic Questions in Theology*, trans. George H. Kehm (Philadelphia: Fortress, 1971), 2:1.

finally Jesus's role in salvation under the rubric of reconciliation (chap. 11). Yet his treatment of these traditional christological loci is unique and betrays his distinctive approach to theology.

Even though Pannenberg's theology is God-centered and focuses on showing how Christian belief in God can illumine human experience of the world, his theology is also firmly anchored in anthropology, the doctrine of humanity. Herein there is commonality with Rahner. One of the basic aims of Pannenberg's approach is to demonstrate that belief in God is not foreign to the structure of the human being. Religiosity is not—as atheistic critics of religion have maintained—something foreign imposed on the human being but rather an essential part of being human. By definition, the human being is open to receive revelation from God/gods. This does not, of course, prove the existence of a distinctively Christian God, but it does show that talk about God is rational and can be advanced within the nature of human existence.

This understanding provides a crucial bridge to Christology. The idea of Christ's humanity is not foreign to theology but rather is an attempt to understand the appearance of Jesus as the revelation and fulfillment of human destiny. Significantly, Pannenberg titles this chapter in his systematics "Anthropology and Christology." He develops the understanding of Jesus's humanity as the fulfillment of human destiny with the help of the Pauline concept of Jesus as the new human or new Adam. Although, as explained above, in his *Systematic Theology* Pannenberg balances the overly from below orientation of his early career, ultimately he still is convinced that the way to affirmation of the deity of Jesus Christ has to go through the humanity of Jesus the man.[71] Whereas tradition locates the deity of Jesus the man in the person of Christ/*Logos*, Pannenberg locates the deity in the humanity of Jesus. According to Pannenberg, the obedient Son did not seek his own glory but rather subjected himself to the service of the Father's kingdom. Pannenberg makes here the brilliant observation that it is precisely in this distinguishing himself from the Father, "in this subordination to the rule of the one God [that he is] the Son."[72] In other words, as the heading in the chapter on the deity of Jesus Christ puts it: "The Self-Distinction of Jesus from the Father [Is] the Inner Basis of His Divine Sonship." By thus submitting himself to the Father, the earthly Jesus also avoided the crime of making himself equal to his Father. In this outlook, differently from tradition, self-emptying is the refusal to equate oneself with the Father rather than being an exercise in renunciation of divine attributes.

---

71. This section is based on Kärkkäinen, *Christ and Reconciliation*, 139–40 particularly.
72. Pannenberg, *Systematic Theology*, 2:373.

While Pannenberg's solution has been welcomed by contemporary theologians, they are concerned that relocating the deity solely to the human life of Jesus the man, while not heretical, may not be sufficient to traditional affirmations. While Pannenberg's view helps avoid one of the major problems of the traditional incarnational model—that is, the robust affirmation of the true humanity of the incarnated Son—it may go too far in making the deity solely the matter of the humanity of Jesus and thus failing to establish a thick account of divinity. This of course has implications for the work of salvation: the death on the cross is merely the death of the human Jesus, who only on account of resurrection will be shown to be the Son of God. The abiding and necessary teaching of Chalcedon is that both the life and death of Jesus Christ are the joint work of the divine and human natures in one person.

For Paul, all humans are to carry the image of the new Adam. From this Pannenberg concludes that as the new Adam, Jesus is the prototype of the new humanity and brings to fulfillment the destiny of humanity. But Jesus is the destiny not only of individual human life. According to Pannenberg, Paul also emphasizes the corporate dimension of the image of Christ as the new Adam. In other words, Jesus is the fulfillment of human destiny with regard to interhuman relationships. As a corollary, no individual person is able to fulfill human destiny; it is possible only in community.

The Resurrection and Jesus's Divinity

For Pannenberg, the resurrection, with its historical factuality, is the key not only to Christ's meaning but also to the whole of Christian theology. It is the "confirmation" of Jesus's claims and his lasting significance:[73]

> The Easter event certainly shed a new light on the death of Jesus, on his earthly ministry, and therefore on his person. But that does not mean that even without the event of the resurrection these would have been what they are when seen in its light. We depreciate the Easter event if we construe it only as a disclosure or revelation of the meaning that the crucifixion and the earthly history of Jesus already had in themselves. Only the Easter event determines what the meaning was of the pre-Easter history of Jesus and who he was in his relation to God.[74]

In other words, resurrection "dispelled and removed the ambiguity that had earlier clung to the person and history of Jesus."[75] Confirmation means that

73. Ibid., 2:45.
74. Ibid., 2:345.
75. Ibid., 2:345–46; see also 283.

what was confirmed at the event of resurrection was something that was there already in the beginning of the history of Jesus.[76]

The incarnate Christ claimed to be the Son sent by his Father to preach about the coming kingdom. Pannenberg begins his consideration of the divinity of Christ right here. Rather than appealing to Christology from above, which presupposes what it argues, Pannenberg begins with the historical foundation of Jesus's claims and their validation by the Father through the raising of Jesus from the dead. Jesus's proclamation of the nearness of the kingdom of God clearly implied a personal claim to authority that went beyond anything a human person can claim for himself or herself; in fact, Jesus proclaimed himself to be the mediator of God's coming lordship, which was already operative in the present. To validate his claims Jesus looked to a future confirmation, the resurrection. For Pannenberg, the event of the resurrection was *the* starting point for the assertion of Jesus's deity, his unity with God.

The assertion of Jesus's deity on the basis of the resurrection is related to the way in which resurrection was understood in the Jewish context. Here the pervasive influence of apocalypticism is the key to understanding the meaning of resurrection. New Testament scholarship agrees that more significant than the presence of several apocalyptic passages—passages that talk about the coming end of the world in terms of cataclysmic cosmic events and divine intervention—is that the whole of the New Testament grew in the soil of apocalypticism. The apocalyptic worldview provides the key to understanding the New Testament significance and meaning of Jesus and his resurrection. Three main features of apocalypticism have special significance here. First, the full revelation of God will not happen until the end of history. Second, the end of history is of universal significance: it involves both Jews and gentiles. At the end, God will be shown to be the God of all people and all creation. And third, the end of history entails a general resurrection of the dead.

If the resurrection of Jesus can be shown to be a historical event—and Pannenberg believes it can be, on the basis of the empty tomb tradition and the existence of a large number of eyewitnesses, the validity of whose testimony was not contested by their contemporaries—then that resurrection means the beginning of the resurrection of all, which will take place at the end. For Pannenberg, Jesus's resurrection is the key to the insight that the human person Jesus is one with God. In raising Jesus from the dead, the Father confirmed Jesus's pre-Easter claims with regard to the coming of the kingdom and the Father's rule; Jesus was shown to be the eschatological Son of Man of the prophecy of Daniel 7:13–14 and the apocalyptic expectation of the time. After

76. Ibid., 2.

Jesus died on the cross, people could not justify belief in Jesus and his claims without divine confirmation. Had there been no resurrection, his opponents would have been correct: his authority claims would have been blasphemous.

According to Pannenberg, we may now apply christological titles to him, such as Son of Man, Lord, and Son of God. Even more, the end of the world has already begun with the resurrection of Jesus. His resurrection is a "prolepsis," a preview of what will apply to all of us at the end. What happened in Jesus's life as a microcosm will apply to the rest of us and to creation. The definitive revelation of God through the resurrection of Jesus took place, even though its final fulfillment awaits the end-time revelation when the God of the Bible shows himself to be the God of all. But already now we may say that if Jesus is ascended to God and the end of the world has begun, then God is ultimately revealed in Jesus.

But what about the cross of Christ? What is the meaning of the cross for the personhood of Christ and our salvation? It has often been noted that Pannenberg so focuses on the resurrection that the cross does not play a crucial enough role in his Christology. It is true that Pannenberg emphasizes resurrection and therefore places less emphasis on the cross. His approach to the cross is through the concept of "inclusive substitution," in contrast to "exclusive substitution." For Pannenberg, in his cross and resurrection Jesus acted as our substitute. Jesus did not die so that we can avoid death, as the exclusive view maintains; instead, in tasting death for us, he radically altered it. No longer do we need to be terrified of death. Because we participate through faith in the new life brought by Christ, we can look forward to participating in God's life beyond death.

Having now considered Orthodox, Roman Catholic, and mainline Protestant Christologies, we turn next to less well-known interpretations in academic theology that, however, exercise great influence among churches, particularly in North America. These are Christologies coming from the so-called evangelical movement and represented here by the Anabaptist/Mennonite Norman Kraus and the late Baptist Stanley Grenz.

Norman Kraus: Disciples' Christology

Christology from the Disciples to the Disciples

It has been customary for the writers of church history and Christian theology either to ignore or to downplay contributions from the "margins," as mainline theologians have seen them. Even in the twentieth century it has not been uncommon for most church historians to divide Western Christianity into Protestant and Catholic types without remainder. An array of legitimate Christian churches and communities have been left out, mainly descendants of the Radical Reformation, such as Anabaptism and later Free Church movements. Whereas Catholics and the Magisterial Reformers regarded the Radical Reformers, the "left-wingers," as dissenters, the latter considered themselves the true church of God on earth, guardians of apostolic doctrine and practice.

American C. Norman Kraus, in his book *Jesus Christ Our Lord*, offers a Christology from a disciple's perspective.[77] Kraus, a theologian who has taught in Asia and Africa and interacts with non-Western concerns in his writings, represents the Anabaptist tradition going back to the time of the Radical Reformation. His focus is on the meaning and significance of Jesus Christ to discipleship, the main emphasis of Anabaptism. For Anabaptism, mere belief or orthodox convictions are not enough; a practical Christian lifestyle in obedience to the Lord's commands must be visible. In addition to interacting with his Anabaptist heritage, Kraus challenges the standard Western interpretations of Christ that use the categories of guilt and penalty and looks at Christ's work in light of the Asian concept of shame. Standing as he is in the tradition of Anabaptism, Kraus also intends to write a "peace theology" from the perspective of Christology. The starting point is the biblical affirmation, "he himself is our peace" (Eph. 2:14).

Kraus finds the concept of self-identity and self-revelation most helpful to his Christology. Jesus, the self-revelation of God to us, is God-giving-himself-to-us. That self-revelation comes to us only in the form of a genuinely personal, historical relationship.

To write a Christology from a disciple's perspective, Kraus begins by listening to the biblical testimony of the first disciples of Christ. Out of that he creates a Christology that is firmly embedded in the existing cultures of the global world. In fact, Kraus writes not only a full-scale Anabaptist Christology but also a prolegomenon, an introduction to Christian theology as a whole. Christology is the gateway to studying God.

Christology or Jesusology?

The nineteenth century and subsequent quest of the historical Jesus raised the question of whether we should talk about Christology or Jesusology. After all, the focus of the quest was to inquire into the historical and psychological origins of the person by the name of Jesus from the town of Nazareth. While Kraus acknowledges the value of the approach from below, in his reading of

77. C. Norman Kraus, *Jesus Christ Our Lord: Christology from a Disciple's Perspective* (Waterloo, ON: Herald Press, 1987).

the New Testament he sees a synthesis of the approaches from below and from above. This is encapsulated in Ephesians 4:20–21, which talks about Christ and "the truth that is in Jesus." In other words, this passage combines the earthly Jesus and the Christ of faith. From this Kraus draws an introductory conclusion, a framework that serves the rest of his Christology:

> Christology begins with the faith conviction that the man Jesus can be rightly understood only in the unique categories of biblical messianism and attempts to explain how and why this is so. But it also begins with the firm conviction that this messianic image must be understood in light of the fact that the Christ is none other than Jesus of Nazareth. Christology moves beyond the biographical categories of a historical Jesus in its attempt to assess his significance, but it must never abandon its historical referent. The historical revelation in Jesus remains the norm for defining the authentic Christ image and the Christian's experience of God.[78]

In trying to understand the Jesus of the first disciples—in an attempt to offer a Christology for current disciples—Kraus asks the following: Why should we not simply read the New Testament Gospels for an account of the historical Jesus? Why must we theologize about Jesus at all? The obvious reason is that the Gospels contain more than one theological picture, more than one interpretation of Christ. Which one should we choose for the purposes of our current needs? The loving Savior blessing the children? The healer and miracle worker? The rabbi-prophet who teaches with authority? The nonresistant suffering servant? Or the preexistent prototype of all creation?

For Kraus, the existence of both a history of Jesus and theological interpretations of its meaning in one and the same canon points to the methodology of Christology: it is not either-or but both-and with regard to the approaches from below and from above. What is clear is the need for multiple, distinctive theological interpretations of Christ to do justice to the varied cultural and religious needs of our times:

> This Christ may come in the semblance of an American savior whose image merges into that of the Statue of Liberty welcoming the distressed of the world to a land of freedom and opportunity. Or he may be presented as the 900-foot-high miracle worker which Oral Roberts claims to have seen in his vision.[79]

78. Ibid., 25.
79. Ibid., 27.

The context for such a search of meaningful contextual Christologies is the missionary work of the church among various cultures of the world. The purpose of disciples' Christology is to help the church understand the implications of its message both for its life of discipleship and for its proclamation of the gospel to the nations. The context and purpose of the original witness to Christ in the Gospels and the rest of the New Testament was missionary proclamation. The task of such a Christology is to employ images and languages of existing cultures to express its message in various culturally appropriate ways. But a criterion is needed, Kraus argues, and that is the New Testament, the testimony to the original disciples' view of Christ. "We need a theological description that will provide a norm for using the New Testament images in shaping the message of the gospel for the many cultures of the world. It must also give a clue to our own self-understanding as followers of Christ and guide us into a relevant discipleship."[80]

The Theological Significance of Jesus's Humanity

It hardly comes as a surprise that Jesus's full humanity is a key point for a disciples' Christology. The Anabaptists of the sixteenth century, who put great emphasis on following Christ in faithful obedience, clearly understood this point. They focused their attention on the sinless and nonviolent humanity of Jesus as the prototype for a new humanity of obedience and purity. Some Anabaptist sources from the seventeenth and eighteenth centuries talk about the "holy Manhood" of Christ. The man Jesus is the gateway to the ethical renewal of humanity. Metaphysical explanations about his divinity were not the focus, even though all Anabaptists strongly affirmed the classical orthodoxy of the creeds.

Anabaptist sources looked at Christ's humiliation, death on the cross, and subsequent descent into Hades as the process of salvation. Salvation does not come by power but by the humble submission of the Servant of God unto death.[81] According to Kraus, implicit in the Anabaptist insistence on the full humanity of Christ are two basic convictions: first, that God is a self-giving Creator who fully identifies with us in our need, and second, that our humanity finds its true fulfillment in this One who is the prototypical image of God. The Word become flesh is not just another kind of "contextual" communication but God's love coming to us as one of us. At the same time, incarnation also affirms the creation of humanity. The humanized Word of God is God's

80. Ibid., 29–30.
81. Ibid., 63.

image and therefore points to the way God wanted human beings to be. This destiny to be like God is the true meaning and destiny of human existence. In this regard, Kraus makes basically the same point as Pannenberg (though without reference to him).

For Kraus, the heart of the Christian message is the conviction that Jesus is the fulfillment and thus the revelation of God's intention for human life. All docetic attempts to attenuate Jesus's humanity detract from this central tenet of Christian theology. The way the sinlessness of Jesus was defended in the past created a problem in appreciating his full humanity. Especially the Augustinian understanding of sin, as sensuality and inherited guilt, motivated theologians to defend Christ from all taint and influence of sin. For Kraus, the focal point of the sinlessness of Jesus is his refusal to assert his self-will in opposition to God's will; this is the core of Jesus's being the perfect image of God, which "from the biblical perspective . . . is what it means to be fully human!"[82] In his humanity, Jesus totally identified himself with humanity. He lived in solidarity with human beings. The cross for Kraus represents the consummation of God's solidarity with the world.

If incarnation is a word about humanity, at the same time it is also a word about God. Incarnation speaks of the self-disclosure of God in the God-man, Jesus Christ. Jesus's claim of unity with God was established and validated by his resurrection from the dead. Here again, Kraus follows the path of Pannenberg; for both of these theologians, the resurrection is the divine confirmation of Jesus's claim that he is the mediator of divine life and the coming kingdom of God. Resurrection for Kraus is *the* sign pointing to the reality of the deity of Christ. Jesus's resurrection also confirms our salvation. Salvation means overcoming death, and had Jesus not been raised from the dead, our hope beyond death would be vain.

The Cross, Shame, and Guilt: Christ in the Asian Context

In his search for appropriate images of salvation, Kraus considers some that are less familiar in standard Christologies. One image that seems to capture much of the *agapē* love of God is the parent-child analogy. The true nature of genuinely moral responses is best seen in our most intimate human relationships, which is why the parent-child metaphor has potential for illuminating God's way with his children. In the New Testament, Jesus's special name for God was the Aramaic *abba*. In light of this, it seems strange that so little use has been made of this metaphor. This approach can illumine the passionate

82. Ibid., 72.

yet mature love of the heavenly Father for his wayward and erring children. Sin means the rejection of love; therefore, Fatherly love means restitution for sin and open arms to the repenting son and daughter.

Kraus uses many other metaphors from the New Testament and Christian tradition that highlight the loving solidarity between Christ and us. One of the main images in the Bible, especially in the New Testament, is the restoration of covenantal relationship. The covenant that God made with Israel and later with us in Christ is an offer of salvation based on the faithfulness of God. It is about relationships, trust, love. Another image, widely employed especially outside Western culture, presents salvation as deliverance from alien authorities. Deliverance from both the power of sin and bondage to the demonic are part of this image.

The Eastern concept of salvation as the renewal of the image of God is one of Kraus's favorite images in his Christology and soteriology. This is understandable in light of the importance he attaches to the humanity of Christ as the fulfillment of human destiny. Early Christian tradition talked about the restoration of the image as divinization or deification: Christ became human so that we may become deified. The moral renewal of Wesleyan and Holiness movements was a later appropriation of this image.

The most distinctive approach to the work of Christ in Kraus's *Jesus Christ Our Lord* is related to Asian cultures, especially the Japanese context.[83] There is a pronounced difference between the Western idea of guilt and the Asian idea of shame as the main category for the human predicament. Guilt focuses on the act; shame focuses on the self. The nature of fault in shame cultures is the failure to meet self-expectations. Guilt arises out of offenses against legal expectations. The internal reactions vary, too. In guilt cultures, there is remorse, self-accusation, and fear of punishment. In shame cultures, embarrassment, disgrace, self-deprecation, and fear of abandonment abound. The remedy for guilt is often a demand for revenge or penalty, while for shame it is identification and communication; love banishes shame, while justification banishes guilt. Out of these two paradigms emerge different views of the cross of Christ. For the Asian, the cross represents an instrument of shame and God's ultimate identification with us in our sinful shame; it is an expression of God's love. In standard Western soteriologies, the cross has often been an instrument of penalty and God's ultimate substitute for our sinful guilt; the cross expresses God's justice.

These two approaches are, of course, not exclusive of each other. The cross of Christ is related to both shame and guilt. Reconciliation means overcoming

83. Ibid., chap. 12.

shame and freedom from guilt. In his self-sacrifice, Jesus acted vicariously for us in two ways. He bore the consequences of our sin in order to be our servant (Mark 10:45). Jesus also took the place of all humankind inasmuch as his revelation is universal. As one totally identified with and representing humanity, he faced his destiny of death on the cross. Furthermore, the crucified Christ not only effects the resolution of shame anxiety but also reveals the normative ethical-social dimensions of shame: "The cross exposes false shame as an idolatrous human self-justification and, in exposing it, breaks its power to instill fear."[84] Shame is expressed in the taboos and norms of society. In theological terms, that means, according to Kraus, that expressions of shame are negative indicators of a society's concept of the image of God reflected in humanity. They define what is considered truly human. Thus, when Christian theology says that the cross exposes false shame and reveals the true nature of human shame, it means that the crucified Christ reveals God's authentic image for humanity. In other words, Kraus concludes, the crucified Jesus demonstrated God's standard of right human relations and became the truly universal norm for humanity.

Stanley Grenz: Evangelical Christology

Theology for the Community of God

The term *evangelical* in its current usage, especially in the English-speaking world, is ambiguous. Following the Reformation, the term meant Protestant theology as opposed to Catholic theology. Another meaning was added in the twentieth century when it came to mean those Protestants who adhered to the more orthodox version of Christianity as opposed to the liberal left wing. Thus, there arose an "evangelical doctrine of Scripture" that held that the Word of God is divine in its origin and trustworthy in all regards. In still more recent decades, the evangelical movement, which is transdenominational and global and represents not only all sorts of Protestants (from Lutherans to Presbyterians to Baptists to Pentecostals) but also Anglicans, has distanced itself from the more reactionary fundamentalism, even though most fundamentalists regard themselves as the true evangelicals. Reference to "evangelical theology" here follows the main usage in the English-speaking world, namely, various Protestant Christian traditions that are open to dialogue with other Christians and cherish classical Christianity as explicated in the creeds and mainstream confessions, yet are also open to new developments in theology and other academic fields.

84. Ibid., 220 (emphasis in original removed).

Stanley Grenz's *Theology for the Community of God*, as the title suggests, approaches the nature and task of systematic theology from the perspective of the community of God, the church.[85] Too often theologies in general and Christologies in particular are written for and from the perspective of individuals in need of salvation. This work attempts to overcome that reductionism and reflect on the communitarian implications of theology and Christology. Christology for Grenz is reflection on the role of Jesus of Nazareth, whom Christians acknowledge as the Christ, "in the reconciling, community-building work of the Triune God."[86]

Grenz's Christology follows the traditional path in that he first considers the divinity of Christ, his humanity, and the union of the two natures before entering into a discussion of the work of Christ in his cross and resurrection.[87] Grenz's treatment is up to date, creative, and open to most current developments in the field while being anchored in basic evangelical convictions. The influence of Wolfhart Pannenberg is visible in the background; this is understandable given that Pannenberg was Grenz's *Doktorvater*, doctoral mentor (even though Grenz rarely refers to Pannenberg).

Characteristic of Grenz's approach is his effort to find a balance between Christology from below and from above. At times he seems to support one-sidedly the approach from below, but in his final conclusions the approach from above is also visible.

The Fellowship of Jesus the Christ with God

If Grenz were a typical evangelical theologian of the past, he would simply allude to biblical statements about the claims, miracles, and other ministries of Jesus to affirm Jesus's unity with God, his deity.[88] But that is not his approach. In the footsteps of his teacher Pannenberg, Grenz sets himself the tedious task of establishing the divinity of Christ on the basis of historical inquiry. Grenz argues that we cannot separate the Christ of faith from the Jesus of history, although that is tempting, because it would free us from historical research.

Grenz considers several proposals as to what aspect of Jesus's life can provide the foundation for his deity. Traditionally, Jesus's sinlessness has been a good candidate. However, this aspect lacks an objective historical foundation

---

85. Stanley Grenz, *Theology for the Community of God* (Grand Rapids: Eerdmans, 1994).
86. Ibid., 244.
87. Christological chapters in Grenz, *Theology for the Community of God*, are chap. 9 (divinity), chap. 10 (humanity), and chap. 11 (union of two natures); chap. 12 deals with atonement.
88. That is the approach of the Conservative Baptist theologian Millard J. Erickson in his massive monograph *The Word Became Flesh: A Contemporary Incarnational Christology* (Grand Rapids: Baker, 1991).

and was questioned even during Jesus's life. An even more serious objection to this proposal is that even if we could establish the claim for Jesus's sinlessness, it would not guarantee his divinity: sinlessness is not the same as being divine. At its best, sinlessness could make a person an extraordinary individual. Using Jesus's teaching as the foundation for his divinity results in the same problems associated with his sinlessness. His teaching was contested during his life, and even had it not been, authoritative teaching does not make one divine.

A weightier proposal concerns the death of the Messiah, which has often been seen as *the* foundation for his deity. His death reveals his identity. As the soldier at the foot of the cross observed, "Surely he was the Son of God!" (Matt. 27:54). However, in isolation, Jesus's death is ambiguous. Was Jesus's death the death of a political victim or a sacrificial martyr? Only in light of a prior faith commitment (the assurance that he was divine) can the death of Christ serve as foundational.

What about his own claim to divinity? Gospel criticism has questioned many, if not most, of the passages that contain such a claim. The scholarly consensus maintains that Jesus was aware of his divinity, but this awareness does not guarantee his divinity; he may have been wrong. Furthermore, other religious leaders have made similar claims. What makes Jesus's claim distinctive, however, is that he looked for a future vindication that would establish the truthfulness of his claim: the resurrection.

The resurrection is, in fact, another aspect that has been seen as the foundation for Jesus's divinity. Resurrection alone would not make a person a god; Lazarus was raised from the dead, but he was not considered divine. What makes resurrection a valid foundation in Jesus's case is its relationship to Jesus's claim of divinity. Grenz concludes that Jesus's claim and his resurrection taken together provide evidence for his divinity. Through his teaching and actions, Jesus made a claim for his own uniqueness; this claim called for a future confirmation. If the resurrection did take place, it constitutes the needed confirmation. And there is also the wider context of the eschatological coming of the kingdom that was inaugurated by the resurrection: "The resurrection is God's declaration that through his ministry, Jesus had indeed inaugurated the divine reign. In him God is truly at work enacting his eschatological purpose, which is the establishment of the community of God."[89] From this we can work backward to other proposals. As divine, Christ is sinless, his teaching has divine authority, and in his death he acted for our salvation.

89. Grenz, *Theology for the Community of God*, 260.

For Grenz, in order for his argumentation to hold, he has to establish the historical nature of the resurrection. Once again, following Pannenberg, he maintains that the empty tomb tradition and the existence of independent witnesses provide historical evidence for the factuality of the Gospel claims. While using the resurrection as the means to establish Christ's deity, however, Grenz also wants to avoid an adoptionistic interpretation according to which Jesus was made God's Son by virtue of the resurrection. Jesus was already divine; the resurrection merely provides the historical evidence for that fact.

In this way, Grenz affirms the fellowship of Jesus Christ with God on the basis of historical inquiry. In addition to the historical evidence, though, the birth of faith also requires personal experience of the living Lord. But even that is based on the conviction of the historical foundation and not vice versa. In 1 Corinthians 15:17–19, the historicity of the resurrection is Paul's criterion for the reliability of the Christian message.

What, then, are the implications of Jesus's unity with God? In theological history, there has been a dualism between two approaches, functional and ontological. The functional approach argues on the basis of the task given to Christ, and the ontological proceeds with reference to his being (ontology is the branch of philosophy that inquires into the question of being). For Grenz, these two options are not mutually exclusive but complementary. The biblical concept of Jesus as the revealer of God (John 14:9–10) has the potential of transcending the function-versus-ontology demarcation. Christological understanding of Jesus is functional in that he reveals God and ontological in that he is the self-revelation of God. To reveal God, Jesus Christ has to be God, ontologically one with God.

In his fellowship with the Father, Jesus reveals to us both God's compassionate, loving heart and his own special *abba* relationship with his Father. As the self-revelation of God, he is able to bring us into the most intimate relationship with the Father. At the same time, Christ also reveals the Father's lordship. Once again, the title "Lord" is both functional and ontological. Because Jesus is one with God, he functions as God present in the world. He is the cosmic Lord (Phil. 2:9–11), the Lord of history, and our personal Lord.

The Fellowship of Jesus the Christ with Humankind

According to Grenz, Jesus is not only essential deity but also essential humanity, "man for us." Jesus shares in our true humanness. Grenz develops this line of thought by looking at Jesus's earthly life. Jesus obviously participated in the conditions of normal human life, experienced growth, and lived the life

of a particular Jewish person at a particular time. The Bible also affirms that
he completely identified with us in all respects (Heb. 2:14, 17).

What is the foundation for affirming Jesus's true humanity? Grenz does not
find the foundation just by considering Jesus's earthly life. The resurrection
in isolation shares the same ambiguity with regard to Jesus's humanity as
with regard to his divinity, but combined with Jesus's claim for true humanity,
it shows that God gave his approval to that claim. Therefore, Jesus's claim
for true humanity in conjunction with his resurrection serves as the needed
historical foundation for Jesus's fellowship with humanity. If there had been
no resurrection following the cross, God's plan for eternal fellowship with
humans would have been made void. But Jesus's resurrection shows what our
path can be, too, in the newness of life. In this context, Grenz talks about
the "paradigmatic nature of Jesus' humanness in an ontological sense": Jesus
reveals the transformed ontological reality that we will one day become.[90]

The fellowship of Jesus Christ with humankind points not only to hope
beyond death but also to God's intent for our future lives, which goes beyond
individual life. It points to community. Jesus is the paradigm for human fellowship. Jesus as the new human expresses the true humanity intended for
us. As such, he shows us the nature of the "universal human" with regard to
the marginalized, women, and the individual. Jesus's humanity encompasses
and gives room to women and men, young and old, rich and poor.

The Fellowship of Deity and Humanity in Jesus

It is one thing to affirm separately the divinity and the humanity of Jesus
Christ and still another to consider the unity of these two natures. For Grenz,
the foundation for affirming the unity lies in two New Testament titles: Word
and Son. The term "word," *logos*, was rooted in both Greek culture and the
corresponding Hebrew term *davar*, which has the dual meaning "word" and
"event." In the first chapter of the Gospel of John, two roles are assigned to
the Word. On the one hand, the Word has a creative role ("through him all
things were made" [1:3]); on the other hand, he has a revelatory role ("we
have seen his glory" [1:14]). Another biblical passage, Colossians 1:15–16,
employs the same idea. For Grenz, the declaration that Jesus is the Word

> therefore constitutes a theological statement concerning the significance of
> this historical life. In him, God's revelation is disclosed and God's power is
> operative. As a result, the title asserts that in Jesus of Nazareth the power of
> God is at work revealing the meaning of all reality—even the nature of God.

90. Ibid., 283.

To refer to Jesus as the Word is to affirm that as this human being, he is the revelation of God.[91]

The related New Testament references to Jesus as the Son are, of course, based on the biblical notion of the "Son of God," which is rooted in the Old Testament and the ancient Near East. In the ancient Near East, the title "son" was given to those thought to be the offspring of the gods, such as kings or those with extraordinary, "divine," powers. To the Hebrews, "son" indicated election to participate in God's work, a special agent elected to carry out God's mission in the world. In the Gospels, the title "Son of God" in reference to Jesus indicated his unique obedience to God's will and mission. On the basis of Jesus's unique sonship and earthly life of obedience, he was seen as divine, as conveyed in the Epistles. The title "Son," therefore, came to carry exalted aspects similar to those of "Word." In fact, Hebrews 1:3–4 shows a connection between the two by describing the Son as the one through whom God made the universe and as the revelation of God's essence.[92]

Taken together, the titles Word and Son offer the basis for explaining the unity of Jesus's two natures. This basis is their common connection with the idea of revelation. As the Word and the Son, Jesus is both essential deity and essential humanity, and he reveals both natures. The unity of the two natures, therefore, is a revelatory unity. As this revelation, Jesus brings the two natures together in his one person. According to Grenz, this appeal to revelation as the focus of the unity of the two natures is not merely functional, as some critics suggest. Inherent in revelation is participation. Jesus not only reveals but also participates in divine and human life. His revelatory unity, therefore, leads to his ontological unity with God and humanity.[93]

Incarnation

When considering the formulation of traditional and evangelical Christology, Grenz is critical of the way the Chalcedonian definition incorporated the central features of what he calls "incarnational" Christology. Incarnational Christology focuses on the condescension and self-humiliation of the divine *Logos*, the Son, in taking to himself human nature. It also includes the exaltation of human nature to inseparable (in technical theological language, hypostatic) communion with the divine *Logos* because of that act. Therefore, in the incarnation

91. Ibid., 301–2.
92. Ibid., 302–3.
93. Ibid., 303–5.

the Son did not unite with a human person, but with human nature, which gained existence in its connection with the Logos (*enhypostasis*). As a consequence of the incarnation, the one person Jesus Christ enjoys the properties of the two natures (*communicatio idiomatum*).[94]

This traditional approach to incarnation shares several common features. Jesus combines in one person a divine and a human nature, and the incarnation was the means of effecting the union of these two natures. This act was the work of the Second Person of the Trinity, the *Logos*, and resulted in a "hypostatic union" of deity and humanity in Jesus. In other words, in this union, the personal center of the earthly life was the eternal Son, with the human nature existing only through its union with the *Logos*. The historical act of incarnation took place in the conception of Jesus in the womb of Mary. While this post-Chalcedonian Christology has good intentions in trying to defend the full humanity and the full divinity of Christ and their coexistence, it is beset with serious problems, Grenz argues, and therefore has to be modified.

Some of the most typical criticisms targeted at incarnational Christology are the following: similarity with other mythological stories of contemporary religions, dangers of docetism (which compromises the full humanity of Christ) or Apollinarianism (which regards the human nature of Christ as nonpersonal), and, the most serious of all, the separation between *Logos* and Jesus. What was the *Logos* doing before the incarnation?[95]

On the way to a more satisfactory formulation of the doctrine of the incarnation, Grenz goes back to the central biblical passages from which theologians have built the concept of incarnation: John 1:1–4 and Philippians 2:5–11. In Grenz's reading of these passages, there was no historical descent of a preexisting divine *Logos*. In fact, Paul does not even mention the *Logos*; rather, he writes about Jesus Christ. The historical person Jesus refused to clutch his divine prerogatives but was God's humble, obedient servant to the point of death, and as a consequence he achieved the highest name. Therefore, Paul drew the incarnation view from the history of Jesus. Similarly, Grenz contends that even John, though he mentions the *Logos*, builds on the historical life of Jesus. John does not mention Jesus's birth as the vehicle that facilitated the incarnate state of the eternal *Logos*. John appeals to eyewitnesses who observed Jesus's earthly life and testified that they "have seen his glory," the glory of the one who became flesh. The Johannine prologue does not focus on how Jesus came into existence. It is a theological declaration of the significance of Jesus's earthly life. When he confesses Jesus as the incarnate

94. Ibid., 306.
95. For his critique of incarnational Christology, see ibid., 308–9.

Word, John is claiming that as this human being, Jesus is divine; he is God's revelation. As a remedy, Grenz suggests once again Christology from below. He searches for the answer to the identity of Jesus by looking at his historical life. The confession of the incarnation, rather than being the presupposition of Christology, is the conclusion drawn from an examination of the earthly life of Jesus Christ, which is the presupposition and beginning of Christology.[96]

The last two Christologies to be discussed in this section on Euro-American Christologies are the most innovative and widely contested. More traditional theologians consider them on the borders (if not even beyond the borders) of Christian tradition. They are the pluralist Christology of Hick and the process Christology of Cobb.

John Hick: Pluralist Christology

The Pluralistic Revolution of Religions

With John Hick, the world's most noted and hotly debated defender of religious pluralism, we enter the domain of theology of religions and comparative theology. As distinct theological disciplines they are more recent, although the kind of work they attempt has been done among theologians here and there throughout the centuries. Theology of religions seeks to investigate the theological value of religions and Christianity's place and function among other religions. Comparative theology builds on that work, as well as the accumulated results of comparative religion—which, as the name indicates, compares religious beliefs and rites—in order to accomplish specific and detailed comparisons among religions. The following example illustrates the differences of these disciplines: whereas the theology of religions may investigate the relationship between Christian tradition (as one of the Abrahamic faiths, along with Judaism and Islam) vis-à-vis Asian traditions (say, Hinduism and Buddhism), a comparative theological exercise could engage the question of similarities and differences between the Christian doctrine of Christ's incarnation and (theistic) Hinduism's notion(s) of divine *avataras* (that is, embodiments of the divine such as the darling figure Krishna, an "incarnation" of Vishnu).

As a philosopher of religion, Hick has significantly advanced the theology of religions quest.[97] Along with that, he has also engaged comparative theology. Hick has gleaned many insights from Asian and Muslim traditions through

96. Ibid., 309–11.
97. Hick's main monograph on that topic is *An Interpretation of Religion: Human Response to the Transcendent, Gifford Lectures 1986–87* (London: Macmillan, 1989), a heavy and complex book, not recommended for beginners! Fortunately, Hick has also written less technical and

his extensive travels along with teaching and research periods in various global locations.

Interestingly enough, Hick began his theological career as a conservative, almost fundamentalist believer following his dramatic conversion experience, but during his years of teaching and doing research in the field of theology, he has become the leading spokesperson for a pluralist theology (of religions). Already in 1970, Hick and his colleagues published a critical manifesto titled "The Reconstruction of Christian Belief for Today and Tomorrow,"[98] in which they questioned the literal meaning of most traditional Christian beliefs, including the Bible as divine revelation, creation *ex nihilo*, the substitutionary death of Christ, the virgin birth, hell, and so forth. Hick also questioned the old paradigm according to which there is no salvation outside the church, which necessitated traditional missionary work with proclamation and desire to convert. A number of well-known factors of the multireligious world inspired and supported his shift from the normativity of Christ to pluralism, such as the link between ethnicity and religion, the lack of missionary success despite massive efforts by the Christian church, the high quality of religious and ethical life in non-Christian religions, and particularly the phenomenological similarity of religions (that is, most religions have scriptures, religious rites and rituals, places of worship, prayers, and so forth).

Hick employs a familiar astronomical model to illustrate his pluralistic theology of religions, namely, the shift from the earth-centered Ptolemaic to sun-centered Copernican model.[99] Rather than Jesus Christ of the traditional view, it is God, the Ultimate Truth, who is the center of all religions, around whom they revolve in the way of planets:

> And the needed Copernican revolution in theology involves an equally radical transformation in our conception of the universe of faiths and the place of our own religion within it. It involves a shift from the dogma that Christianity is at the center to the realization that it is God who is at the center, and that all the religions of mankind, including our own, serve and revolve around him.[100]

---

more accessible works, such as his widely read *God and the Universe of Faiths: Essays in the Philosophy of Religion*, 2nd ed. (Oxford: One World, 1993).

98. John Hick, "The Reconstruction of Christian Belief for Today and Tomorrow," *Theology* 73 (1970): 339.

99. For a detailed discussion and documentation, see Kärkkäinen, *Trinity and Revelation: A Constructive Christian Theology for the Pluralistic World* (Grand Rapids: Eerdmans, 2014), 2:343–47. Therein I acknowledge my debt to Matti T. Amnell, *Uskontojen Universumi: John Hickin uskonnollisen pluralismin haaste ja siitä käyty keskustelu*, Suomalaisen Teologisen Kirjallisuusseuran Julkaisuja 217 (Helsinki: STK, 1999).

100. John Hick, *The Second Christianity*, 3rd ed. of *Christianity at the Centre* (London: SCM, 1983), 82. More technically put, the essence of pluralism means that there is "both the

The challenge to Christian theology, as well as, for example, to Hindu or Buddhist theology, is to move away from the "Ptolemaic" view in which Christianity or any other religion stands at the center and in which other religions are judged by the criteria of that center. To accomplish this task Hick contends that the views of the adherents of religions cannot be taken at face value; rather, each religion has to deemphasize its own absolute and exclusive claims.

To illustrate his point, Hick uses an allegory from Buddhist sources according to which ten blind men touch an elephant and each describes what an elephant is on the basis of his limited experience. Various conceptions of God/god(s)/divine such as Yahweh, Allah, or the Holy Trinity are but aspects of the Divine. They are like maps or colors of the rainbow.[101] Later in his career, to do justice to his understanding of the nature of religious language, Hick shifted from speaking about "God" to "the (Ultimate) Reality," a term that is more flexible than the personal term "God." For Hick, the great religions of the world are different—and one may say complementary—ways of approaching this Reality, which exists beyond the human capacity of knowing.

An important asset for Hick in his turn to a pluralistic theology in general and Christology in particular is a careful analysis of the nature of religious language. Whereas in the past Christian theology took the biblical and doctrinal claims such as virgin birth, incarnation, and resurrection as factual (technically put, "propositional") claims,[102] along with classical liberals and, say, Bultmann, Hick considers them merely a myth. Or, as he puts it, the "myth" is based on "metaphor," which means that we speak "suggestive of another."[103] Take for example incarnation: rather than a one-time, unique event manifested by Jesus of Nazareth two millennia ago, "incarnation" may mean the presence of divine (love) among many, or perhaps (to a varying extent) all, human beings.

---

one unlimited transcendent divine Reality and also a plurality of varying human concepts, images, and experiences of and responses to that Reality" (83).

101. Hick, *God and the Universe of Faiths*, 140–41.

102. That said, classical theology also understood clearly that these kinds of claims concerning the divine "things" and particularly the life of God are but human constructs, and therefore one has to be careful in their application. The term *analogical* means exactly that: on the one hand, there is a true correspondence between, say, the claim to God's fatherhood and human fatherhood. On the other hand, this correspondence is only relative. As a philosopher of religion, unfortunately, Hick seems not to make much of that nuancing in classical theology.

103. John Hick, *The Metaphor of God Incarnate: Christology in a Pluralistic Age* (London: SCM; Louisville: Westminster John Knox, 1993), 99. For a detailed discussion of metaphor (and myth) in Hick, see Kärkkäinen, *Christ and Reconciliation*, 215–18.

"Mythical" Christology

With his turn to a pluralistic notion of the deity and mythical/metaphorical view of religious language, Hick constructs a pluralistic Christology. Building on (and also creatively reworking) the heritage of classical liberalism (and aspects of the original quest), he considers incarnation, or virgin birth, or resurrection, as myths rather than historical records. Unabashedly, he represents "low Christology," in which incarnation means that all human beings, who only differ from one another in degree, are "Spirit-filled, or Christ-like, or truly saintly."[104] Hick calls this the "mythical" or metaphorical understanding, as presented in his main christological monograph, *The Metaphor of God Incarnate: Christology in a Pluralistic Age*.

The reason incarnation has to be made a myth or metaphor has to do with the simple observation that as long as the traditional viewpoint is maintained, it leads to rejection of other faiths' claims to "incarnation(s)." In traditional Christianity, incarnation language has been taken for granted, and it entails exclusivism: God is present in Christ in a specific, unique way. In the mythical interpretation, on the other hand, incarnation is not about a god becoming a human being; that kind of idea is totally repulsive to contemporary people. The *Logos* for Hick transcends any particular religion and is present in all of them. As a result, as mentioned above, the notion of incarnation becomes elusive and loose.

Hick also rejects Jesus's sinlessness and other similar claims. In summary form, some leading arguments of Hick's pluralistic Christology can be presented in the following manner:[105]

1. Jesus did not teach that he himself was God incarnate.
2. The Chalcedonian two-natures doctrine of the person of Christ cannot be expressed in a religiously adequate fashion.
3. The historical and traditional two-natures doctrine has been used to justify great evils, such as wars, persecution, repression, and genocide.
4. The notion of incarnation is better understood as a metaphor rather than as expressing some literal, metaphysical truth about the person of Christ.

104. Cited in Gerald O'Collins, SJ, "The Incarnation: The Critical Issues," in *The Incarnation: An Interdisciplinary Symposium on the Incarnation of the Son of God*, ed. Stephen T. Davis et al. (Oxford: Oxford University Press, 2004), 2 (and wrongly attributed to John Hick, "Incarnation," *Theology* 80 [1977]: 205; I have been unable to find the original reference).

105. Kärkkäinen, *Christ and Reconciliation*, 218–19, based on Oliver D. Crisp, *Divinity and Humanity: The Incarnation Reconsidered* (Cambridge: Cambridge University Press, 2007), 155–56.

5. The life and teaching of Jesus challenge us to live a life pleasing to God. Jesus is the Lord who makes God real to Christians.

6. This metaphorical understanding of the incarnation fits with a doctrine of religious pluralism, whereby Christ's life and teaching are seen as one example of the religious life that can also be found, in different ways and forms, in other major world religions.

A fitting nomenclature for Hick's pluralistic Christology is "degree" Christology, as opposed to the "substance" Christology of Chalcedon and classical Christianity. In degree Christology, as illustrated best in Hick's view of incarnation, Jesus Christ differs from other (religious) figures only in degree and is not in his own unique category, as in traditional theology. The following quotation illustrates this well:

> Incarnation, in the sense of the embodiment of ideas, values, insights in human living, is a basic metaphor. One might say, for example, that in 1940 the spirit of defiance of the British people against Nazi Germany was incarnated in Winston Churchill. Now we want to say of Jesus that he was so vividly conscious of God as the loving heavenly Father, and so startlingly open to God and so fully his servant and instrument, that the divine love was expressed, and in that sense incarnated, in his life. This was not a matter (as it is in official Christian doctrine) of Jesus having two complete natures, one human and the other divine. He was wholly human; but whenever self-giving love in response to the love of God is lived out in a human life, to that extent the divine love has become incarnate on earth.[106]

Instead of *homoousios*, the term of the ancient creeds that establishes the divinity of Christ and his equality with the Father, Hick prefers the term *homoagapē*; that is, in Jesus, rather than a unity of divine-human natures, a God-kind of love comes to manifestation. This of course makes traditional trinitarian doctrine both useless and obsolete.

In that light, it can be thought that the development of classical Christology was a historical accident. Had it spread to the East, it might have taken another path of development. Hick's vision for an Eastern Christ is this:

> Instead of Jesus being identified as the divine *Logos* or the divine Son he would have been identified as a Bodhissattva who, like Gotama some four centuries earlier, had attained to Buddhahood or perfect relationship to reality, but had in compassion for suffering mankind voluntarily lived out his human life in order to show others the way to salvation.[107]

106. John Hick, *God Has Many Names* (Philadelphia: Westminster, 1982), 58–59.
107. Hick, *God and the Universe of Faiths*, 117.

John Cobb: Process Christology

Process Thought in Search of a New Worldview

In a marked deviation from much of contemporary Euro-American theology, with its rejection of or disdain for metaphysics (that is, the philosophical inquiry into "ultimate reality"), American process theology, based on the groundbreaking work of the late British-American mathematician-turned-philosopher Alfred Whitehead, makes it a theological theme.[108] In process metaphysics, change, becoming, dynamism, and relationality seek to replace the static substance ontology and atomism of both classical philosophy (as exemplified by the medieval masters) and (Newtonian) modern science. Soon Whitehead's work was picked up by theologians under the tutelage of his pupil Charles Hartshorne, including Schubert Ogden, W. Norman Pittenger, John B. Cobb Jr., and Marjorie Hewitt Suchocki.[109]

Whitehead intuited in his dynamic understanding of reality that some kind of "subjective experience" (which he also calls "feeling") is present not only in humans but in all reality.[110] For Whitehead, everything has meaning and significance within the framework of a whole. There are no bare facts without meaning and significance, and that significance is related to the significance of every other moment and the total movement.[111] For the sake of explaining process theology's Christology, there is no need to delve into the idiosyncratic and complex terminological apparatus coined by Whitehead. Let it suffice to discern the dynamic, process-oriented, relational, and "living" intuition of the world and its processes. Leading process thinker Marjorie Hewitt Suchocki puts it nontechnically:

> Process theologies are relational ways of thinking about the dynamism of life and faith. Process-relational theologians integrate implications of a thoroughly interdependent universe into how we live and express our faith. We are convinced

108. On the relationship between his role as a mathematician and a philosopher-theologian, see Ralph M. Martin, "On the Whiteheadian God," in *God in Contemporary Thought: A Philosophical Perspective*, ed. Sebastian A. Matczak (New York: Learned Publications, 1977), 615–18.

109. A reliable and accessible exposition is John B. Cobb Jr. and David Ray Griffin, *Process Theology: An Introduction* (Philadelphia: Westminster, 1976). For a helpful survey of its Christology, see chap. 4 in William J. LaDue, *Jesus among the Theologians: Contemporary Interpretations of Christ* (Harrisburg, PA: Trinity Press International, 2001).

110. Whitehead develops this new metaphysics in his *Adventures of Ideas*, originally published in 1933 and now available as a reprint (New York: Free Press, 1967), and in his massive magnum opus (which goes well beyond the beginner level), *Process and Reality*, corrected ed. by David R. Griffin and Donald W. Sherburn (New York: Free Press, 1978).

111. Owen Sharkey, "Mystery of God in Process Theology," in *God in Contemporary Thought: A Philosophical Perspective*, ed. Sebastian A. Matczak (New York: Learned Publications, 1977), 686–88.

that everything is dynamically interconnected; that everything matters; that everything has an effect.[112]

On the theology side, one has to note that in this process orientation there is no doctrine of creation *ex nihilo* ("from nothing") but rather a vision of world and God co-evolving, God being the source and inspiration of evolution. Neither is there an idea of definite eschatological consummation after classical theology; even God, albeit the biggest, wisest, and most loving "entity," cannot guarantee a certain outcome but only provide a "lure," an invitation. In that real sense, even God is "inside" the world process, unlike in classical theism, in which there is a radical distinction (although not separation) between the (uncreated) God and (created) world.

Process Christ: Differing Interpretations

Although sharing the general intuitions and vision of Whitehead, various process scholars have understandably developed diverse theological interpretations of Christology.[113] It is safe to say that all of them value highly the humanity of Jesus. Yet the mere interest in the history of Jesus in the line of the quest is hardly on the agenda of process Christology.[114] David Griffin's important work, *A Process Christology*, brings together several traditions: the new quest of the historical Jesus, neo-orthodoxy (Karl Barth), the existentialism of Paul Tillich and Rudolf Bultmann, and the process philosophy of Whitehead and others, such as Charles Hartshorne.[115]

Although process theologians writing on Christ are in no way dismissive of classical christological traditions, neither are they bound to those confessions. Theirs is a robustly constructive theological approach. For a theologian such as Norman Pittenger, a pioneer christologist in the camp, Christ seems to be mainly an extraordinary person rather than a special revelation in the classical sense of the term. Or how else could we understand this statement in *Christology Reconsidered*, his mature work?

Jesus, in the dynamic existence which was his, fulfilled the potentialities which were also his in a manner that impressed those who companied with him as

112. Marjorie Hewitt Suchocki, "What Is Process Theology? A Conversation with Marjorie," *Process & Faith* (2003): 3, available at http://oldsite.processandfaith.org/sites/default/files/pdfs /What_Is_Process_Theology.pdf.

113. Though somewhat outdated, still a useful and reliable guide is H. D. McDonald, "Process Christology," *Vox Evangelica* 20 (1990): 43–56.

114. For details and references to Pittenger, see ibid., 45.

115. David Griffin, *A Process Christology* (Philadelphia: Westminster, 1973).

being extraordinary without being a violation of the ordinary conditions of manhood. . . . His degree of realization was not the same as that of other men whom his companions knew; it was immeasurably different yet not utterly removed from the experience of manhood elsewhere seen.[116]

It seems to me Marjorie Hewitt Suchocki's definition of Jesus's "divinity" represents the same kind of orientation:

Jesus represents God for us, because we see him consistently responding positively to God's moment by moment call to him. That call is that he live as God would have him live in each and every situation. He conforms himself so thoroughly to the will of God that in and through his person and his actions, we see clearly what God is like.[117]

Our focus in this section is on the Christology of leading American process theologian John Cobb, which, similarly, is definitely constructive yet quite keen on following the intuitions of some key classical traditions (even when they are reformulated in his system).

Christ in a Pluralistic Age

Although titled *Christ in a Pluralistic Age*, the important christological contribution of John B. Cobb Jr., the late formative American process theologian, does not represent a typical pluralistic agenda after Hick and others.[118] The reason is that, while not equating the more universal sphere of *Logos* and its more particular manifestation in the life of Jesus of Nazareth, John Cobb's version of process Christology also keeps them together in an important way. On the one hand, he treats *Logos* as if it were a cosmic or universal principle that has had a number of manifestations in arts, theology, the Freudian concept of "conscience," and so forth.[119] Speaking of "Christ as the Logos *incarnate* in the world as creative transformation" certainly points to both classical liberals and pluralists such as Hick. On the other hand, differently from pluralists, Cobb maintains that "Christ is indissolubly bound up with Jesus."[120] He even maintains that "unless the power of creative transformation discerned in art and theology is also the power that was present in him and that continues

116. Norman Pittenger, *Christology Reconsidered* (London: SCM, 1970), 119–20; see also the similar kind of statement on "three essential elements in the christological enterprise" (6–7).
117. Suchocki, "What Is Process Theology?," 14.
118. This section is based on Kärkkäinen, *Christ and Reconciliation*, 213–14.
119. John B. Cobb Jr., *Christ in a Pluralistic Age* (Philadelphia: Westminster, 1975), 82–83; more widely part 1.
120. Ibid., 62.

to operate through his word, the affirmations [about the manifestations of *Logos* in arts and elsewhere] . . . cannot stand."[121]

Rather than pushing away the centrality of Christ, as pluralists such as Hick would do, Cobb attempts to widen the meaning of Christ as "Creative Transformation," manifested in areas such as the arts, cosmic realities, psychology, and future hope, which so far have been marginal in traditional Christian interpretations.[122] Ultimately, this is to find a better way to relate to other religions.

Following process thought, which rejects all notions of "substance," Cobb cannot of course subscribe to the creedal confession of *homoousios* (of the same "essence"). The way he attempts to express the current meaning of the ancient formula, gleaning also from his earlier work *The Structure of Christian Existence*,[123] means that the incarnation of the *Logos* would be manifested in the constitution of selfhood, in a way that "the 'I' in each moment is constituted as much in the subjective reception of the lure to self-actualization that is the call and presence of the logos as it is in continuity with the personal past. This structure of existence would be the incarnation of the Logos in the fullest meaningful sense."[124] Although for Cobb *Logos* "is incarnate in all human beings and indeed in all creation,"[125] it is only in Jesus that the presence of God is incarnated in the way explained above. Other human beings experience "the new possibility ['lure'] provided by the Logos as challenging it from without," and they conform to it in varying degrees.[126]

Having now scrutinized a number of leading Euro-American christological interpretations, the discussion in the two subsequent chapters moves into the global context and consults scholars from Africa, Asia, and Latin America, as well as those Euro-American views that are usually called contextual.

121. Ibid., 97.
122. See especially ibid., 61.
123. John B. Cobb Jr., *The Structure of Christian Existence* (Philadelphia: Westminster, 1967).
124. Cobb, *Christ in a Pluralistic Age*, 140.
125. Ibid., 138.
126. Ibid., 139.

6

Christologies from the Global South

Christologies in Global Contexts: Radical Challenges to Theology

The world in which Christian faith is lived out, churches do their ministry, and theology is practiced has dramatically changed since the second half of the last century.[1] Theologies are yet to fathom the implication of the "globalization" of the church.[2] Indeed, we can speak of the "Macroreformation"[3] taking place before our very eyes as Christianity is moving from the Global North (Europe and North America) to the Global South (Africa, Asia, Latin America). This demographic shift has turned the tables:[4] by 2050, only about

1. For these and similar facts and analyses, see the detailed report "Christianity in Its Global Context, 1970–2020," by Gordon-Conwell Theological Seminary (June 2013), available at www .gordonconwell.edu/ockenga/research/documents/ChristianityinitsGlobalContext.pdf. This section is based on Kärkkäinen, *Christ and Reconciliation: A Constructive Christian Theology for the Pluralistic World* (Grand Rapids: Eerdmans, 2013), 16–21.

2. The reason "globalization" is in quotation marks is that it is a highly contested and widely debated issue among philosophers, sociologists, scholars of (international) politics, and others—the details of which we are not examining in an introductory survey text. In this book, the term is used in its everyday meaning, that is, that theologies and churches find themselves in a world in which various cultures, nations, and influences interact closely with one another.

3. Justo L. González, *Mañana: Christian Theology from a Hispanic Perspective* (Nashville: Abingdon, 1990), 49.

4. For a current, short statement, see John Parratt, "Introduction," in *An Introduction to Third World Theologies*, ed. John Parratt (Cambridge: Cambridge University Press, 2004), 1.

one-fifth of the world's three billion Christians will be non-Hispanic whites. The typical Christian in the first decades of the third millennium is a non-white, non-affluent, non-Northern person, more often female than male. "If we want to visualize a 'typical' contemporary Christian, we should think of a woman living in a village in Nigeria or in a Brazilian *favela*,"[5] as "the centers of the church's universality [are] no longer in Geneva, Rome, Athens, Paris, London, New York, but Kinshasa, Buenos Aires, Addis Ababa and Manila."[6] As a result, "Christianity is no longer exclusively identified as a Western religion . . . [but] also a world Christianity. This means Christianity cannot be understood exclusively from a Western perspective."[7]

So far it has been taken for granted that the male-dominated, Euro-American way of doing theology is the only normative way. This has meant the suppression and marginalization of other viewpoints. Consider the statement of Cuban-born American church historian Justo González:

> North American male theology is taken to be basic, normative, universal theology, to which then women, other minorities, and people from the younger churches may add their footnotes. What is said in Manila is very relevant for the Philippines. What is said in Tübingen, Oxford or Yale is relevant for the entire church. White theologians do general theology; black theologians do black theology. Male theologians do general theology; female theologians do theology determined by their sex. Such a notion of "universality" based on the present unjust distribution of power is unacceptable to the new theology.[8]

To make a difference in the way theology is practiced calls for the cultivation of "multiperspectivalism" and inclusivity. This kind of attitude allows for diverse, at times even contradictory and opposing, voices and testimonies to be part of the dialogue.[9] Malaysian-born, Chinese American, Pentecostal theologian Amos Yong reminds us that it means "taking seriously the insights of all voices, especially those previously marginalized from the theological conversation—for instance, women, the poor, the differently abled or disabled, perhaps even the heretics!"[10]

Perhaps no other field of study in theology is as integrally connected to culture and worldview as Christology. The foreword to a recent study in

5. Philip Jenkins, *The Next Christendom: The Coming of Global Christianity* (Oxford: Oxford University Press, 2011), 2.

6. John Mbiti, quoted in Kwame Bediako, *Christianity in Africa: The Renewal of a Non-Western Religion* (Edinburgh: University Press; Maryknoll, NY: Orbis, 1995), 154.

7. Jung Young Lee, *The Trinity in Asian Perspective* (Nashville: Abingdon, 1999), 11.

8. González, *Mañana*, 52.

9. See Amos Yong, *The Spirit Poured Out on All Flesh: Pentecostalism and the Possibility of Global Theology* (Grand Rapids: Baker Academic, 2005), 239–40.

10. Ibid., 240.

intercultural Christologies encapsulates well the significance of cultural context for Christologies in various global settings:

> If any single area of theology is especially poised to raise questions about the nature and practice of inculturation [the influence of culture on theology and vice versa], it is surely Christology. The fact of the Incarnation itself places us already on a series of boundaries: between the divine and the human, between the particular and the universal, between eternity and time. The questions raised for culture span the entire range of Christological discourse, from what significance Jesus' having been born in a specific time and place might have, to the cultural and linguistic differences that plagued the Christological controversies of the fourth and fifth centuries.[11]

The term *contextual* implies that the Christologies to be studied in this section are firmly anchored in a specific context, be it cultural, intellectual, or related to a specific worldview.[12] To call these Christologies contextual does not mean that the Christologies already studied are free from contextual influences, however. Even classical Christologies in the West, including the classical christological creeds, are not immune to surrounding philosophical, religious, social, and political influences. Ironically, the more that Western theologians have studied theologies outside the West, the more knowledgeable they have become about their indebtedness to factors in the context in which the early creeds and christological interpretations arose. However, it has become commonplace to use the term *contextual* for theologies not based, more or less, on classical Western ones. These theological interpretations, emerging from new contexts and questions, most of which were unknown when the basic christological formulations were developed, are important topics of current theology.

> The task before us is complicated and challenging because Christian difference is always a complex and flexible network of small and large refusals, divergences, subversions, and more or less radical alternative proposals, surrounded by the acceptance of many cultural givens. There is no single correct way to relate to a given culture as a whole, or even to its dominant thrust; there are only numerous ways of accepting, transforming, or replacing various aspects of a given culture from within.[13]

11. Robert J. Schreiter, foreword to Volker Küster, *The Many Faces of Jesus Christ: An Intercultural Christology*, trans. John Bowden (Maryknoll, NY: Orbis, 2001), xi.

12. For a useful discussion, see Küster, *Many Faces of Jesus Christ*, 15–36.

13. Miroslav Volf, "When Gospel and Culture Intersect: Notes on the Nature of Christian Difference," in *Pentecostalism in Context: Essays in Honor of William W. Menzies*, ed. Wonsuk Ma and Robert P. Menzies (Sheffield: Sheffield Academic, 2008), 233.

Contextual theology means opening up to the diversity of interpretations and the widening of one's own horizons. On the one hand, it requires—as German male theologian Jürgen Moltmann aptly puts it—that the theologian "recognizes the conditions and limitations of his own position, and the relativity of his own particular environment."[14] On the other hand, it also means that one does not have to bracket, so to speak, the limitations and specificity of one's own contextuality. Rather, again citing Moltmann, who is speaking of himself in the third person, "For him this means a critical dissolution of naïve, self-centered thinking. Of course he is a European, but European theology no longer has to be Euro*centric*. Of course, he is a man, but theology no longer has to be *androcentric*. Of course he is living in the 'first world,' but the theology which he is developing does not have to reflect the ideas of the dominating nations."[15]

Among the growing "contextual" and intercultural interpretations of Christ, the following ones have been chosen as representative examples.[16] Chapter 6 will tap into the rich resources of theologizing about Jesus Christ among Latin American, African, and Asian theologians, conveniently named theologians from the Global South. In keeping with the more communal orientations of most cultures in those continents, the survey is not focused on individual theologians, even though, for the sake of accuracy and specificity, a number of particular theologians will be mentioned and analyzed. Following the survey of Christologies from the Global South, in the next chapter the discussion zooms in on the so-called contextual Christologies that are found mainly in the Global North (Europe, North America). That includes various types of female theologians' views of Christ, as well as black and womanist (female African American), Latino/a, postcolonial, and queer theologies of Christ.

An important word of warning before proceeding is in order. Doing theology in a way that highlights contemporary intercultural and contextual diversity is not meant to imply that Christian tradition is to be undervalued. That would be not only naive but also counterproductive. Much of contemporary theology in particular locations and contexts draws its energy from a careful, painstaking, and often tension-filled dialogue with and response to tradition. Theological tradition is the heritage of the whole church of Christ on earth, not only of the church in the Global North. Irenaeus, Augustine, Aquinas, Calvin, and Schleiermacher have contributed—and are contributing—to the growing living tradition

14. Jürgen Moltmann, *The Trinity and the Kingdom of God: The Doctrine of God*, trans. Margaret Kohl (San Francisco: Harper & Row; London: SCM, 1981), xii.
15. Ibid. (emphasis original).
16. For concise discussions, see also Kärkkäinen, "Christology in Africa, Asia and Latin America," in *Blackwell Companion to Jesus*, ed. Delbert Burkett (Hoboken, NJ: Wiley-Blackwell, 2010), 375–93.

of Christian theological reflection in all locations in our shrinking globe, albeit differently depending on the context. Therefore, this volume is also critical of those kinds of "contextual" or "intercultural" theologies that simply naively dismiss tradition and claim to begin from scratch, in other words, merely from the "context(s)." A landmark volume written by two leading Roman Catholic missiologists in the United States titled *Constants in Context* accurately illustrates the need for Christian theology to negotiate the *constant* features of Christian beliefs and doctrines in changing, diverse, and often perplexing *contexts*.[17] Christian theology has tried more than one way to "accommodate" to the cultural challenge; some approaches have been less than successful.

Christologies from Latin America: Christ the Liberator

In Search of the Christ of the Poor and Marginalized

The problems of colonialization and subjugation of the indigenous peoples of South America go far back in history.[18] At the end of the fifteenth century when South America was "discovered" under the leadership of Christopher ("The-Christ-Bearer") Columbus and taken over by the *conquistadors* (Spanish soldiers), the Christ presented to the Indians represented the side of the powerful and the ruler.[19] At the same time, the figure of the suffering Christ was portrayed in popular piety:

> The two images [of Christ presented to the Indios] are to some degree two sides of the one coin of colonialist propaganda. The dying or dead Christ is an offer of identification in suffering, without arousing hope—the resurrection is distant. Even today, in the popular Catholicism of Latin America, Good Friday is the greatest day of celebration. The other side, Christ the ruler, is embodied in the Spanish king and the colonial rulers, to whom the Indios are to bend the knee in veneration. In both cases the christology degenerates into an instrument of oppression. At an early stage resistance against it grew.[20]

With this long history of pain and suffering, liberation theologians of various stripes have sought to correct and "polish" the picture of Christ for

17. Stephen B. Bevans and Roger P. Schroeder, *Constants in Context: A Theology of Mission for Today* (Maryknoll, NY: Orbis, 2004).

18. For an accessible account, see Küster, *Many Faces of Jesus Christ*, 41–46.

19. For political and religious motifs behind the conquest, see Anton Wessels, *Images of Jesus: How Jesus Is Perceived and Portrayed in Non-European Cultures* (Grand Rapids: Eerdmans, 1990), 58–61.

20. Küster, *Many Faces of Jesus Christ*, 42.

that continent.[21] Vatican II (1962–65) was a key moment in the evolvement and formulation of that consciousness. Soon after the council, Catholic bishops stated as their goal the work for liberation: "Action on behalf of justice and participation in the transformation of the world fully appear to us as a *constitutive dimension of the preaching of the Gospel*, or, in other words, of the church's mission for the redemption of the human race and its liberation from every oppressive situation."[22] CELAM, the Second Conference of Latin American Bishops at Medellín, Colombia (1968), placed three interrelated themes on its agenda: efforts for justice and peace, the need for adaptation in evangelization and faith, and the reform of the church and its structures.[23]

Out of liberation theologies' struggle for freedom, justice, and economic sharing arose a new type of ecclesiological experimentation that has contributed to the renewal of the church in Latin America, namely, base Christian communities. The term *base* means the poor, the oppressed, and the marginalized. These communities, in which lay leadership and lay ministries have taken on a new significance, represent a grassroots cry for the liberation of the poor and other outcasts in society. According to Leonardo Boff, one of the leading liberationists, these communities "deserve to be contemplated, welcomed, and respected as salvific events."[24] Base communities not only identify with the poor and the weakest in society but *are* a church of the poor. As such, base communities resist the widespread Christian ethos of reducing Christianity to the intimate sphere of private life. "Jesus preached and died in public, out in the world, and he is Lord not only of the little corners of our hearts, but of society and the cosmos as well."[25] The preaching of the gospel, good news to the poor, kindles in the poor the fire of hope and transforms their lives.

Jesus and "Integral Liberation"

According to Brazilian Leonardo Boff, there are two current approaches to liberation Christology.[26] The "sacramental approach" aims to offer a rein-

---

21. In the section on Latin American Christology, I am indebted beyond the number of direct references to chap. 5 in William J. LaDue, *Jesus among the Theologians: Contemporary Interpretations of Christ* (Harrisburg, PA: Trinity Press International, 2001).

22. "Declaration from the Roman Bishops Synod of 1971," in *Mission Trends*, ed. Gerald H. Anderson and Thomas F. Stransky (New York: Paulist Press, 1975), 2:255 (emphasis added).

23. For details, see the documentation "Medellin 1969 (excerpts)," available at www .geraldschlabach.net/medellin-1968-excerpts.

24. Leonardo Boff, *Ecclesiogenesis: The Base Communities Reinvent the Church*, trans. Robert R. Barr (Maryknoll, NY: Orbis, 1986), 1.

25. Ibid., 38.

26. This section is based on Kärkkäinen, *Christ and Reconciliation*, 86–90.

terpretation of Christology in terms of classical dogmas and concepts with some liberationist orientation. Boff thinks that even though it is helpful in its acknowledgment of the need for liberation, this type of Christology falls short in its analysis of the situation of the Latin American context and is not able to remedy its massive social and political challenges. The second type of liberation Christology is called a "socioanalytical presentation of Christology." This is genuinely liberationist in that it not only offers an incisive analysis but also attempts sociopolitical structural change. This type of liberation theology makes critical use of the tools of social and political sciences and is not afraid to borrow from socialist or Marxist analyses of society. In this latter approach, social, economic, and political liberation is seen as constitutive of the preaching of the kingdom of God. In light of the socioanalytical approach, for example, the exploitative nature of capitalism with the corollary problem of economic dependency is exposed, and measures are taken to counteract it. Socioanalytical Christology aims for liberating *orthopraxis* (literally, "right action") rather than *orthodoxy* (literally, "right worship," though the current meaning is "right belief").[27]

In order to respond to the many charges against complacency toward the issues of poverty and social inequality, the term "integral liberation" was coined in the so-called Puebla Document subsequent to the Medellín conference in 1968. It denotes Jesus's liberating ministry that takes into consideration different dimensions of life—whether social, political, economic, or cultural—and the whole web of factors affecting human life. Gustavo Gutiérrez has called this liberationist orientation a "theology from the underside of history."[28] The idea of integral liberation insists that "spiritual" and "earthly" belong together and can never be divorced from each other, as has often happened in classical theology. This is in keeping with the Christology of the New Testament: the emancipatory power of the gospel of the kingdom of God—God's righteous and just rule—was manifest in the ministry of Jesus of Nazareth. Those whom Jesus delivered—the sick, the demon possessed, those outside the covenant community—became signs of the coming kingdom and its power of liberation and reconciliation.[29]

---

27. Leonardo Boff, *Jesus Christ Liberator: A Critical Christology for Our Time*, trans. Patrick Hughes (Maryknoll, NY: Orbis, 1978), 269–78. Leonardo's brother, Clodovis Boff, speaks of the "socioanalytic mediation" of theology, a robust interaction with social sciences as an aid to analyze appropriately sociopolitical conditions for theology. Clodovis Boff, *Theology and Praxis: Epistemological Foundations*, trans. Robert R. Barr, rev. ed. (Maryknoll, NY: Orbis, 1987).

28. Gustavo Gutiérrez, *The Power of the Poor in History: Selected Writings*, trans. Robert R. Barr (Maryknoll, NY: Orbis, 1983), 169.

29. See further Priscilla Pope-Levison and John R. Levison, *Jesus in Global Contexts* (Louisville: Westminster John Knox, 1992), 36.

In order to orient our way of reading the Bible in the liberationist manner, Latin American liberationists have proposed a new hermeneutic to guide theological work that is liberationist in its nature and goals.[30] The starting point is the context rather than the text. With this insight, the "hermeneutical circle" takes place in four interrelated stages:

1. Ideological suspicion: an emerging notion that perhaps something is wrong in society, especially among the underprivileged
2. Analytical reflection on the social-value system: asking penetrating questions, such as whether a situation is justified by Scripture and whether God's purposes are fulfilled in it
3. Exegetical suspicion: an acknowledgment of the fact that theology is not relevant because of a one-sided and biased style of reading the Bible that neglects the perspective of the poor and oppressed
4. Pastoral action: articulating an appropriate response to what is determined to be one's personal biblical responsibility[31]

The following section seeks to illustrate the importance of a liberationist hermeneutic.

A Hispanic Rereading of the History of Christological Doctrine: An Exercise in Liberative Hermeneutics

A wonderful way to illustrate the importance of hermeneutics, including ideological suspicion, with regard to not only the biblical text but also the history of the doctrine, is provided by Justo L. González, a Cuban American liberation historian-theologian. He offers a liberationist rereading of the development of the christological doctrine in the early church.[32] He begins with analysis of the appeal of gnosticism and considers it a hidden way of justifying the conditions of oppression by making evil and injustice a matter of this-worldly affairs and looking for "salvation" in another world. As a result, no opposition to evil structures or work for liberation was needed:

> The Gnostics were well aware of the evil and injustice that abound in this world. Their solution, however, was not to oppose that evil but rather to surrender this

30. For an accessible account of Leonardo Boff's and Jon Sobrino's approaches, see Küster, *Many Faces of Jesus Christ*, 47–55.

31. Juan Luis Segundo, *The Liberation of Theology*, trans. John Drury (Maryknoll, NY: Orbis, 1976), 39–40.

32. González, *Mañana*, chap. 10.

world to the powers of evil. And to turn to a wholly different realm for their hope for meaning and vindication. According to them, original reality—and therefore also ultimate reality—was purely spiritual. The physical world is not part of a divine plan of creation but is rather the result of a mistake. In this world, and in the material bodies that are part of it, our souls are entrapped, although in truth they belong to the spiritual world. Salvation thus consists in being able to flee this material world.[33]

Similarly, docetism was found appealing: in that heresy, Jesus was not a real human being; he only appeared to be so. True divinity can never appear in the form of evil matter, flesh. Similarly to gnosticism, in docetism evil and all else in this world are not significant; what matters is the other world. In other words, gnosticism and docetism were found appealing by those who suffered: instead of resisting the evil and working for liberation, they dreamed of another world. Orthodox Christology, however, ruled against these heresies and deemed them unsatisfactory: Jesus suffered and fought against the evil. What about the appeal of adoptionism? González's view is that

adoptionism is the Christological expression of a myth that minorities and other oppressed groups have always known to be oppressive. This is the myth that "anyone can make it." Those who belong to the higher classes have a vested interest in this myth, for it implies that their privilege is based on their effort and achievement. But those who belong to the lower classes and who have not been propagandized into alienation from their reality know that this is a myth, and that the few that do make it are in fact allowed to move on in order to preserve the myth.[34]

In other words, adoptionism is seen as an alienating doctrine by those who realize that their society is in fact closed.

González also considers the implications of other early heresies, such as Apollinarianism, whose danger from the Hispanic vantage point is that such a doctrine would undo the saving power of Jesus. If the human mind is not in need of salvation, as Apollinarianism implies, then problems in life are relegated to the bodily nature as opposed to the spiritual.

Nestorianism, however, in González's estimation, has not been a problem to Hispanics because its robust distinction (if not separation) between the two natures allows for us to "assert that the broken, oppressed, and crucified Jesus is God . . . [and as such] the sign that God suffers with us."[35]

33. Ibid., 140–41.
34. Ibid., 144.
35. Ibid., 148.

The Jesus of Real History

Rather than "theory," the preferred term of liberation theology is "praxis." Liberationists look at what Jesus did and taught as the template for Christian life. The focus is placed on the historical Jesus, who lived a real life under real human conditions. Interest in the historical Jesus leads to the study and appropriation of the Gospels. That shifts the focus from abstract speculations to the study of Jesus's earthly life with implications for healing, liberation, affirmation of life, and other liberative impulses. No wonder the historical Jesus and the Gospels are in the forefront.[36] Latin American liberationists usually prefer Mark and Luke to Matthew and John.

That said, it has to be noted at the outset that the interest of liberation theologians in the Jesus of history differs from the quest of the historical Jesus among the theologians of classical liberalism. For liberationists, the focus is not the historical facts of the life of Jesus as such, as in the main drive of the quest, but rather understanding the relevance of the history of Jesus to the struggles in Latin America. "*Understanding* Jesus, as opposed to recovering Jesus, requires holding together in creative fusion two distinct horizons: the historical Jesus of the Gospels and the historical context of contemporary Latin America."[37] As the name "liberation theology" suggests, the main role in which Jesus Christ is depicted is that of Liberator. Jesus's ministry encompasses several forms of liberation, beginning with the fight against unjust economic structures, which liberationists see evident in the parable of the workers who labored for different lengths of time but earned the same wage (Matt. 20:1–16). Jesus also fought social structures by inviting those who were outside the religious law, such as prostitutes and tax collectors, into table fellowship. In that culture, as in many non-Western cultures even today, table fellowship is the most honoring and inclusive means of welcoming another person. Indeed, Jesus

> fought dehumanization by placing human need above even the most sacred traditions such as Sabbath purity (Mark 2:23–3:6). Therefore the oppressed were conscientized in his presence. Blind Bartimaeus, whom the crowds silenced, was given voice and healed by Jesus (Mark 10:46–52). An unnamed woman with a flow of blood and no financial resources touched Jesus and subsequently "told him the whole truth" (Mark 5:25–34). Jesus fought sin by denouncing

---

36. See, e.g., Jon Sobrino, *Christology at the Crossroads: A Latin American Approach* (Maryknoll, NY: Orbis, 1978), 10.

37. Pope-Levison and Levison, *Jesus in Global Contexts*, 31.

everything—whether religious, political, economic, or social—that alienated people from God and from their neighbor.[38]

This is the thrust of the book *Jesus Christ Liberator* by Leonardo Boff, who has experienced great pressure not to speak for the poor and other marginalized. Christ's message concerning the kingdom of God actually amounted to the promise of the full realization of the whole of reality. Boff complains that the revolutionary message of Christ has been reduced in many cases to a decision of faith made by individuals without much relation to the social and political aspects of life. Boff argues that the liberation proposed by Jesus relates to the public realm as well as to the personal sphere. He even contends that "over the years the church has fallen into the temptation of adopting the customs of pagan society, with authority patterns reflecting domination, and with the use of lofty and honorific titles by those in positions of power over others."[39] By doing so, the church has been hiding its true identity as the community of Christ.

As mentioned, according to González, the interpretation of Christ became tuned in with the wishes and hopes of the ruling class, and the role of Christ as the one who identifies with the outcasts, the poor, and the oppressed lost its dynamic:

—◦ NOT *REALLY*

> Great pains were taken to mitigate the scandal of God's being revealed in a poor carpenter. His life and sayings were reinterpreted so as to make them more palatable to the rich and powerful. Innumerable legends were built around him, usually seeking to raise him to the level that many understood to be that of the divine—that is, to the level of a superemperor. Art depicted him as either the Almighty Ruler of the universe, sitting on his throne, or as the stolid hero who overcomes the suffering of the cross with superhuman resources and aristocratic poise.[40]

But even so, González reminds us, there still remained the very real and very human figure of the carpenter, crucified by the ruling powers, crying when abandoned by God and his fellow people, yet being "very God." Liberation Christology has had to remind traditional theology of the inadequacy of its categories and orientations with regard to uncovering the biblical message about Christ.

Liberationists remind the rest of us that it is in the "faces of the poor" that the marginalized Christ can be seen most clearly. This principle might

38. Ibid., 35.
39. As paraphrased by LaDue, *Jesus among the Theologians*, 170.
40. González, *Mañana*, 140.

be a modern version of Luther's basic hermeneutical principle that God is to be seen in his opposites, namely, suffering and shame.[41] The affirmation of the presence of Christ in the midst of the poor is significant because today, as in Jesus's time, the poor and outcast make up the majority of the world's population. The Spanish-born Jesuit liberationist who served decades in Latin America, Jon Sobrino, rightly concludes, "If Christianity is characterized by its universal claims, whether made on the basis of creation or of the final consummation, what affects majorities should be a principle governing the degree of authenticity and historical verification of this universalism. . . . Otherwise, the universality it claims will be a euphemism, an irony, or a mythified ideologization."[42]

Salvation as Liberation

As mentioned earlier, Christology has traditionally been divided into two sections: Christology proper, which deals with the person of Christ, and soteriology, which deals with the work of Christ, the salvation Christ accomplished. Naturally, these two areas are integrally related; what one believes about the person of Christ carries over to what one affirms about the nature of salvation in Christ. In liberation theology, this connection between Christology and soteriology comes to focus in that, as a result of looking at the person of Christ from the perspective of liberation, salvation is understood as liberation. The term *liberation* here does not necessarily mean only this-worldly social and political liberation, as liberation theologians are sometimes unjustly charged of believing, especially by their more conservative colleagues. Rather, it emphasizes that salvation is not *only* about saving the soul.

Salvation in the biblical sense of the term—based on the Old Testament concept of *shalom*, "peace," "well-being," "harmony"—is a multidimensional and inclusive concept. It bridges otherworldly and this-worldly dimensions. Liberationists rightly remind Christian theologians of the often-too-narrow outlook on salvation and insist that sociopolitical aspects not be overlooked. In Gutiérrez's terminology, traditional theology errs in viewing salvation as exclusively "quantitative," that is, as "guaranteeing heaven" for the greatest number. According to him, in the Latin American context there is an urgent need to reinterpret salvation in qualitative terms, as a way of social, political, and economic transformation. The careful analysis of Gutiérrez leads him to the conclusion that the Christian sense of salvation has three interrelated facets:

41. Küster, *Many Faces of Jesus Christ*, 55.
42. Jon Sobrino, *Jesus in Latin America* (Maryknoll, NY: Orbis, 1987), 141.

1. Personal transformation and freedom from sin
2. Liberation from social and political oppression
3. Liberation from marginalization (which may take several forms, such as unjust treatment of women and minorities)[43]

This wider and more "earth-centered" vision of salvation can be discerned time after time in investigating Christologies from the Global South.

Christologies from Africa: Christ the Ancestor

Christ and the Most "Christianized" Continent

The radical transformation of the Christian church during the second half of the twentieth century has made Africa—formerly a "mission land"—the major Christian center. Indeed, according to analysts, by about 2020 Africa will house more Christians than any other continent![44] Although some theological topics, such as the Trinity, may not be focused on much in African Christian spirituality, "Christology . . . at the very heart of all Christian theology . . . is particularly true for African Christian theology."[45]

In that light we may ask the following: In what way can Jesus Christ be an African among the Africans according to their own religious experience? Who is Christ for Africans, and what is the impact of this Christ? "For too long, embracing Christ and his message meant rejection of African cultural values. Africans were taught that their ancient ways were deficient or even evil and had to be set aside if they hoped to become Christians."[46] The irony, of course, is that African values and customs are often closer to the world of the Bible and its cultures than is the Western form of Christianity that has often been forced on the African mind-set. Yet, historically, it is also true that "Jesus was in Africa even before the rise of Christianity" in that his family found a hiding place in Egypt and that one of the first converts was Ethiopian, among other early allusions.[47] Furthermore, much of early Christian theology

43. Gustavo Gutiérrez, *A Theology of Liberation: History, Politics, and Salvation*, rev. ed., trans. and ed. Sister Caridad Inda and John Eagleson (Maryknoll, NY: Orbis, 1988), xxxviii.

44. For these and similar facts and analyses, see "Christianity in Its Global Context, 1970–2020."

45. John Onaiyekan, "Christological Trends in Contemporary African Theology," in *Constructive Christian Theology in the Worldwide Church*, ed. William R. Barr (Grand Rapids: Eerdmans, 1997), 356.

46. Robert J. Schreiter, "Jesus Christ in Africa Today," in *Faces of Jesus in Africa*, ed. R. J. Schreiter (Maryknoll, NY: Orbis, 1991), viii.

47. Wessels, *Images of Jesus*, 98–99.

in general and Christology in particular was shaped by North African theologians such as Tertullian, Cyprian, and Augustine.[48]

The rich cultural background of Africa contributes to its variety of christological approaches and trends. Furthermore, Africa has been influenced by different Christian traditions, which adds to the proliferation of conceptions and images of Jesus Christ. Generally speaking, Roman Catholic theology has found it easier than Protestant traditions to make Christian sense out of African rituals and symbols.

Distinctive Roles of Christ in African Christian Spirituality

Similarly to the New Testament and later Christian tradition, Jesus Christ appears in African Christianity in many roles and under many titles. Some of them are similar to received Christian tradition, while others are novelties. The title "Servant of God," for example, is found in some African cultures, as is "Redeemer": the Redeemer is welcomed as he who rescues us from the enslavement of the evil forces that surround us. Other christological titles with parallels in the African environment include "Conqueror" and "Lord." The title "Lord" denotes authority and power in the same way as the "Lord on the hills" of the people of Kabba, one of the Yoruba tribes. The New Testament title "Son of God" is understandable in the African context in that the idea of God sending a son to the world makes good sense for a culture used to divinities and the Supreme Being. Even though the idea of "Savior" is not so prevalent in most African cultures, it is not totally foreign to them either, as is evident in the Yorubas' expectation of the divinities (*Orisha*) to save them.[49]

Related to the central role of the community in most African cultures are family-related images of Christ drawn from African cultures and employed by African Christologies. Christ as the Elder Brother, an idea that can also be found in the biblical account of Christ as the "firstborn" (Col. 1:15–20), relates to the African conception of the family and the village as the primary network of life. Personality for Africans does not denote individuality but belonging to community. This idea comes to focus, for example, in the Akan conception of the human being, who is able to fulfill himself or herself only

48. True, by the time of the Islamic invasion in the seventh century, both Christian theology and churches had virtually disappeared from African soil, and it took until the beginning of the modern missionary movement in the nineteenth century to reintroduce Christianity on any significant scale to Africa. This sweeping historical note, however, is not meant to dismiss the sporadic presence of Christianity in Africa between these two periods; the Portuguese reintroduced Christianity to Congo before the time of the Reformation, and so forth.

49. For a useful and succinct discussion of these and other titles, see Charles Nyamiti, "African Christologies Today," in *Faces of Jesus in Africa*, 3–23.

in society. J. S. Pobee has suggested that what is most distinctive about Akan Christology is its emphasis on Christ's kinship, circumcision, and baptism as rites of incorporation into the community.[50]

A prominent role of Jesus is that of Healer, another key New Testament description of Jesus's ministry.[51] In Africa, health means not only lack of sickness but also well-being in a holistic sense. Sickness is not primarily a result of physical symptoms but is deeply spiritual. For many African christologists, healing is the central feature of the life and ministry of Jesus Christ. Aylward Shorter has compared Galilean healers, whose techniques were adopted by Jesus, with traditional African medicine men and has discovered many similarities between the two traditions.[52] Both practice a holistic form of healing on the physical, mental, social, and even environmental levels.[53] But in contrast to the healers both of Jesus's time and in the African context, Christ was the "wounded healer" who became a healer through the pain and suffering of the cross.

Unlike their counterparts in the West, African Christians reject both the secularist worldview as well as missionaries' thin Western conceptions of reality and spirit. "Orthodoxy" has left Christians helpless in real life, and so an alternative theology has been needed that relates to the whole range of needs, which includes the spiritual but is not limited to abstract, otherworldly spiritual needs.

Of all Christian traditions, Pentecostalism and later charismatic movements have focused most on the role of Jesus Christ as the Healer. A rapidly growing "Pentecostalization" is going on in Africa, with many traditional churches adopting Pentecostal-type worship patterns, prayer services, and healing ministries. A major attraction for Pentecostalism in African contexts has been its emphasis on healing. In these cultures, the religious specialist or "person of God" has power to heal the sick and ward off evil spirits and sorcery. This holistic function, which does not separate the "physical" from the "spiritual," is restored in Pentecostalism, and many indigenous peoples see it as a "powerful" religion to meet human needs.[54]

50. As discussed in ibid., 6–7.

51. This subsection is based on Kärkkäinen, *Christ and Reconciliation*, 63; see also the important discussion on the wider topic of Christ as healer in Timothy C. Tennent, *Theology in the Context of World Christianity: How the Global Church Is Influencing the Way We Think about and Discuss Theology* (Grand Rapids: Zondervan, 2007), 109–22.

52. Aylward Shorter, *Jesus and the Witchdoctor: An Approach to Healing and Wholeness* (Maryknoll, NY: Orbis, 1985).

53. See further Cece Kole, "Jesus as Healer?," in *Faces of Jesus in Africa*, 128–50.

54. See further Allan H. Anderson, "The Gospel and Culture in Pentecostal Mission in the Third World," *Missionalia* 27, no. 2 (1999): 220–30.

Then there are titles that are African context–specific, such as "Chief,"[55] prominent, for example, among Bantu Christians.[56] Christ is called Chief because he has conquered and triumphed over Satan and is thus a hero (cf. Col. 2:15). Christ is also called Chief because he is the son of the Chief, of God. The belief that God is the Chief of the whole universe is part of Bantu religion. Perhaps the most prominent—and at the same time most novel—of all African designations of Christ is "Ancestor," which will be taken up in the following section.

Before that, however, note that along with particular titles and metaphors, the Gospels' narrative about the life of Christ as such represents local African theologies. Several episodes in the life cycle of Christ, such as birth, baptism, and death, have meaning to Africans, who celebrate and honor crucial turning points of life with the help of various rites, from circumcision to dedication in the temple, to growing into puberty and later into adulthood. Parallel to distinctive Jewish rites that Jesus experienced, various African cultures celebrate these points of transition. Even Jesus's washing the feet of his disciples at the Last Supper is seen as an initiatory gesture: Jesus, the Master, initiates his followers into his own lifestyle. As such, Christ acts as the Head and Master of initiation: having been made perfect, he becomes the Head of those who obey him (Heb. 5:9). In general, African Christology discovers in Christ's life a gradual movement toward a goal, toward perfection, as mentioned in Hebrews 5:8.[57]

Jesus Christ as the Ancestor

While not limited to the African context,[58] a distinctive feature of African Christologies is engagement with the ancestors.[59] The reason is simple: "In many African societies ancestral veneration is one of the central and basic traditional and even contemporary forms of cult."[60] Catholic Charles Nyamiti, author of the widely acclaimed *Christ as Our Ancestor* (1984), succinctly summarizes the significance of the ancestor theme for the African context:[61]

55. See, e.g., Wessels, *Images of Jesus*, 11–12.

56. Francois Kabasele, "Christ as Chief," in *Faces of Jesus in Africa*, 103–15.

57. Kärkkäinen, *Christ and Reconciliation*, 74.

58. From an Asian perspective, see, e.g., J. Y. Lee, "Ancestor Worship: From a Theological Perspective," in *Ancestor Worship and Christianity in Korea*, ed. J. Y. Lee, Studies in Asian Thought and Religion 8 (Lampeter, UK: Mellen House, 1988), 83–91.

59. See Bediako, *Christianity in Africa*, 84–86; F. Kabasele, "Christ as Ancestor and Elder Brother," in *Faces of Jesus in Africa*, 116–27. This section is based on Kärkkäinen, *Christ and Reconciliation*, 74–77.

60. Charles Nyamiti, "African Ancestral Veneration and Its Relevance to the African Churches," *African Christian Studies* (Nairobi) 9, no. 3 (1993): 14.

61. Charles Nyamiti, "The Trinity from an African Ancestral Perspective," *African Christian Studies* 12, no. 4 (1996): 41.

- kinship between the dead and the living kin
- sacred status, usually acquired through death
- mediation between human beings and God
- exemplarity of behavior in community
- the right to regular communication with the living through prayer and rituals

An important characteristic of the sacred status of the ancestor is also the possession of "superhuman vital force" deriving from the special proximity to the Supreme Being. That gives the ancestor the right to be a mediator.

Ghanaian Kwesi Dickson reminds us of the significance of the role of ancestors in representing the sense of community and the "concept of corporate personality," a theme familiar from the Old Testament and key to understanding African culture.[62] Ancestors, as well as those not yet born, are regarded as part of the community, and by their presence they express the solidarity of the community. The spirits of the ancestors use their power for the well-being of the community. Ancestors are called on at the important moments of life.[63]

A relational, familial version of the ancestral theme is Christ as "Brother Ancestor,"[64] a metaphor with links to the naming of Jesus Christ as "our brother" in the book of Hebrews (2:10–12). According to Benezet Bujo of the Democratic Republic of the Congo (formerly Zaire), the idea of Jesus as the "Proto-Ancestor," the unique ancestor, the source of life and highest model of ancestorship,[65] is a legitimate way to illustrate the central New Testament idea of Word becoming flesh (John 1:14).[66] In Jesus we see not only one who lived the African ancestor-ideal in the highest degree, but one who brought that ideal to an altogether new fulfillment. He performed miracles such as healing the sick, opening the eyes of the blind, and raising the dead to life. In short, he brought life, and life-force, in its fullness.[67]

Linked with the title "Ancestor" is that of "Kinsman," which can be seen as parallel to the New Testament idea of Christ as "the firstborn over all

62. Kwesi A. Dickson, *Theology in Africa* (London: Darton, Longman & Todd, 1984), 170; see also 172–74.

63. Peter Fulljames, *God and Creation in Intercultural Perspective: Dialogue between the Theologies of Barth, Dickson, Pobee, Nyamiti, and Pannenberg* (Frankfurt am Main and New York: Peter Lang, 1993), 47.

64. Charles Nyamiti, *Christ as Our Ancestor: Christology from an African Perspective* (Gweru, Zimbabwe: Mambo Press, 1984), 74–76.

65. Bénézet Bujo, *African Theology in Its Social Context* (Maryknoll, NY: Orbis, 1992), 79. On the ancestral theme, see 79–121 especially.

66. Ibid., 83.

67. Ibid., 79.

creation" (Col. 1:15). Born of God (John 1:13), in participation with our Kinsman, we have the hope of becoming "children of God" and thus acquiring the status of kinship with Jesus. African kinship leads to a relationship of strong solidarity both horizontally and vertically.

The diverse African cultural matrix has produced ever-new applications of Christ's meaning. Just consider the following: to the tribe of Ewe-Mina, Christ represents *Jete*-Ancestor, the source of life. "An ancestor is, according to the Ewe-Mina, co-fecundator of birth and is capable of providing to many newly born children the necessary vital energy for his apparition in them. Christ as *Jete*-Ancestor means that he is the Ancestor who is the source of life and the fulfillment of the cosmotheandric relationship in the world."[68]

Christologies from Asia: Christ the Universal Savior

The Breathtaking Diversity of the Asian Context

There is a quiet determination among Asian Christians that their commitment to Jesus Christ and their words about Jesus Christ must be responsible to the life they live in Asia today. Such theology is called a living theology. . . . Asian theology seeks to take the encounter between life in Asia and the Word of God seriously.[69]

With these words, Kosuke Koyama, one of the best-known Asian theologians from Japan, introduces an anthology of essays on the themes of emerging Asian theologies. While Asia is the cradle of most of the major religions in the world, it was not until the last part of the twentieth century that contributions to Christian theology began to emerge there on a large scale. What is distinctive about the Asian context is the continuous correlation between Christian theology and the pluralism of Asian religiosity. As Sri Lankan Catholic liberationist Aloysius Pieris states, "The Asian context can be described as a blend of a profound religiosity (which is perhaps Asia's greatest wealth) and an overwhelming poverty."[70]

How do we approach Asia theologically? How do we make sense theologically of Asia—the world's largest and most populated continent—as a

68. Ibid., 5.

69. Kosuke Koyama, "Foreword by an Asian Theologian," in *Asian Christian Theology: Emerging Themes*, ed. Douglas J. Elwood (Philadelphia: Westminster, 1980), 13.

70. Aloysius Pieris, "Western Christianity and Asian Buddhism," in *Dialogue* 7 (May–August 1980): 60–61.

theological "unit"? Merely for heuristic purposes, something like the following description of its theological orientations and representatives may be legitimate:

> On the forefront of Asian theological reflection have been India and Sri Lanka with the strong Hindu influence. Theologians such as Raimundo Panikkar, Swami Abhishiktananda, M. M. Thomas, Stanley J. Samartha, and Aloysius Pieris are well known figures in the wider international theological academia. A rising center of theological thinking is Korea, with its phenomenal church growth. There is a strong proliferation of Korean theology ranging from fairly conservative evangelical theology that cuts across denominational boundaries to a more liberal strand of Asian pluralism and Minjung theology. In another cluster of Asian countries, Buddhism has played a major role: China, Taiwan, Thailand, and Japan. The Japanese theologian Kosuke Koyama, who spent several years as missionary-theologian in Thailand, is well known among his peers, as is also the Taiwanese-born Choan-Seng Song. Like so many of their counterparts, both of these Asian theologians teach currently in the USA and contribute to the emerging Asian-American theological guild. The predominantly Catholic Philippines stands in its own category, as does Indonesia, which is strongly influenced by Islam but also in some areas by Hinduism and Buddhism.[71]

In nearly every Asian country, Christians are the minority.[72] This fact has implications for Asian theologies when compared to European and US theologies, which are often written from the standpoint of Christianity being a major force in society. The thrust of Asian theology is to inquire into the identity of Christianity vis-à-vis other religious confessions. Koyama aptly notes the various forces that shape Asian Christianity as Asians address the question "Who do you say I am?" (Matt. 16:15):

> This question comes to Asian Christians, who live in a world of great religious traditions, modernization impacts, ideologies of the left and right, international conflicts, hunger, poverty, militarism, and racism. Within these confusing and

71. Veli-Matti Kärkkäinen, *The Trinity: Global Perspectives* (Louisville: Westminster John Knox, 2007), 309, which uses and adapts the classification by George Gispert-Sauch, SJ, "Asian Theology," in *The Modern Theologians: An Introduction to Christian Theology in the Twentieth Century*, ed. David F. Ford, 2nd ed. (Cambridge: Blackwell, 1997), 456. See also John Parratt, ed., *An Introduction to Third World Theologies* (Cambridge: Cambridge University Press, 2004), which divides the presentation of Asian theologies into two camps, India and east Asia—for which see Kirsteen Kim, "India," 44–73, and Edmond Tang, "East Asia," 74–104.

72. Even in South Korea, which is known for its substantial Christian presence and growth of the church in the latter part of the twentieth century, Christians represent less than one-third of the whole population. Only in the Philippines do Christians outnumber others.

brutal realities of history the question comes to them. Here the depth of soul of the East is challenged to engage in a serious dialogue with the Word of God. Jesus refuses to be treated superficially.[73]

Although Asian Christianity, similarly to the rest of the Global South, has been dominated by Euro-American influences until recently,[74] this continent has also produced a rich Asia-based theology. Choan-Seng Song, from Taiwan, who has done much of his lifework in the United States, encourages Asians to write "theology from the womb of Asia."[75] His theology, called "third eye" theology, is tuned into seeing Christ not only through Chinese, Japanese, and other Asian eyes but also through African, Latin American, and other eyes; "third eye" refers to the Buddhist master who opens eyes to see areas that have been unknown. The goal of this kind of authentic Asian theology is "the freedom to encounter Jesus the savior in the depth of the spirituality that sustains Asians in their long march of suffering and hope."[76] Several Asian theologians talk about the "critical Asian principle" as the main guide to their theology. Following this principle, they seek to identify what is distinctively Asian and to use this distinctiveness in judging matters dealing with the life and mission of the Christian church and theology.

One of the distinctive features of Asian thinking is reluctance to employ the Western either-or dialectic. Instead, most Asians feel comfortable thinking in terms of yin-yang inclusiveness. This term goes back to Taoism and Confucianism in their Chinese forms. According to such philosophies, change is the interplay of yin and yang. These two terms, crucial to much of Eastern thought (and expressed in different Asian languages and thought forms in varying terminology), mean female-male, weak-strong, light-dark, and so on. But these poles are seen not as opposites but as complements. One can easily imagine how this kind of inclusive thinking might affect one's Christology:

> Jesus as the Christ, as both God and man, cannot really be understood in terms of either/or. How can man also be God? In the West we have to speak in terms of paradox or mystery in order to justify the reality of Christ. However, in *yin-yang* terms, he can be thought of as both God and man at the same time. In him God is not separated from man nor man from God. They are in complementary relationship. He is God because of man: he is man because of God.[77]

73. Koyama, "Foreword by an Asian Theologian," 14.
74. For comments and analyses by leading Asian theologians, see Kärkkäinen, *Trinity*, 309–10 particularly.
75. Choan-Seng Song, *Theology from the Womb of Asia* (Maryknoll, NY: Orbis, 1986).
76. Ibid., 3.
77. Jung Young Lee, "The Yin-Yang Way of Thinking," in *Asian Christian Theology*, 87.

Rather than in any way encyclopedic or comprehensive, the following survey seeks to highlight some distinctive Asian contributions to the understanding of Christ.[78]

Christ in Interpretations of the Neo-Hindu Reform

In the subcontinent of India during the heights of the colonial enterprise started at the end of the nineteenth century, there emerged a new wave of interpretations of Christ among the representatives of the so-called Indian Renaissance or neo-Hindu reform.[79] Contemporary (to us) Indian theologian Stanley J. Samartha describes the Christ acknowledged by neo-Hinduism as an "unbound" Christ. What he means by that is that while many Indians were attracted by the person of Jesus Christ, they also detached that person from the institutional church.[80] For nineteenth-century Hindu Keshub Chunder Sen, Christ was the focus of personal devotion (*bhakti*). Sen summed up his Christology as a "doctrine of the divine humanity." In this outlook, Christ as "the medium is transparent, and we clearly see through Christ the God of truth and holiness dwelling in him."[81]

Although denying the Christian understanding of Christ's deity, several Hindu writers were drawn to Christ's ethical-social teachings.[82] Swami Prabhavananda's *Sermon on the Mount according to Vedanta* considers the famous ethical Sermon as the "essence of Christ's Gospel."[83] His spiritual teacher, Swami Prahmananda, who himself had seen Jesus in a vision, taught him to regard highly Christ's teaching. During Prabhavananda's first days in the monastery of the order of Sri Ramakrishna, on Christmas Day, the monks were advised to "meditate on Christ within and feel his living presence." "An intense spiritual atmosphere pervaded the worship hall," Swami Prabhavananda reminisces, which led to the realization for the first time that "Christ

---

78. Throughout this section on Asian Christologies, I am indebted to Levison-Pope and Levison, *Jesus in Global Contexts*, chap. 3; Küster, *Many Faces of Jesus Christ*, section D (77–134).

79. This section is based on Kärkkäinen, *Christ and Reconciliation*, 277–80.

80. For a short statement and sources, see Jacques Dupuis, *Jesus Christ at the Encounter of World Religions* (Maryknoll, NY: Orbis, 1991), 15.

81. Cited in ibid., 24. Keshub Chunder Sen, *Keshub Chunder Sen's Lectures in India*, 2nd ed. (Calcutta: The Brahmo Tract Society, 1886), 290.

82. Note that whereas it is not a problem for a theistic Hindu to envision a person such as Jesus Christ as divine, similarly to pantheons of similar kinds of divine figures in their own tradition, that affirmation has little to do with the unique Christian confession of Christ's deity.

83. Swami Prabhavananda, *Sermon on the Mount according to Vedanta* (Hollywood, CA: Vedanta Society of Southern California, 1992 [1963]), 7.

was as much our own as Krishna, Buddha, and other great illumined teachers whom we revered."[84]

As is well known, for Mahatma Gandhi, Jesus was an ethical teacher who expresses the ideal of a new community and way of life. Therein, Gandhi saw the same principles that guided his own pacifist fight for the liberation of the Indian people. As deeply as Gandhi was committed to the teaching of Jesus, especially the Sermon on the Mount, he was never ready to make a personal commitment to the person of Christ, let alone the community of the Christian church.

> The message of Jesus, as I understand it, is contained in his Sermon on the Mount. The Spirit of the Sermon on the Mount competes almost on equal terms with the Bhagavadgita for the domination of my heart. It is that Sermon which has endeared Jesus to me. . . .Though I cannot claim to be a Christian in the sectarian sense, the example of Jesus' suffering is a factor in the composition of my underlying faith in non-violence, which rules all my actions, worldly and temporal.[85]

There are also a few famous Hindus who have become Christians in belief but have claimed not to leave behind Hinduism. The best known of these is Brahmabandhab Upadhyaya, whose spirituality is based on a deep personal experience of the person of Jesus the Son of God, who becomes at once his guru and his friend. Whether Jesus was divine is not the point; what matters is that Christ claimed to be the Son of God.[86] Of this orientation to Christ, late Catholic expert Jacques Dupuis says aptly:

> The Christ acknowledged by Hinduism is often a churchless Christ. For that matter, the Christ acknowledged by Hinduism is often a Christ delivered from the encumbrances of numerous "bonds" with which he is laden by traditional Christianity—whether it be a matter of applauding his message while rejecting the Christian claim to his person, or of receiving him as one divine manifestation among others in a catalog of divine descents (*avatara*) as varied as it is extensive.[87]

The diversity of christological portraits and interpretations in neo-Hindu reform is beautifully reflected in the different, yet complementary, titles of

84. Ibid., 8–9.

85. Mohandas K. Gandhi, *The Message of Jesus Christ* (Bombay: Bharatiya Vidya Bhavan, 1963), cover page and 79, respectively.

86. For a brief discussion, see Jacob Kavunkal, "The Mystery of God in and through Hinduism," in *Christian Theology in Asia*, ed. Sebastian C. H. Kim (Cambridge: Cambridge University Press, 2008), 28–30.

87. Dupuis, *Jesus Christ*, 15.

current interpreters: Raimundo Panikkar's *The Unknown Christ of Hinduism* and M. M. Thomas's *The Acknowledged Christ of the Indian Renaissance*.[88]

One Christ—Many Religions

Although most Christians today are unwilling to take a totally negative attitude toward neighbors of other faiths, there seems to be a good deal of hesitation on the part of many to reexamine the basis of their exclusive claims on behalf of Christ. The place of Christ in a multireligious society becomes, therefore, an important issue in the search for a new theology of religions.[89]

Ordained in the Church of South India and involved in theological teaching in his earlier years, Stanley J. Samartha has exercised considerable influence through his post as director of the World Council of Churches Dialogue Programme, which he initiated.[90] Throughout his life Samartha has advocated dialogue among world religions as the demand of our age. Samartha began his theological thinking with moderate christocentrism but later moved toward a more clearly pluralistic model. In *One Christ—Many Religions: Toward a Revised Christology*, he argues that christocentrism is applicable only to Christians; it can never be considered the only way to the mystery of the divine.[91] Christocentrism, therefore, cannot be the norm by which various religious traditions are valued.

Behind Samartha's theology of religions is his idea of the Divine as "mystery." This also shapes his Christology:

This Mystery, the Truth of the Truth (*Satyasya Satyam*), *is* the transcendent Center that remains always beyond and greater than apprehensions of it even in the sum total of those apprehensions. It is beyond cognitive knowledge (*tarka*) but it is open to vision (*dristi*) and intuition (*anubhava*). It is near yet far, knowable yet unknowable, intimate yet ultimate and, according to one particular Hindu view, cannot even be described as "one." It is "not-two" (*advaita*), indicating thereby that diversity is within the heart of Being itself and therefore may be intrinsic to human nature as well.[92]

88. M. M. Thomas, *The Acknowledged Christ of the Indian Renaissance* (London: SCM, 1969).
89. Stanley J. Samartha, "The Cross and the Rainbow: Christ in a Multireligious Culture," in *The Myth of Christian Uniqueness*, ed. J. Hick and P. Knitter (Maryknoll, NY: Orbis, 1987), 69.
90. See Konrad Raiser, "Tribute to Stanley J. Samartha" (World Council of Churches, 2002), available at www.wcc-coe.org/wcc/what/interreligious/cd38-02.html.
91. Stanley J. Samartha, *One Christ—Many Religions: Toward a Revised Christology* (Maryknoll, NY: Orbis, 1991).
92. Samartha, "Cross and the Rainbow," 75.

Samartha argues that the nature of mystery makes inadmissible any claim on the part of one religious community to have exclusive or unique knowledge.[93] While Christ remains central in this conception, he is not so exclusively. "This Other [God as the Mysterious Other] relativizes everything else. In fact, the willingness to accept such relativization is probably the only guarantee that one has encountered the Other as ultimately real."[94] Samartha observes that a process of rejecting exclusive claims and seeking new ways of understanding the relationship of Jesus Christ to God and humanity is already under way. A shift is taking place from the "normative exclusiveness" of Christ to what he calls the "relational distinctiveness" of Christ. The term *relational* refers to the fact that Christ does not remain unrelated to neighbors of other faiths, while *distinctiveness* denotes the recognition that the great religious traditions are different responses to the mystery of God.[95]

As a result, for Samartha the incarnation is a symbol of the divine rather than a normative historical happening. Also, the death and resurrection of Christ, even though they are revelations of who God is, are not to be treated as a universally valid paradigm. Samartha has no problem affirming the humanity and divinity of Jesus Christ, but he is not willing to affirm the orthodox teaching that Christ is God. The reason is simply that "an ontological equation of Jesus Christ and God would scarcely allow any serious discussion with neighbors of other faiths or with secular humanism."[96]

Samartha relativizes all particular religious expressions and forms in history, the incarnation of Christ included, but is not willing to deny their necessity. The Mysterious Other must confront us through particular mediations. Therefore, Samartha does not naively assume the equality of all religions. What he claims is that each and every religion and its figures are limited: "A particular religion can claim to be decisive for some people, and some people can claim that a particular religion is decisive for them, but no religion is justified in claiming that it is decisive for all."[97]

For Samartha, classical theology runs the danger of "christomonism" in its insistence on the absolute finality of Jesus Christ. It turns Jesus into a kind of "cult figure" over against other religious figures. Instead of a christomonistic approach to other religions, Samartha advocates a theocentric approach, which

93. For details, see Kärkkäinen, *Trinity and Revelation*, 341–43.
94. Stanley J. Samartha, *Courage for Dialogue: Ecumenical Issues in Inter-Religious Relationships* (Maryknoll, NY: Orbis, 1982), 151–52.
95. Samartha, *One Christ—Many Religions*, 77.
96. Samartha, "Cross and the Rainbow," 80.
97. Samartha, *Courage for Dialogue*, 153; see also Stanley J. Samartha, "Unbound Christ: Towards Christology in India Today," in *Asian Christian Theology*, 146.

is more consistent with the God-centered message of Jesus of Nazareth. He tries to hold in tension the normative significance of Christ as the revelation of God and the need for openness in relation to other faiths:

> No one could have anticipated in advance the presence of God in the life and death of Jesus of Nazareth. There is an incomprehensible dimension to it. That Jesus is the Christ of God is a confession of faith by the Christian community. It does indeed remain normative to Christians everywhere, but to make it "absolutely singular" and to maintain that the meaning of the Mystery is disclosed *only* in one particular person at one particular point, and nowhere else, is to ignore one's neighbors of other faiths who have other points of reference. To make exclusive claims for our particular tradition is not the best way to love our neighbors as ourselves.[98]

The "Cosmotheandric" Vision of Christ

The theology of "Hindu-Catholic"[99] Raimundo Panikkar is a unique blending of Hindu and Christian insights as well as diverse other influences.[100] His most distinctive contribution is the term "cosmotheandric," which shapes his whole theology and worldview. From the three words—"God," "human," and "cosmos"—it speaks of the coming together of the three. Or, as Panikkar puts it succinctly, "the cosmotheandric principle could be formulated by saying that the divine, the human and the earthly—however we may prefer to call them—are the three irreducible dimensions which constitute the real, i.e., any reality inasmuch as it is real."[101] For Christians the cosmotheandric principle is expressed in their most distinctive doctrine, namely, the Trinity. Incarnation, the coming of the divine to dwell in the human, is its focal point.

Now, importantly for the pluralistic world, Panikkar argues that while a distinctively Christian way of speaking of cosmotheandrism, Trinity is not an exclusively Christian reality. Rather, Trinity is "a junction where the authentic spiritual dimensions of all religions meet."[102] In other words, the Christian

98. Samartha, "Cross and the Rainbow," 76.

99. The oft-quoted autobiographical comment—according to which he "left" Europe as a Christian, "found" himself as a Hindu, and "returned" as a Buddhist—fittingly illustrates this diverse background and varied orientations. Raimundo Panikkar, *The Intrareligious Dialogue* (New York: Paulist Press, 1978), 2.

100. This section is based on Kärkkäinen, *Christ and Reconciliation*, 226–29.

101. R. Panikkar, *The Cosmotheandric Experience: Emerging Religious Consciousness*, ed. Scott Eastham (Maryknoll, NY: Orbis, 1993), ix.

102. R. Panikkar, *The Trinity and the Religious Experience of Man: Icon-Person-Mystery* (Maryknoll, NY: Orbis; London: Darton, Longman & Todd, 1973), 42.

doctrine of the Trinity is naming "Christianly" cosmotheandrism, and other faith traditions use their distinctive nomenclatures and perspectives.

Panikkar's thinking is complex and elusive. With regard to Christian faith's relation to other faith traditions, he seems to hold two kinds of orientations in a dynamic tension. On the one hand, differently from fellow pluralists such as Hick, Panikkar is not ready to leave behind the distinctive features of Christian confession of Christ, although he also sees the coming convergence of religious intuitions. While Christianity can learn from others, it also has a significant role to play in leading "to the *plenitude* and hence to the *conversion* of all religion."[103] In the final analysis, the end of this process (and the goal of Christianity) is "humanity's common good." Christianity "simply incarnates the primordial and original traditions of humankind."[104]

On the other hand, in his most significant christological monograph, the revised version of *The Unknown Christ of Hinduism* in 1981, Panikkar has undoubtedly moved toward a pluralistic version of Christology. Therein he rejects all notions of Christianity's superiority over or fulfillment of other religions by arguing that the world and our subjective experience of the world have radically changed since the Christian doctrine concerning Christ was first formulated. Not unlike many fellow pluralists, he makes a distinction between the universal Christ and the particular Jesus. "Christ is . . . a living symbol for the totality of reality: human, divine, and cosmic."[105] With Catholic theology he affirms that the *Logos* or Christ has been incarnated in Jesus of Nazareth. But he departs from orthodoxy by denying that this incarnation has taken place solely and finally in Jesus. Arguing for the opposite of what he argued in the first edition of *The Unknown Christ of Hinduism*, in which he posited a unity between Christ and Jesus, he now rejects it. According to his revised Christology, no historical form can be the full, final expression of the universal Christ. Panikkar claims that "Christ will never be totally known on earth, because that would amount to seeing the Father whom nobody can see."[106]

Lotus and Cross

Chinese American Choan-Seng Song has attempted to establish bridges between Buddhist and Christian religions. He wonders whether the Buddhist

103. Ibid., 4 (emphasis original).
104. R. Panikkar, "The Jordan, the Tiber, and the Ganges: Three Kairological Moments of Christic Self-Consciousness," in *Myth of Christian Uniqueness*, 102.
105. R. Panikkar, *The Unknown Christ of Hinduism: Towards an Ecumenical Christophany*, rev. ed. (Maryknoll, NY: Orbis, 1981), 27.
106. Paul F. Knitter, *No Other Name? A Critical Survey of Christian Attitudes toward the World Religions* (Maryknoll, NY: Orbis, 1985), 156.

lotus and the Christian cross could exist side by side. As the cross of Christ has been the focus of Christian spirituality and theology, so the image of Buddha seated cross-legged on the lotus has symbolized Buddhist devotion. But the symbols differ: the lotus springs from fertile water and symbolizes serenity, while the cross, a rugged piece of wood cut off from its roots and placed on a stony hill, represents cruelty and shame. Yet they are united in that they are responses to the question of suffering: "Asian Buddhists enter human suffering through the lotus, and Christians through the cross."[107]

Song's *Jesus, the Crucified People* penetrates deeply into the suffering and death of Christ. He also offers a revised interpretation by emphasizing human participation in the event of crucifixion, with his stress on "crucified people" rather than "crucified God," and speaks of "human beings abandoning human beings" rather than the Second Person of the Trinity having been forsaken by the First Person.[108] Indeed, differently from mainline Christian tradition, Song seeks "to work toward the abolition of the cross" because of its cruel nature and thus its incapacity to help tackle the issues of the real world, such as suffering, poverty, and injustice.[109]

A distinctive term in Song's theology is "transposition"—a transposition from the Israel-centered view of history to the view that regards other nations as constitutive parts of God's design of history.[110] In this view, Israel's role as the people of God was symbolic, illustrating the way God would also deal redemptively with other nations. Asian nations have their own specific moments of salvation history parallel to Israel's exodus, giving of the law, captivity, and so on. Furthermore, the savior figures of Asian religions parallel the savior figure of the Christian faith, Jesus Christ:

> The expression of Buddha's compassion for the masses in his vows and the way he toiled unselfishly for their emancipation from pain and suffering are not without redemptive significance. Can we not say that Buddha's way is also a part of the drama of salvation which God has acted out fully in the person and work of Jesus Christ?[111]

107. Choan-Seng Song, *Third-Eye Theology: Theology in Formation in Asian Settings* (Maryknoll, NY: Orbis, 1979), 123.

108. Choan-Seng Song, *Jesus, the Crucified People* (New York: Crossroad, 1990), 88–89.

109. Choan-Seng Song, "Christian Mission toward Abolition of the Cross," in *The Scandal of a Crucified World*, ed. Yacob Tesfai (Maryknoll, NY: Orbis, 1994), 130–48.

110. Choan-Seng Song, *The Compassionate God: An Exercise in the Theology of Transposition* (London: SCM, 1982). For a succinct exposition, see Hwa Yung, *Mangoes or Bananas? The Quest for an Authentic Asian Christian Theology* (Oxford: Regnum, 1997), 168–71 particularly.

111. Choan-Seng Song, "From Israel to Asia: A Theological Leap," in *Mission Trends*, 212. For a useful discussion on "Christology in the Context of Buddhism," see chap. 8 in Küster, *Many Faces of Jesus Christ*.

Consequently, the task of the proclamation of Christ on Asian soil is not one of conversion but of growing with Asians in their knowledge and experience of God's saving work in the world. The contribution of Christian missions is to inform Asian spirituality, shaped by Asian cultures and religions, of the love of God in Jesus Christ. This helps to move Asian society toward freedom, justice, and love, Song believes.[112]

"Asia's Struggle for Full Humanity: Toward a Relevant Theology"

Liberation theology and the yearning for freedom are not limited to Latin America, the cradle of liberationism. Asian Christians have joined forces to develop authentically liberationist Christologies. In 1979 the Asian Conference of Third World Theologians held a consultation in Sri Lanka under the rubric of "Asia's Struggle for Full Humanity: Toward a Relevant Theology." The consultation took notice of problems such as poverty, unemployment, child labor, and the exploitation of women and committed to furthering a "radical transformation" of theology. That kind of theology "must arise from the Asian poor with a liberated consciousness."[113] What CELAM, the Latin American Catholic Bishops' Conference, was for Latin America, the Asian Conference of 1979 was for Asia. Its point of departure was the Asian context and dialogue with local culture, Asian religious traditions, and the life of the people, especially the poor. Asian bishops affirmed that, with the local church as the focus of evangelization and dialogue as its essential mode, they would help Asian Christians work for salvation and solidarity with the poor and oppressed as well as attempt a true dialogue with the ancient religions of the area.[114]

With some exceptions, most Asian countries are poor. From the Western viewpoint, it is painful to acknowledge that one—if not *the*—major reason for poverty in too many Asian countries is the tragic history of colonialization. This historical fact should make Western preachers of Christ aware of the difficulty with which many Asians hear their message, the message of their former masters.

The most noted theologian in Asia who has attempted to draw implications from Christology for the struggle of humanization is M. M. Thomas, a layperson of the Mar Thoma Church of southern India. He entered theology

112. See the useful discussion in Küster, *Many Faces of Jesus Christ*, 129–33.

113. Quoted in Donald K. McKim, *The Bible in Theology and Preaching* (Nashville: Abingdon, 1994), 160.

114. *Asia's Struggle for Full Humanity: Toward a Relevant Theology; Papers from the Asian Theological Conference, January 7–20, 1979, Wennappuwa, Sri Lanka*, ed. Virginia Fabella (Maryknoll, NY: Orbis, 1980).

through the gateway of political and social consciousness, coming as he did from Marxist philosophy. The title of his main book, *Salvation and Humanization*, reveals the central orientation of his thinking.[115] For Thomas, the validity of Christology is based less on its doctrinal orthodoxy than on its contribution to the human quest for a better quality of life and social justice. In *Risking Christ for Christ's Sake*, Thomas attempts to develop a "Christ-centered humanism" based on a syncretistic view of religions.[116] The source of strength for this risky ecumenical and interreligious work comes from the cross and resurrection of Jesus Christ. In it he puts forth a liberation theology with the purpose of explicating in real life the implications of faith in Christ.

Thomas's theology recognizes the presence of Christ in all struggles for justice, whether Christian or not. Moreover, it acknowledges the presence of Christ in all spiritualities that inspire struggles for justice. Christ is present in these struggles as the cosmic lord of history. Not only Christianity but also Asian religions provide a spiritual basis for striving for justice. On the basis of Colossians 1 and Ephesians 1, Thomas argues that if Christ as the principle and goal of creation is present in all creation, then every attempt to better creation and the life of creatures is related to Christ, whether so acknowledged or not by the agents of change. There is a curious dialectic in Thomas's understanding with regard to how people recognize the power of Jesus at work in the world: "Christ makes use of worldly and non-worldly forces for this purpose. The notion that Christ is at work only in the church and Christians is foolish and nonsensical. But it is the church and the Christians who can recognize Christ in the efforts and events of our time."[117]

Thomas's Christ, the cosmic lord of history, is related not so much to the mystery of the divine (as in many other Asian interpretations of Christ) as to the historical plane, the struggle for equality, justice, and peace. Thomas's liberation theology is for Asia:

> Thomas' Christology does not deny the importance of history in order to provide a common basis for all religions. Rather, the cosmic lord of history becomes the meeting point of religions as they struggle for justice. Christ is present not so much in ahistorical mystery as in the human quest for a better life. Therefore,

115. M. M. Thomas, *Salvation and Humanization: Some Crucial Issues of the Theology of Mission in Contemporary India* (Madras: Christian Institute on the Study of Religion and Society, 1971).

116. M. M. Thomas, *Risking Christ for Christ's Sake: Towards an Ecumenical Theology of Pluralism* (Geneva: WCC, 1987).

117. Cited in Küster, *Many Faces of Jesus Christ*, 84; this section is indebted to his succinct account; see 79–81, 83–88.

for Thomas, the cosmic lord of history and the historical Jesus, who labored among the poor, are one and the same, sharing an identical purpose.[118]

Another christologist who has labored in the area of social justice is Aloysius Pieris, a Sri Lankan Jesuit and director of a local research institute that promotes Christian-Buddhist dialogue. Like Thomas, he criticizes other liberation movements for their inability to recognize the liberative force of other religions. Naming Christianity the specifically liberationist religion too easily leads to the implication that other religions are not and thus fosters an unhealthy isolation of Christianity from other religions.

Pieris links Asia's poverty and spirituality to Jesus's "double baptism" in "the Jordan of Asian religions and the Calvary of Asian poverty."[119] Jesus's baptism and death immersed him in the Asian context and life. By submitting to baptism by John the Baptist, Jesus refused the ideology of the Zealot movement, the radical political left wing of his day, and the appeal to power and privileges of other contemporary movements, such as that of the aristocratic Sadducees. Instead, he identified himself with the powerless margins of society. Jesus pointed to the ascetic John as the archetype of the true spirituality of the kingdom of God and denounced striving for the accumulation of wealth and placing one's trust in mammon. Jesus's radical social program, in Pieris's analysis, led him finally to the cross, on which he was executed by the powerful elite. The powerful crucified him on "a cross that the money-polluted religiosity of his day planted on Calvary with the aid of a colonial power (Luke 23:1–23). This is where the journey, begun at Jordan, ended."[120]

Christ, *Minjung*, and *Dalit*

An authentically Asian Christology cannot help but delve into the suffering and wounds of Asian people. Chi-Ha Kim, a Korean poet, wrote a play titled *The Gold-Crowned Jesus*.[121] The scene plays in front of a Catholic church, where there is a cement statue of Jesus wearing a golden crown. It is a cold winter day, and beggars are lying beneath the statue. Looking at the gold-crowned Jesus, one of them wonders what the relevance of such a savior figure might be for a beggar with no place to go. In the midst of his

---

118. Pope-Levison and Levison, *Jesus in Global Contexts*, 73.
119. Aloysius Pieris, *An Asian Theology of Liberation* (Maryknoll, NY: Orbis, 1988), 48.
120. Ibid., 49.
121. For details, see Chi-Ha Kim, *The Gold-Crowned Jesus and Other Writings* (Maryknoll, NY: Orbis, 1978).

anguish, the beggar feels something wet dropping on his head. Looking up, he sees the cement Jesus weeping. Noticing that the golden crown might be of value, the beggar is about to take it for himself when he hears the voice of Jesus: "Take it, please! For too long a time have I been imprisoned in this cement. Eventually you have come and made me open my mouth. You have saved me."[122]

It is the task of Asian Christology to free Jesus for the common people. The term *minjung* means "mass of people." It is also the name of a Korean liberation movement for people who since the 1960s have lived under a military dictatorship and have been exploited economically and alienated sociologically, without due rights for social action. The *minjung* movement stands for human rights, social justice, and democratization.[123]

Byung-Mu Ahn, the most famous theologian related to this movement, argues that it is time for Christian theology to free Christology of the *kerygma* from Western enslavement and put the living Jesus in contact with the common people. The living Jesus lived with the poor, the sick, and women, healing them, feeding them, and defending them. According to Ahn, Jesus's action is incessant. Unlike the "Christ of the *kerygma*," Jesus does not remain seated, immovable on his unshakable throne within the church. On the contrary, Jesus associates and lives with the *minjung*. The Gospel of Mark especially highlights Jesus's association with the *ochlos* (the Greek term for "common people"), but the other Gospels have the same emphasis.

The main difference between traditional Christology and *minjung* Christology, as developed by Ahn, is that the former depicts Jesus as the true Messiah in the sense that he obeyed and fulfilled God's will. *Minjung* Christology does not deny this aspect of obedience, but there is another tradition that

> conveys an absolutely different image of Jesus, who identifies with the cries and wishes of the suffering Minjung. It is particularly the healing-stories that expose this image of Jesus. The Jesus who heals the sick people is by no means described as someone who fulfills a pre-established program. Jesus never seeks for the sick persons voluntarily, nor does he follow an earlier intention (plan) for helping them. On the contrary, the request always comes from the Minjung's side first. And accordingly, Jesus' healing activities appear as him being obedient to the wishes of the patients. . . . Jesus' healing power, which has a functional

122. Quoted in Byung-Mu Ahn, "Jesus and the People (Minjung)," in *Asian Faces of Jesus*, ed. R. S. Sugirtharajah (Maryknoll, NY: Orbis, 1995), 163–64.
123. For a diverse collection of essays by a group of globally diverse scholars, see Paul S. Chung, ed. and trans., with Kim Kyoung-Jae and Veli-Matti Kärkkäinen, eds., *Asian Contextual Theology for the Third Millennium: Theology of Minjung in Fourth-Eye Formation* (Eugene, OR: Pickwick, 2006).

relation to the suffering of the Minjung, can be realized only when it is met by the will of the Minjung.[124]

Jesus, as the spokesperson for the sick, the poor, the alienated, and women, speaks to God on behalf of the *minjung*. Christian faith does not constitute "a manufactured product" given to human beings from heaven to possess but rather involves the "salvation that Jesus realized in the action of transforming himself, by listening to and responding to the cry of Minjung."[125]

Japanese theologian Koyama, who has worked with the exploited and poor rural people of northern Thailand, strikes the same chord when talking about the crucified Christ challenging human power. Christ exposes human power not from the luxury of an armchair but by abandoning himself to human dominance, even to crucifixion. No one can mutilate him, Koyama says, because he is already mutilated. No one can crucify him, because he is already crucified. "In the crucified Christ we are confronted by the ultimate sincerity of God."[126]

Another Asian Christology that focuses on the least in society comes from India. *Dalit* is currently the self-designation of Indian outcastes. Arvind Nirmal, who coined the term "*dalit* theology" at the beginning of the 1980s, enumerates six meanings of the term: "(1) the broken, the torn, the rent, the burst, the split, (2) the opened, the expanded, (3) the bisected, (4) the driven asunder, (5) the downtrodden, the crushed, the destroyed, (6) the manifested, the displayed."[127] *Dalit* Christology represents a liberation movement for these people at the bottom of society. Indeed, Nirmal argues that Jesus himself was a *dalit*. Jesus identified with the "*dalits*" of his day, and in his "Nazareth Manifesto" (Luke 4:18–19) he promised liberation for the prisoners. On the cross "he was the broken, the crushed, the split, the torn, the driven asunder man—the dalit in the fullest possible meaning of that term." Therefore, it is "precisely in and through the weaker, the downtrodden, the crushed, the oppressed and the marginalized that God's saving glory is manifested or displayed. This is because brokenness belongs to the very being of God."[128]

124. Ahn, "Jesus and the People (Minjung)," 169.
125. Ibid.
126. Kosuke Koyama, "The Crucified Christ Challenges Human Power," in *Asian Faces of Jesus*, 149.
127. Cited in Küster, *Many Faces of Jesus Christ*, 164.
128. Cited in ibid., 172.

7

"Contextual" Christologies in the Global North

Having investigated some representative christological interpretations among some Latin American, African, and Asian theologians and theological movements, we continue probing into the riches of diverse "contextual" theologies of Christ by first focusing on female theologians' views, with particular emphasis on Caucasian (white) women who have been in the forefront. As the reader might have noticed, so far among the "intercultural" theologians women's views were not accounted for. To correct that omission, female voices will be highlighted robustly in this chapter. After feminist voices, the discussion will draw from a reservoir of other diverse "contextual" theologies from North American (and to some extent European) soil, beginning with African American (black) Christologies, done by both men and women. Thereafter, Hispanic or Latino/a interpretations will be considered. The discussion in this chapter ends with a look at postcolonial theologies of Christ, in which particular attention will be given to Asian American female contributions.

Feminist Christologies

The Diversity of Female Theologies and Approaches

Not long ago it was customary to speak of "feminist" Christologies when referring to all theological approaches by and from the perspective of female theologians. Currently that is both reductionist and illegitimate, as there are so many different and differing approaches that might be labeled (for the purposes of the current discussion) "female" Christologies. While united in the central task of liberation, women's voices in theology no longer form a united front but rather display the kind of variety that can be expected of any theology in the beginning of the third millennium. Therefore, to speak of "feminist" theology in generic terms is quite misleading.

The term "feminist" refers to white women's approaches; "womanist" to African American; and *mujerista* to Latina women. The proliferation of views is enhanced by the emergence of women's voices from Africa, Latin America, and Asia. That white women's voices are more loudly heard (even in this text) is not because of their superiority but the simple fact that so far they have had the luxury (academic, financial, and social) to develop distinctively female interpretations. Without in any way lumping together these diverse groups, it is also the case that "even with all their diversity, feminist, womanist, and *mujerista* theologies have one thing in common: they make the liberation of women central to the theological task."[1]

It should be noted that not all feminist theologians are convinced that the "masculinist predominance of Logos-centered theology" can be redeemed.[2] Some feminists have lost all hope of Jesus Christ being able to "symbolize the liberation of women"—so much so that, "in order to develop a theology of women's liberation, feminists have to leave Christ and Bible behind."[3] The majority of female theologians, however, believe that the corrective, balancing, and reorienting task is both possible and desirable. Those theologians do not leave behind the rich tradition of christological reflection—as male dominated as it may be—but seek to renew and reorient it.

The first major section of this chapter focuses mostly on feminist interpretations, and other female voices will be heard in subsequent sections, including womanist along with black theologies, *mujerista* with Hispanic or Latino/a Christologies, and so forth. That way we do not have to repeat the specific contextual information in each case. This will also show the linkage of specific female interpretations with their respective constituencies and partially explain the diversity itself.

    1. Mary McClintock Fulkerson, "Feminist Theology," in *The Cambridge Companion to Postmodern Theology*, ed. Kevin J. Vanhoozer (Cambridge: Cambridge University Press, 2003), 109.
    2. This formulation comes from Wonhee Anne Joh, *Heart of the Cross: A Postcolonial Christology* (Louisville: Westminster John Knox, 2006), 93. Joh herself does not fully support this criticism.
    3. Naomi Goldenberg, *Changing of the Gods: Feminism and the End of Traditional Religions* (Boston: Beacon, 1979), 22; see also Daphne Hampson, *After Christianity* (Valley Forge, PA: Trinity Press International, 1996).

Male-Exclusive Christology and the Experience of Women

I have always found it difficult to walk away from the church, but I have also found it difficult to walk with it. . . . The alienation is shared with many other women and men whose pain and anger at the contradictions of church life lead them to challenge the very idea of talking about a feminist interpretation of the church. It is also increased by knowledge of the disdain and anger of those theologians and church officials who consider women like me to be the problem rather than the church itself.[4]

This quotation from a leading American feminist theologian, Letty M. Russell, reveals the anguish many women feel concerning the way the Christian church and theology have treated women. At the same time, she confesses, "It is impossible for me and for many other alienated women and men to walk away from the church, however, for it has been the bearer of the story of Jesus Christ and the good news of God's love."[5]

Living as we do in an age of "hermeneutics of suspicion," we find many conventional ways of talking about religion threatening. Many feminist thinkers insist that the personification of God as Father is a form of patriarchy that makes mechanisms for the oppression of women appear justified; from this grows male dominance. There is no denying that most images of God in religions reflect the hierarchical structures of the society.[6] Even though, generally speaking, it may be an overstatement that the symbol of divine fatherhood has been the source of the misuse of power for violence, rape, and war, it is true that language not only reflects reality but also constructs it.

Although women's experiences vary from culture to culture and context to context, there are some uniting features, three of which seem to have the greatest implications for Christology. First, women from different situations have experienced their embodiment as something negative in many Christian traditions. Western theology in particular has been based on a dualistic worldview that placed soul over body and male over female. Female caricatures in early Christian writings abound. For example, women were called "the gateway to hell" and "less than male." Even though Christianity is an incarnational religion, it has too often been uncomfortable with the body, especially with the task of women to give birth to the next generation. With regard to the doctrine of the incarnation, Jesus's maleness has often been used as an argument against the full humanity of women. "The doctrine that

---

4. Letty M. Russell, *Church in the Round: Feminist Interpretation of the Church* (Louisville: Westminster John Knox, 1993), 11.

5. Ibid.

6. See Rosemary Radford Ruether, *Sexism and God-Talk* (Boston: Beacon, 1983).

only a perfect male form can incarnate God fully and be salvific makes our individual lives in female bodies a prison against God and denies our actual, sensual, changing selves as the locus of divine activity."[7]

Second, women from different contexts have experienced oppression. Patterns of domination and submission vary, but they are present worldwide. The headship of Christ over his body the church, reflected in the headship of the husband over his wife, has often legitimized the subordination of women.

Third, interrelatedness has been part of the experience of women. Women have traditionally found identity in relation to others as mothers, wives, sisters, daughters. In the past, a single male individual could represent all humanity. In current times, however, the interrelatedness of all life, including creation, has come to the fore; one impetus has been the emergence of process thought, as discussed above. In line with the idea of interrelatedness, Jürgen Moltmann places the question of sexism in relation to God in a wider perspective, that of community. Theologically, it is not enough to criticize traditional theologies for neglecting feminine terminology and attempt to replace the masculine terms with other limited, exclusive terms. Moltmann insists that according to biblical ideas, what makes us *imago Dei* is not the soul apart from the body. The image of God consists of men and women in their wholeness, in their full, sexually specific community with one another. God is not known in the inner chamber of the heart or at a solitary place but in the true community of women and men. As a result, the experience of God is "the social experience of the self and the personal experience of sociality."[8] One could also express the core of feminist ecclesiology by describing the church as "connective"; in it there is a living, dynamic connection between men and women and between God and human beings. "If the table is spread by God and hosted by Christ, it must be a table with many connections."[9]

"Can a Male Savior Save Women?"

Questions posed by feminist theologians with regard to Christology are pointed: Is it possible for the Son of God to be a Savior and representative of God's sons *and* daughters? How does Jesus's "maleness" relate to women? Is God the Son masculine or feminine or beyond? The image of Christ is ambiguous for many contemporary women because it has served both as

7. Rita Nakashima Brock, "The Feminist Redemption of Christ," in *Christian Feminism: Visions of a New Humanity*, ed. Judith L. Weidman (San Francisco: Harper & Row, 1984), 68.

8. Jürgen Moltmann, *The Spirit of Life: A Universal Affirmation*, trans. Margaret Kohl (Minneapolis: Fortress, 1992), 94.

9. Russell, *Church in the Round*, 18.

the source of life and as the legitimator of oppression. Some extreme voices ask whether Christian theology can ever overcome this built-in tension. According to Naomi Goldenberg, "Jesus Christ cannot symbolize the liberation of women. A culture that maintains a masculine image for its highest divinity cannot allow its women to experience themselves as the equals of its men. In order to develop a theology of women's liberation, feminists have to leave Christ and the Bible behind."[10] This "critical principle" of feminist analysis, which has liberation and equality as its goal, borrows from liberation theologies of various sorts; it is what liberationist Gustavo Gutiérrez has called "theology from the underside of history."[11] Feminist thinkers join this liberation tradition in moving from the questions of those at the center of society to the questions of those considered less than human because they are powerless and unimportant.

Feminist Rosemary Radford Ruether's now classic question, "Can a male savior save women?"[12] serves as a clarion call for female reflection on Christ's meaning in our globalized world. One of the key challenges in this reflection has to do with the language we use of the Triune God. Roman Catholic feminist Elizabeth Johnson laments the "normative speech about God in metaphors that are exclusively, literally, and patriarchally male"[13] because that usage begins to shape our view of reality. Over the years, Christians begin to imagine and feel that "God is male, or at least more like a man than a woman, or at least more fittingly addressed as male than as female."[14]

The root cause for these unfortunate effects is literal understanding of God-talk, which may also lead to exclusivity and thus patriarchalism. For the moderate feminist Johnson, the option is not the denial of the legitimacy of male symbols but rather balancing them with female ones. Female images are needed to both challenge and correct the prevailing structures of patriarchalism[15] by introducing alternative symbols and metaphors of the divine, "discourses of emancipatory transformation."[16] After all, as all theology has

---

10. Goldenberg, *Changing of the Gods*, 22.

11. Gustavo Gutiérrez, *The Power of the Poor in History: Selected Writings* (Maryknoll, NY: Orbis, 1983), 183.

12. Rosemary Radford Ruether, *To Change the World: Christology and Cultural Criticism* (New York: Crossroad, 1981), 45–56. This section is based on Kärkkäinen, *Christ and Reconciliation: A Constructive Christian Theology for the Pluralistic World* (Grand Rapids: Eerdmans, 2013), 79–84.

13. Elizabeth Johnson, *She Who Is: The Mystery of God in Feminist Theological Discourse* (New York: Crossroad, 1993), 44.

14. Ibid., 5, 36–37.

15. Ibid., 33; see also 4–5.

16. Ibid., 33; see also 8–9, 17, 31. The phrase "discourses of emancipatory transformation" is attributed to Rebecca Chopp, as cited in ibid., 5.

always insisted, "the holy mystery of God is beyond all imagining."[17] Thus, any talk about God only approximates the reality of the Divine.

Reinterpretations of the "*Logos* Becoming Flesh"

The foundational christological confession in the New Testament is that the "Word [*Logos*] became flesh" (John 1:14). The whole Chalcedonian definition is but its exposition. Are there any implications here for the issues of inclusivity? Elizabeth Johnson argues that in keeping with the inclusive, metaphorical use of language, it means celebrating one, yet multidimensional, human nature in an interdependence of multiple differences, neither "a binary view of two forever predetermined male and female natures, nor abbreviation to a single ideal, but a diversity of ways of being human: a multipolar set of combinations of essential human elements, of which sexuality is but one."[18] In a brilliant sentence Johnson turns the maleness of Jesus into a constructive critique against patriarchalism and exclusion: "the heart of the problem is not that Jesus was a man but that more men are not like Jesus, insofar as patriarchy defines their self-identity and relationships."[19]

Whereas in the New Testament, *Logos* is linked with Jesus of Nazareth, its Old Testament background also appears in the concept of Wisdom, which is of course not gender specific—any more than "Spirit," an important biblical way of speaking of the presence of the divine in Jesus Christ. Especially in the Old Testament Wisdom literature, *hokmah* is a highly developed personification of God's presence, and Johnson finds its use in the Bible suggestive of many female traits such as "sister, mother, female beloved, chef and hostess, preacher, judge, liberator, establisher of justice, and a myriad of other female roles."[20] While there is no consensus among commentators on whether *Sophia* (the Greek term for Wisdom) is best depicted as a male or female symbol, Johnson finds credible the option that considers Sophia a female personification of God.[21] Along with other titles, Divine Sophia can be utilized in speaking of Jesus Christ. Furthermore and importantly, Johnson notes that many of the actions attributed to "Jesus-Sophia" include

17. Ibid., 45.
18. Ibid., 155.
19. Ibid., 161.
20. Ibid., 87.
21. Ibid., 91. With reference to female theologians such as Elisabeth Schüssler Fiorenza, Johnson argues that Jewish wisdom writers—differently from the classical prophetic traditions—were not afraid of employing the goddess traditions of the surrounding cultures to bring home the idea of the female side of God (93).

preaching, ingathering, and confronting, as well as dying and rising, activities that are as much female as male. In all of these activities, Jesus-Sophia is also linked with the female figure of personified Wisdom.[22] After all, the *Logos* as the universal principle of reality (used of Jesus the Christ in the New Testament) is beyond sexism.

Furthermore, we have to note that had the incarnation of the *Logos* happened in the form of the female gender, the corresponding problem would be how to include the male gender. Hence, replacing male-dominated talk about the divinity with female-dominated talk is not only unnecessary but a thoroughly counterproductive exercise. It would sharpen rather than help resolve the issue of lack of inclusivity. A true human being can only exist as either male or female. Both sexes are fully human beings, created in the image of God. Thus, either male or female has the capacity to fully represent the human person and humanity. In that light, the unfortunate argument in the Roman Catholic statement in support of male-only ordination is highly problematic, as widely acknowledged, as it takes the male priest as the only valid representative of Christ.[23]

Black and Womanist Christologies

Black Experience and Theology

Black Christology refers to a varied group of theological approaches found mainly in the African American context but also in Africa—for example, in South Africa. These approaches address Christology in light of the challenges faced by people of African descent. Though it is often unclear whether black Christology includes only African American Christologies or also African Christologies, this chapter focuses on the African American context. The final section considers black Christology in the South African context as an example of the shared values of black theology in various parts of the world.

The starting point for black theology in general and black Christology in particular is black experience. The proponents of this contextual theological movement argue for the uniqueness of black history and current experience, which have to be taken into consideration in doing theology. Too often, they say, theology has been done by white males of the West,

22. Ibid., 165–67.
23. "Declaration on the Admission of Women to the Ministerial Priesthood," October 15, 1976, Sacred Congregation for the Doctrine of the Faith, section 5 particularly, available at www.ewtn.com/library/curia/cdfinsig.htm.

and Christianity has justified black suffering.[24] Therefore, the liberation of African Americans stands at the center of black theologies. James Cone, a senior scholar and one of the defining pioneers, defines liberation as working so "that the community of the oppressed will recognize that its inner thrust for liberation is not only consistent with the gospel but is the gospel of Jesus Christ."[25]

Black theology differs from traditional theology in much the same way as African American Christianity differs from the Christianity of Europe and white North America. It is based on African heritage and cultural roots. Perhaps the most distinctive features of that heritage are the legacy of slavery and the struggle to survive under harsh and unjust oppression. "African slaves who embraced Christianity also modified and shaped it to meet their existential needs and saw, even in the contorted presentations of the gospel by some white people, a continuity between what they knew of God in Africa and the God of the Bible."[26] Black theologians believe that "God has revealed Godself to the black community and that this revelation is inseparable from the historic struggle of black people for liberation."[27]

Black theology is a creative, engaging, responsible dialogue with several sources and influences. According to Cone, there are six sources:

1. Black experience: the totality of black existence in a white world of oppression and exploitation; blacks making decisions about themselves, affirming the value of blackness

2. Black history: not only how whites have treated blacks but also how blacks have resisted that oppression

3. Black culture: the self-expression of the black community in music, art, literature, and other kinds of creative forms

4. Revelation: not only a past event (and Cone emphasizes the nature of revelation as an *event*) but also God's present redemptive activity on behalf of blacks

5. Scripture: in line with the neo-orthodox, Barthian view, Cone thinks that the Bible is not to be identified with revelation; the Bible has the

---

24. The defining work on American (and South African) black theology is Dwight N. Hopkins, *Black Theology USA and South Africa: Politics, Culture, and Liberation* (repr., Eugene, OR: Wipf & Stock, 2005). Part 1 provides the background and part 2 almost an encyclopedic treatment of main figures and themes.

25. James H. Cone, *A Black Theology of Liberation*, 2nd ed. (Maryknoll, NY: Orbis, 1986), 1.

26. James H. Evans Jr., *We Have Been Believers: An African-American Systematic Theology* (Minneapolis: Fortress, 1992), 3.

27. Ibid., 11.

capacity to become revelation in the event when God and human beings meet in an event initiated by God. The Bible is a testimony and guide to God, who acts as the liberator.

6. Tradition: a critical appropriation of how the church has understood the gospel in varying contexts[28]

Black Christ?

James Cone sets the tone for black Christology by making this programmatic statement and challenge:[29]

> If Jesus Christ is to have any meaning for us, he must leave the security of the suburbs by joining blacks in their condition. What need have we for a white Jesus when we are not white but black? If Jesus Christ is white and not black, he is an oppressor, and we must kill him. The appearance of black theology means that the black community is now ready to do something about the white Jesus, so that he cannot get in the way of our revolution.[30]

Although the mature Cone has softened his rhetoric against the "white Christ," the underlying opposition to its dominance still energizes much of the agenda of black Christologies. Behind it is the conviction that the *"norm of all God-talk which seeks to be black-talk is the manifestation of Jesus as the black Christ who provides the necessary soul for black liberation."*[31]

Cone is not alone in the insistence on the blackness of Jesus. As early as 1829, Alexander Young's "Ethiopian Manifesto" envisioned a black Messiah. The first book to set forth a detailed presentation of the meaning of a black Messiah for African American theology was Howard Thurman's *Jesus and the Disinherited*, in 1949.[32] Differently from Cone and others, Thurman's approach draws heavily from *African* experience of African American Christology. Another difference from Cone is that Thurman's Christology did not make a direct reference to political activism but rather to the idea of the kingdom of God in Jesus "in us." Its emphasis lies in the role of Jesus the Messiah in bringing about liberation by virtue of being a mediator between the forces of evil, the effects of sin, and the powers of redemption. In that sense, his Christology takes a more "spiritual" (as opposed to sociopolitical) orientation.

28. Cone, *Black Theology of Liberation*, 33–34.
29. This section is based on Kärkkäinen, *Christ and Reconciliation*, 84–86.
30. Cone, *Black Theology of Liberation*, 117.
31. Ibid., 38 (emphasis original).
32. Howard Thurman, *Jesus and the Disinherited* (Nashville: Abingdon, 1949).

Political orientation came to the fore in Albert Cleage's *The Black Messiah* (1968).[33] The most controversial claim of Cleage is that Jesus of Nazareth was literally black. He even insisted that the Bible was written by black Jews. He also argued that Jesus identified himself with the ultranationalistic Zealot movement committed to bring about a black nation of Israel. Understandably, the scholarly guild, including African Americans, has not been convinced; there simply is no historical support for this claim.

Better received is the moderate counterpart, Tom Skinner's *How Black Is the Gospel?*[34] Differently from Cleage, Skinner's "Black Messiah" is beyond racial divisions. Christ is liberator but does not identify with any particular color of people. Jesus's only allegiance was to his Father and the kingdom of God he preached.[35] The same kind of moderate, balanced approach is evident in J. Deotis Roberts's *Black Theology in Dialogue* (1987), which (similar to Cone) utilizes the so-called correlational model of Paul Tillich.[36] In line with Tillich's theological method, Roberts intuited the "Black Messiah" symbolically rather than as literally/historically black. The black Messiah is a mythical construct that helps to overcome the negative associations of being black. But ultimately, the black Messiah has to give way to a "colorless Christ."

Black Christology from South Africa

Many of the leading ideas of Cone and his colleagues found their way into the church in South Africa under the oppression of apartheid.[37] Yet many South Africans, especially Allan Boesak, have also taken a critical stand against some of the ideas presented by Cone.[38] Boesak, who at one point was sentenced to prison, is a South African pastor who also was the president of the World Alliance of Reformed Churches from 1982 until 1991. For him, black theology is the theological reflection of black Christians on the situation in which they live in South Africa. Blacks ask what it means to believe in Jesus Christ when

33. Albert Cleage, *The Black Messiah* (New York: Sheed & Ward, 1968).

34. Tom Skinner, *How Black Is the Gospel?* (New York: J. B. Lippincott, 1970).

35. Many other black Christologies fall between the extremes of Cleage and Skinner. A moderate viewpoint is represented in J. Deotis Roberts's *Black Theology in Dialogue* (Philadelphia: Westminster, 1987), which, as the name suggests, seeks to facilitate dialogue among whites and blacks about the meaning of Christ.

36. For Tillich, the method of theology had to do with the "correlation" of philosophy and culture. Whereas philosophy/culture posed the questions, theology was seeking for answers.

37. For a detailed account, see part 3 in Hopkins, *Black Theology USA and South Africa*; for a shorter, informative discussion, see Priscilla Pope-Levison and John R. Levison, *Jesus in Global Contexts* (Louisville: Westminster John Knox, 1992), 97–117.

38. For a useful comparison between Cone and Boesak, see Volker Küster, *The Many Faces of Jesus Christ: Intercultural Christology* (Maryknoll, NY: Orbis, 2001), 145–51.

one is black and lives in a world controlled by white racists. Boesak is not prepared to separate the reality of the historical Jesus from the reality of his presence in the world today. In line with Cone, Boesak also affirms that the idea of liberation is not just *part* of the Christian gospel; it *is* the gospel of Christ. For Boesak, Christ is the center not only of Christology but also of all theology. He even uses the expression "christological theology."

Boesak offers his understanding of the terms "black consciousness" and "black power." He says that confining black consciousness to the process of discovering one's black identity limits the concept. It should also lead to the act of overcoming the institutionalized oppression of apartheid in South African society. To clarify his view, he criticizes Cone's understanding of black theology. According to Boesak, Cone makes the black experience "revelatory" in the sense that he bases his theology on that experience rather than on the revelation of God in Christ and therefore virtually identifies black power with the gospel. Not all agree with this reading of Cone's position; Boesak's criticism reflects his own struggle to find a balance that he sees lacking in Cone. But the way in which Boesak finally conceives of black power remains unclear. For example, he does not clearly present his standpoint concerning the use of violence. He is not an advocate of violence, but to what extent he would allow its use is not clear in his writings. What is clear is that he is critical of the tendency of white theologians to make the issue of violence *the* theme of black theology.

The central feature of Boesak's thought is the idea of Christ as the reconciler of both black and white. "Liberation and reconciliation presuppose one another."[39] For reconciliation to happen, white racism must be abolished. In agreement with Cone, Boesak maintains that blacks must drop their internalized slave mentality and accept themselves in their blackness. They can then claim the promise of God for their own dignity before God in Christ.

Womanist Liberating Christology

How do black women (womanists) speak of Jesus Christ as their Savior?[40] While some black female scholars may not see a need for a distinctively black "feminist" theology, many do. Naturally, emerging black feminist Christologies share the overall concern of black theology: to liberate from white oppression

39. Allan A. Boesak, *Farewell to Innocence: A Socio-Ethical Study on Black Theology and Black Power* (Maryknoll, NY: Orbis, 1977), 92.

40. A short, useful introduction is provided by Victor I. Ezigbo, *Introducing Christian Theologies*, vol. 1, *Voices from Global Christian Communities* (Eugene, OR: Cascade, 2013), 179–82.

and to cry for freedom and self-fulfillment. They also share the general aim of feminist theologies: to set women free from patriarchy and male dominance.[41]

An important corollary to black feminism is the longing for a holistic theology and Christology that integrate into a single theological vision all aspects of human life. African American cultures, like most two-thirds world cultures, lean toward holism more than most dualistic Western worldviews. At the same time, womanist theologians often remind their white female colleagues of the difference of focus of liberation: for them it is less about gender equality, although it is also about that, and has much to do also with socioeconomic, educational, and work-opportunity issues, and related matters. Some womanists also critique their black male counterparts for propagating and enforcing attitudes of inequality and inferiority within black communities.

Kelly Brown Douglas's *The Black Christ* reminds us that much more important than the details of creedal sophistications are the Gospel narratives about the ministry of Jesus. This is not to leave behind Nicene and Chalcedonian traditions but rather to put them in perspective.[42] Similarly, Jacquelyn Grant's *White Women's Christ and Black Women's Jesus*—a telling title!—shifts the main focus onto Jesus's humanity and earthly ministry.[43] In line with many other types of liberationists, womanist theologians prefer the from below approach to the study of Christology, as it focuses on the "deeds of the historical Jesus and not the idealized Christ, in keeping with the liberative traditions of the religious community."[44] In doing so, however, they are less concerned about the traditional methodological questions in their pursuit of from below insights in the service of liberation, inclusivity, and equality. Douglas surmises that mainline theology, with its focus on incarnation and other classical topics, has also made the ruling class totally blind to the sins of slavery and oppression. Jesus's "ministry to the poor and oppressed is virtually inconsequential to this interpretation of Christianity."[45]

Black female theologians appreciate greatly the New Testament narrative about Jesus who was inclusive in his love toward women and other marginalized

---

41. An early formative work is Delores S. Williams, *Sisters in the Wilderness: The Challenge of Womanist God-Talk* (Maryknoll, NY: Orbis, 1993). A useful survey is Stephanie Y. Mitchem, *Introducing Womanist Theology* (Maryknoll, NY: Orbis, 2002).

42. Kelly Brown Douglas, *The Black Christ* (Maryknoll, NY: Orbis, 1994), 111–13.

43. Jacquelyn Grant, *White Women's Christ and Black Women's Jesus: Feminist Christology and Womanist Response* (Atlanta: Scholars Press, 1989), 217.

44. JoAnne Marie Terrell, *Power in the Blood? The Cross in the African American Experience* (Maryknoll, NY: Orbis, 1998), 108.

45. Douglas, *Black Christ*, 13.

people in the society. According to Jacquelyn Grant, black women found a Jesus they could claim, and whose claim for them affirms their dignity and self-respect. Jesus means several things to black people; chief among these, however, is belief in Jesus as the divine cosufferer who empowers them in situations of oppression. Black women

> identified with Jesus because they believed that Jesus identified with them. As Jesus was persecuted and made to suffer undeservedly, so were they. His suffering culminated in the crucifixion. Their crucifixion included rapes, and husbands being castrated (literally and metaphorically), babies being sold, and other cruel and often murderous treatments. But Jesus's suffering was not the suffering of a mere human, for Jesus was understood to be God incarnate.[46]

Jesus is seen not only as the divine cosufferer but also as the one who empowers the weak. His love is not sentimental, passive love but a tough, active love. Thus, not only Jesus's divinity but also his life has immense meaning in black feminist thought and spirituality. Jesus was a political Messiah whose task was to set all people free.

Hispanic American and Latino/a Christologies

Theology at the "Borders"

North Americans of Hispanic or Latino/a origin—most of whom are *mestizos*, persons of mixed race—may often feel that they are neither part of the dominant white population in North America nor South Americans nor Mexicans.[47] Not without reason, Hispanic American or Latino/a theology has been called a "border theology."[48] As a "hybrid" expression, this dynamic and lively tradition of *mestizo* Christianity carries much potential to enrich both Protestant and Catholic theologies.[49]

Hispanic and Latino/a theology in North America shares with other immigrant theologies the struggle of marginalization and identity formation. Even though Hispanics/Latinos are not newcomers to North

46. Jacquelyn Grant, "Womanist Theology: Black Women's Experience as a Source for Doing Theology, with Special Reference to Christology," in *Constructive Christian Theology in the Worldwide Church*, ed. William R. Barr (Grand Rapids: Eerdmans, 1997), 346–47.

47. Virgilio P. Elizondo, foreword to Justo L. González, *Mañana: Christian Theology from a Hispanic Perspective* (Nashville: Abingdon, 1990), 13–14.

48. Ibid., 19.

49. González, *Mañana*, 13–14; for the background concerning Hispanics in North America, see chap. 2.

America—indeed, it is the currently dominant population, Caucasians, who are the newcomers historically[50]—they have had to struggle to establish their own theology over against Latin American theology in general and liberation theology in particular. This is not to say that many Hispanic and Latino/a theologians in North America do not share the basic agenda of liberation theologies. Often, however, their approach and methods differ significantly from their Latin American counterparts—and their location is different as well.

The rise of distinctively Hispanic voices in America in the 1950s was connected to the Hispanic *movimiento* for civil rights in society and the church, especially the Roman Catholic Church. The formative phase of Latino/a theology in North America began in the late 1960s under the leadership of Virgilio Elizondo, whose *Galilean Journey: The Mexican-American Promise* focused on the popular piety of Hispanic Catholics as a powerful theological resource.[51] The early 1980s saw several crucial developments, such as the founding of the theological journal *Apuntes*, which until the 1993 appearance of the *Journal of Hispanic/Latino Theology* was the only scholarly venue for this type of theology. The emergence of the Academy of Catholic Hispanic Theologians in the United States (ACHTUS) was also a major event at that time. Women, who constitute roughly one-fourth of all American Latino/a theologians, participated in the development of *mujerista* theology and other feminist Hispanic views (to be studied below).[52] What are some of the contributions of Hispanic and Latino/a Christologies?[53]

A "Biased" Christology

Above we discussed the ways that senior Cuban American historian-theologian Justo L. González's *Mañana: Christian Theology from a Hispanic*

50. Yolanda Tarango and Timothy Matovina, "US Hispanic and Latin American Theologies: Critical Distinctions," *Catholic Theological Society of America: Proceedings* 48 (1993): 128. See also M. Shawn Copeland, "Black, Hispanic/Latino, and Native American Theologies," in *The Modern Theologians: An Introduction to Christian Theology in the Twentieth Century*, 2nd ed., ed. David F. Ford (Cambridge: Blackwell, 1997), 367.

51. See Allan Figueroa Deck, ed., *Frontiers of Hispanic Theology in the United States* (Maryknoll, NY: Orbis, 1992), xii–xiii.

52. See Copeland, "Black, Hispanic/Latino, and Native American Theologies," 367–72.

53. A rich (though diverse and somewhat uneven) resource is the collection of essays in *Jesus in the Hispanic Community: Images of Christ from Theology to Popular Religion*, ed. Harold Joseph Recinos and Hugo Magallanes (Louisville: Westminster John Knox, 2009). A noteworthy contribution by a younger Pentecostal scholar is Sammy Alfaro, *Divino Compañero: Toward a Hispanic Pentecostal Christology* (Eugene, OR: Pickwick, 2010).

Perspective critiqued the ideological ramifications of some key christological heresies. This is an indication of the biased—and thus, contextual (that is, shaped by the context)—nature of all theology, including Christology. The biased nature of any human way of doing theology, however, is not only an obstacle. Somewhat counterintuitively, González argues that there is also something like a legitimate bias for theology. That comes to the fore even in the Bible. "God has certain purposes for creation and is moving the world and humankind toward the fulfillment of those purposes. This means that, in a sense, God is biased against anything that stands in the way of those goals, and in favor of all that aids them."[54] The biased nature of the Bible is accentuated by its "preferential option for the poor," a model to be followed when "reading the Bible in Spanish."[55]

Continuing his critical and "biased" reading of the development of christological traditions from a Hispanic or Latino/a perspective, González laments the fact that despite the emphasis of the Gospels on the suffering and death of Jesus, early on opposition to that kind of "weak" God-man arose in Christology. The Hellenistic aversion to all notions of God/the Deity being able to suffer almost blocked the way for early theology to think of God's real dealings with the fragile and transitory world. Arianism is of course the showcase here. In González's view, the "Arian impassible God . . . was more supportive of imperial authority than the living God of Scripture, even in the mitigated Nicene form."[56] In that light, González thinks it is no wonder that patripassianism appealed to the masses. Patripassianism, the modalistic idea that God in fact suffered in the Son, showed

> clearly that God was one of their number. God was not like the emperor and his nobles, who had an easy life in their lofty positions. God had toiled and suffered even as they must toil and suffer every day. On this point, it would seem that the Patripassianist had an insight into the nature of the biblical God that the more powerful leaders of the church had begun to lose.[57]

Even though González regards the rejection of patripassianism a correct theological choice, he believes that the underlying motive behind its appeal, namely, asserting the suffering of God, must not be ignored. Highly interestingly, this prominent historian of Christian doctrine puts the "orthodox" solutions to heresies in a proper sociopolitical and theological perspective:

54. González, *Mañana*, 21–22.
55. The title of chap. 5 in González, *Mañana*.
56. Ibid., 108–9.
57. Ibid., 109.

The triumph over Arianism ensured that even amid the majority church of the
Middle Ages and of modern times, the voice could be heard of the minority God
who was made flesh in a humble carpenter belonging to an oppressed nation.
The victory over Patripassianism assured Christians of all ages that suffering,
oppressions, and despair do not have the last word, for behind the suffering
Son and suffering humankind stands the One who vindicates the Son and all
those who, like him, suffer oppression and injustice; that at the right hand of
the throne of glory stands the Lamb of God, in representation of all those who
are like lambs taken to the slaughter. But the profound insight of this Nicene
faith was often overshadowed by the fact that Christians had now become a
powerful body and would soon be literally a majority.[58]

Christological Images from the Latina *Mujerista* Perspective

The book that brought the agenda of female Hispanic scholars, Latinas,
to public notice was *Hispanic Women: Prophetic Voice in the Church*, edited
by Ada María Isasi-Díaz and Yolanda Tarango.[59] This was the first attempt
to gather together leading ideas of Latina theology, called *mujerista* theology.
"A *mujerista* is someone who makes a preferential option for Latina women,
for our struggle for liberation."[60] Another hybrid concept, it brings together
the *mestizaje* (mixed white and native people in Latin America) and *mulatez*
(mixed black and white people) and their condition as racially and culturally
mixed people.[61] *Mujerista* is an attempt for a "theology *from* the perspective
of Latinas."[62] Unlike mainline academic theology, which often regards popular
religion as primitive, *mujerista* theology "recognizes popular religion as a
credible experience" of the divine.[63]

In her *En la Lucha: A Hispanic Women's Liberation Theology*, Isasi-Díaz,
currently the leading thinker of the movement, regards highly "grassroot Latinas' religious understanding and the way those understandings guide their
daily lives," because "those religious understandings are part of the ongoing
revelation of God, present in the midst of the community of faith and giving
strength to Hispanic Women's struggle for liberation."[64] *La lucha*, "struggle,"

58. Ibid., 110.

59. Ada María Isasi-Díaz, *Mujerista Theology: A Theology for the Twenty-First Century*
(Maryknoll, NY: Orbis, 2001), 61; for a pioneering Latin American contribution, see Maria Pilar
Aquino, *Our Cry for Life: Feminist Theology from Latin America* (Maryknoll, NY: Orbis, 1993).

60. Isasi-Díaz, *Mujerista Theology*, 62–63.

61. Ibid., 71–72.

62. Ibid., 129–30.

63. Ibid., 174.

64. Ada María Isasi-Díaz, *En la Lucha [In the Struggle]: A Hispanic Women's Liberation
Theology* (Minneapolis: Fortress, 1993), 21.

is the mode of God-talk in Latina theology. Jesus's suffering is the model, but Isasi-Díaz does not believe that Jesus suffered more than all other human suffering or that God, whom Jesus called Father, demanded that Jesus suffer to fulfill his mission on earth. Suffering may be inevitable, but in itself it is not good, nothing to be desired.[65]

Although Latina theological perspectives are emerging—some of them identifying themselves with the concept of the *mujerista*, others not—a distinctively Latina Christology is only taking baby steps at the time of this writing. Pioneering in this field, Isasi-Díaz has coined an exciting new term to speak of the center of Christ's message, the kingdom of God: she names it the "kin-dom" of God. Whereas the traditional name is laden with connotations and history of male domination and political abuse of power, the neologism relates to the community, household, sharing—values dear to all Latinas.[66] It relates to the need for Latinas to cultivate a "deep, intimate relationship"[67] with God, at both the personal and the communal level.

In a recent programmatic constructive essay in search of a Latina Christology, Alicia Vargas establishes a robust theological connection with the painful location of Hispanic women on the "borderlands" and Christ's suffering and resurrection:

> The discourse of the life of Latinas in the United States is an ever-continuing project of de- and reconstruction, of shifting contextual identities. The simultaneously painful and life-giving experience of perennially critiquing, confronting, and constructing new personal and communal perspectives on our continuously conflicting contexts is especially enfleshed for Latinas in the life and resurrection of Jesus Christ. The human pain of Jesus on the cross accompanies the pain of Latinas at deconstructing our own inheritance as Latin American and American cultural products and the racist systems that render us marginal both within the secular community at large and in the community of Christians in the U.S. Christ's resurrection makes itself manifest in us, too, as we continuously reconstruct our fragmented identities to live abundantly in the simul world of our deaths and new life.[68]

Similarly to many other marginalized people, for many Latinas faith in Christ and his resurrection is a powerful energizer and aid in self-affirmation:

65. Isasi-Díaz, *Mujerista Theology*, 163.
66. Ada María Isasi-Díaz, "Christ in Mujerista Theology," in *Thinking of Christ: Proclamation, Explanation, Meaning*, ed. Tatha Wiley (New York: Continuum, 2003), 160–64.
67. Ibid., 172.
68. Alicia Vargas, "The Construction of Latina Christology: An Invitation to Dialogue," *Currents in Theology and Mission* 34, no. 4 (2007): 271–77.

"Latinas' faith in Jesus Christ as our Savior empowers Latinas to take action for individual and communal self-affirmation and responsibility and to deconstruct through our diverse praxis the oppressive categories that attempt to trap us."[69] And even beyond that, "the christological perspective of Latinas empowers us to survive the indeterminacy of cultural and social identity and even our marginalization by racist and sexist systems."[70] This kind of Christology can be called simply "praxis"[71]—and brings to mind Moltmann's call for "Christopraxis," discussed above. It is less interested in speculations concerning doctrinal nuances and more about a proper narrative of Christ, similarly to the Gospel writers, a "religious narrative that can help us not only to understand Christian faith but also to deal with the struggle for liberation-fullness of life we face everyday."[72]

Postcolonial and Queer Christologies

Emerging Postcolonial Consciousness and Hybridity

One of the ways postcolonial thinkers, including Christian theologians, seek to describe the bewildering diversity of societies and communities of the third millennium—in terms of cultures, nationalities, races, identities, and other such markers that used to be easily identifiable—is with the term "hybrid" (and hybridity). In this "new" and complex hybrid world, "the international blurs into the national. 'We' do not quite know who is 'us' and who is 'them.' Neither race nor language can any longer define nationality."[73] Pioneering postcolonial theorist Homi K. Bhabha launched the terms "interstitial perspective," to denote the in-between spaces, borderlands, and "interstitial subjectivity," to refer to the complex and undefined ways of seeing identities.[74] An illustration of the complexity could be the subway in a metropolitan area, "like a great subterranean serpent . . . in the maze beneath the city," full of people of different and mixed colors, races, attire, languages, dialects, and other characteristic features.[75]

69. Ibid., 273.
70. Ibid., 274.
71. Isasi-Díaz, "Christ in Mujerista Theology," 158.
72. Ibid., 159.
73. Catherine Keller, Michael Nausner, and Mayra Rivera, eds., "Introduction: Alien/Nation, Liberation, and the Postcolonial Underground," in *Postcolonial Theologies: Divinity and Empire* (St. Louis: Chalice, 2004), 1.
74. Homi K. Bhabha, *The Location of Culture* (London: Routledge, 1994).
75. "The Subway" is the first subheading in Keller, Nausner, and Rivera, "Introduction," 1. This section is based on Kärkkäinen, *Christ and Reconciliation*, 90–92.

A number of theologians have tapped into the resources of the postcolonial analysis. One group consists of immigrant theologians to whom the "on-the-border" existence is a defining moment—a manifestation of hybridity. Japanese American Rita Nakashima Brock's preferred expression to describe the in-betweenness of Asian American women is Bhabha's term "interstitial."[76] Some other Asian Americans mean the same by different terminology: Korean American theologian Sang Hyun Lee speaks of the marginality of his own people in terms of "liminality," which refers to "the situation of being in between two or more worlds, and includes the meaning of being located at the periphery or edge of a society."[77] Vietnamese American Peter C. Phan uses the phrase "to be betwixt and between," that is, "to be neither here nor there, to be neither this thing nor that."[78]

Whereas liberation theologies of various stripes focus on sexism, poverty, other socioeconomic problems, and political oppression, postcolonial theologies attempt to look at these and similar kinds of issues against the wider horizon of colonialism in its different forms. Although colonialism of the nineteenth century may by and large be over, different types of forces of subjugation, oppression, and abuse are still at work: just think of the economic disparity between the "haves" and "have-nots"; inequality concerning educational and social opportunities; the privilege of language—English as the lingua franca; the all-encompassing influence of mass media, entertainment, forms of commercial culture, and so forth. As a result, there is a need for the "Postcolonial Feminist Rethinking of Jesus/Christ."[79] Although the emerging postcolonial paradigm of Christology does not debunk typical feminist theology, to which "the central problems of Christianity were that the savior was male and that the foundational Christian symbol was androcentric,"[80] it also considers the feminist approach limited as it is occupied merely with the gender issue. (Postcolonialists also bring to the question new dimensions, as the discussion below of hybrid and queer Christology illustrates.) The basic challenge for the postcolonial framing of Christology is this, as formulated by Chinese American Kwok Pui-lan:

76. Rita Nakashima Brock, "Interstitial Integrity: Reflections Towards an Asian American Woman's Theology," in *Introduction to Christian Theology: Contemporary North American Perspectives*, ed. Roger Badham (Louisville: Westminster John Knox, 1998), chap. 13.

77. Sang Hyun Lee, *From a Liminal Place: An Asian American Theology* (Minneapolis: Fortress, 2010), x.

78. Peter C. Phan, "Betwixt and Between: Doing Theology with Memory and Imagination," in *Journeys at the Margin: Toward an Autobiographical Theology in American-Asian Perspective*, ed. Peter Phan and Jung Young Lee (Collegeville, MN: Liturgical Press, 1999), 113.

79. Subheading in Kwok Pui-lan, *Postcolonial Imagination and Feminist Theology* (Louisville: Westminster John Knox, 2005), 169.

80. Ibid., 168.

How is it possible for the formerly colonized, oppressed, subjugated subaltern to transform the symbol of Christ—a symbol that has been used to justify colonization and domination—into a symbol that affirms life, dignity, and freedom? Can the subaltern speak about Christ, and if so, under what conditions? . . . Alternatively, if we need to ground our reflections in the culture and religiosity of our people, how can we avoid the pitfalls of cultural essentialism, nativism, and nationalistic ideologies? What makes it possible to say something new about Jesus/Christ?[81]

The Quest of the Hybridized Jesus

But why should Christian theology of Christ be concerned about and interested in the postcolonial challenge and its notion of hybridity? Are there theological reasons for it? There are at least two important considerations (beyond the more general observation that at all times Christian theology, in order to transcend its own borders, has engaged existing philosophical and cultural phenomena). First, the "ancient church was born a hybrid of the Jewish religion with the plurality of cultures mingling within the Roman Empire. . . . Today, another global hybridity, with both its wounds and its potentiality, is again redefining Christianity" as the church grows and expands, particularly in the Global South.[82] Just think of the beginning of Christianity in Asia. Even though "it was on a hill in Asia, at the far western edge of the continent, that Jesus said to his disciples, 'Go ye into all the world and preach the gospel' (Mark 16:15),"[83] and even though Jesus was Asian—western Asian, to be more precise—it is also true that "it was in *Roman* Asia that Jesus Christ was born." Similar to the Greeks before, the Romans were intruders in the continent.[84] This means that Jesus lived under colonialism and under hybridity when it comes to cultures, politics, identities, allegiances. Second, Christology "offers as its central doctrine the symbol of a divine/human hybrid, at once mimicking and scandalizing the operative metaphysical binaries of the time."[85] Hence, as Kwok Pui-lan brilliantly coins it, there is a need for *the quest of the hybridized Jesus*—after *the quest of the historical Jesus*.[86]

A profound current example of a hybrid interpretation is Jesus as an Afro-Asiatic Jew. Behind this conjecture is the conviction that the Semite Hebrews

81. Ibid., 168–69.
82. Keller, Nausner, and Rivera, "Introduction," 4.
83. Samuel Hugh Moffett, *A History of Christianity in Asia*, vol. 1, *Beginnings to 1500* (San Francisco: HarperSanFrancisco, 1992), 4.
84. Ibid., 1:6.
85. Keller, Nausner, and Rivera, "Introduction," 13.
86. Pui-lan, *Postcolonial Imagination*, 170.

are less a race and more a mixed crowd of people, including those of African descent.[87] Similarly, the metaphor of Jesus as the "Corn Mother" is one of the ways to release American Indians from the "cultural frame of reference that necessitated self-denial and assimilation to the language and social structures of the conqueror."[88] Similarly to the Johannine Christians who looked for the *Logos* that is not necessarily limited to male figures, leading American Indian theologian George Tinker intuits that Native Americans may look for the mythic image of the Corn Mother, who transcends conventional binary sexual limitations. Corn Mother's suffering and self-sacrifice provide food and sustenance for the people.[89]

Whatever the specific context, hybridity pushes Christian theology beyond its comfort level and reminds it of the need to continually appreciate the complexity and subtle nature of diversity built into the biblical narrative of Christ and the subsequent history of global Christian tradition. The notion of hybridity also makes contemporary theology uneasy about being stuck with conventional interpretations and formulations of Christ. This does not mean leaving behind the doctrinal guidelines as set forth in the creedal tradition, but rather calls for commitment to continuous reevaluation and reconsideration of current formulations in light of the complexity of the world.

Unlike much of modernist theology, which is built on "universal" categories, postcolonialists (with postmodernists and others) remind us of the importance of particularity. In order to honor that wish, the presentation of postcolonial Christologies in this section focuses on two specific examples: first, postcolonial interpretations of Christ in Asian American interpretations, both female and male (this is also to offset the lack of a separate section on Asian American theologies); second, the most novel and most widely debated postcolonial construct, queer (or hybrid) Christologies.

Jesus in Postcolonial Asian American Perspectives

Korean American female theologian Wonhee Anne Joh seeks to construct a postcolonial Christology, employing two concepts from her culture of origin: *han* and *jeong*. According to her, *han* is a multifaceted concept that denotes

87. Karen Baker-Fletcher and Garth Kasimu Baker-Fletcher, *My Sister, My Brother: Womanist and Xodus God-Talk* (Eugene, OR: Wipf & Stock, 2002).

88. George Tinker, "Jesus, Corn Mother, and Conquest: Christology and Colonialism," in *Native American Religious Identity: Unforgotten God*, ed. Jace Weaver (Maryknoll, NY: Orbis, 1998), 139.

89. Ibid., 151–52.

suffering and pain, "a sense of unresolved resentment against injustices suffered, a sense of helplessness, . . . a feeling of acute pain and sorrow in one's guts and bowels."[90] According to prominent Korean American theologian Andrew Sung Park, that concept helps bring home the meaning of Jesus's life for the marginalized and suffering ones. Not only the sufferings of the cross but all of Jesus's life represented divine *han*:

> Jesus' birth bespeaks of the han of God for the children of the poor. According to the birth story, there was no room at the inn and Mary delivered the baby in a manger (Lk. 2:7). . . . The han of God persists in the fact that there is no room available in the world for thousands of babies whom God has created. . . . Jesus' suffering for three hours on the cross was one thing; his many years' suffering . . . was a profound source of Jesus' han.[91]

Importantly, Park reminds us, "It is not right to limit the crucifixion of Jesus Christ to the three hours of suffering on the cross. The crucifixion of Jesus must be understood as extending to his whole life. Jesus lived the life of taking up his cross everyday."[92] The concept of *han* also highlights the true nature of God as manifested in his suffering and identification with us:

> The all-powerful God was crucified. The cross is the symbol of God's han which makes known God's own vulnerability to human sin. . . . The cry of the wounded heart of God reverberates throughout the whole of history. God shamefully exposes the vulnerability of God on the cross, demanding the healing of the han of God. The cross is God's unshakable love for God's own creation. Like parents who give birth to and then love children, God is wrapped up in a creational love with humanity.[93]

Linked with *han* is another Korean cultural symbol, *jeong*. Joh tells us that "the power of the cross also points simultaneously to the possibility of a radical form of love that can be linked with the Korean concept of *jeong*." That crucial cultural concept "encompasses but is not limited to notions of compassion, affection, solidarity, relationality, vulnerability, and

---

90. Joh, *Heart of the Cross*, xxi. (Joh attributes this definition to Han Wan Sang but gives a mistaken reference to another author; I was unable to trace the original source.) A careful discussion of the many meanings of *han* can be found in Andrew Sung Park, *The Wounded Heart of God: The Asian Concept of Han and the Christian Doctrine of Sin* (Nashville: Abingdon, 1993), chap. 1 and throughout.

91. Park, *Wounded Heart of God*, 125.

92. Ibid., 124.

93. Ibid., 123.

forgiveness."[94] In sum, "the cross works symbolically to embody both the horror of *han* and the power of *jeong*."[95]

In keeping with the "on the border" nature of all immigrants, including Asian Americans, Joh reports that for Korean American Christians the cross is both an empowering and a disempowering symbol: "The cross continues to empower people as it signifies radical solidarity with their experience of *han* and *jeong* as embodied in their lived immigrant experiences. However, it continues to be disempowering to many . . . because of its traditional interpretation of self-abnegation and its acceptance of sacrifice even unto death, as Jesus is understood to have demonstrated on the cross."[96]

A Queer Jesus?

Whereas traditional feminist Christology seeks to find ways to make the maleness of Jesus less exclusivistic, the postcolonial approach goes further in its project of "Engendering Christ."[97] While the above-quoted question of Ruether—"Can a male savior save women?"—"implicitly consents to the fact that the savior is male, and the question then becomes what has a male savior to do with women," postcolonialists wonder what would happen if they "problematize the gender of the savior."[98] Hence, "marginalized images of Jesus/Christ" have been proposed, including the "Theological Transvestite" and "Jesus as Bi/Christ."[99] The latter metaphor of "Bi" comes from the influential work of Argentinean Marcella Althaus-Reid, who wants to include in theology and Christology sex and sexuality along with gender. For her it is not enough to have that discussion in gay and lesbian theologies. Her proposal of Bi/Christ is not about alleged sexual activity but rather about "people's sexual identity outside heterosexualism and 'a pattern of thought for a larger Christ outside binary boundaries.'"[100]

94. Joh, *Heart of the Cross*, xiii. For a succinct account, see her "The Transgressive Power of Jeong: A Postcolonial Hybridization of Christology," in *Postcolonial Theologies: Divinity and Empire*, ed. Catherine Keller, Michael Nausner, and Mayra Rivera (St. Louis: Chalice, 2004), 149–63.

95. Joh, *Heart of the Cross*, xiv.

96. Ibid., 71.

97. Title of chap. 7 in Pui-lan, *Postcolonial Imagination*.

98. Pui-lan, *Postcolonial Imagination*, 169–70.

99. The first phrase in quotation marks in this sentence is a subheading in Pui-lan, *Postcolonial Imagination*, 174; the discussion of the two hybrid concepts of Jesus appears on pp. 179–82. I am indebted to Pui-lan for some bibliographic references in this section.

100. As paraphrased by Pui-lan, *Postcolonial Imagination*, 181; citation comes from Marcella Althaus-Reid, *Indecent Theology: Theological Perversions in Sex, Gender, and Politics* (London: Routledge, 2001), 117.

From this postcolonial hybrid soil has emerged queer Christology,[101] part of a larger effort to construct a distinctively queer theological tradition.[102] The elusive and somewhat contested term "queer" refers to "those identifying as gay, lesbian, bisexual, transgendered, intersexual, supportively heterosexual or a combination thereof."[103] The main opposition facing those who attempt queer Christologies has to do with a "heteropatriarchal logic manifested in both individual and institutionalized homophobia," which in turn has led to "christophobia" among homosexuals.[104]

Are the advocates of queer theology arguing that Jesus of Nazareth was queer or homosexual/bisexual? No, but they are resisting essentialism, that is, the mind-set that a certain sexual orientation (namely, heterosexuality) makes a "normal" person.[105] Some claim that sexuality, differently from gender, is a social construct rather than a biological necessity.[106] Thomas Bohache defines succinctly the main goal of queer Christology:

> A queer Christology will not try to argue for or against the gayness of Jesus, but will seek rather to determine what his Christ-ness says to marginalized peoples of all generations, including today's queer community. . . . The Queer Christ articulates a solidarity with the marginalized of his day and our day, in order to show that the God consciousness of each person goes beyond the limitations of their physical existence.[107]

An emerging orientation in theological studies and constructive theological reflection, it is yet to be seen what its final shape and contribution will be.

101. Important recent primers include Thomas Bohache, *Christology from the Margins* (London: SCM, 2008) (which also deals with other contextual and global Christologies but focuses on queer theology). Another recent one is Patrick S. Cheng, *From Sin to Amazing Grace: Discovering the Queer Christ* (New York: Seabury, 2012). Significant earlier works include Robert Goss, *Jesus ACTED UP: A Gay and Lesbian Manifesto* (New York: Harper-Collins, 1993); Goss, *Queering Christ* (Cleveland: Pilgrim Press, 2002); Althaus-Reid, *Indecent Theology*.

102. A succinct introduction and survey is Patrick S. Cheng, *Radical Love: Introduction to Queer Theology* (New York: Seabury, 2011).

103. Thomas Bohache, "Embodiment as Incarnation: An Incipient Queer Christology," *Theology & Sexuality* 10, no. 1 (September 2003): 9. This section is largely based on his essay and the book mentioned above.

104. Ibid., 12, 13.

105. Ibid., 17–18. As representative of a tiny minority of those who really argue for the queer nature of Jesus, see Robert Williams, *Just as I Am: A Practical Guide to Being Out, Proud, and Christian* (New York: Crown Publishers, 1992), 116–23.

106. Most famously argued by Judith Butler, *Gender Trouble: Feminism and the Subversion of Identity* (New York: Routledge, 1990).

107. Bohache, "Embodiment as Incarnation," 19.

Similarly to many other recent movements in theology, it is also interested in interfaith dimensions.[108]

Having now investigated contemporary Christologies at the global level, paying special attention to diverse and unique interpretations coming from various locations and contexts, it is time to widen the conversation even more: Christian Christology is placed in the interfaith context. Jewish, Muslim, Hindu, and Buddhist accounts of Jesus Christ will be the focus of the last part of the book.

108. From the Jewish perspective, see Rabbi Rachel Barenblat, "Negotiating Identities: Queer Interfaith Couples Share Their Stories," in *Interfaith Family: Supporting Interfaith Families Exploring Jewish Life* (June 2003), at www.interfaithfamily.com/relationships/marriage _and_relationships/Negotiating_Identities_Queer_Interfaith_Couples_Share_their_Stories .shtml.

PART 4

JESUS CHRIST AMONG RELIGIONS

Diversity without Unity

If globalization was the biggest and most dramatic challenge to much of twentieth-century theology and Christology, in the beginning of the third millennium it is interfaith issues and religious pluralism(s). Globalization and religious plurality of course belong together and feed each other.

Christian faith can no longer be taken as the "religion of the land" either in North America or Europe—and Christian faith has never been dominant in the Global South[1] (with the caveat that, as mentioned, in a few years Africa will be the most Christianized continent). When the Pew Forum on Religion and Public Life (2008) reported that "the United States is on the verge of becoming a minority Protestant country,"[2] the implication was not that other Christian churches, even the Roman Catholic Church, are becoming the major religious player in North America (although the Catholic Church still

1. Diane L. Eck, *A New Religious America: How a "Christian Country" Has Become the World's Most Religiously Diverse Nation* (San Francisco: HarperCollins, 2001), 5–6, 61–65.
2. Pew Forum on Religion & Public Life, "U.S. Religious Landscape Survey: Religious Affiliation: Diverse and Dynamic," February 2008, 5–7, http://religions.pewforum.org/pdf/report-religious-landscape-study-full.pdf.

holds a considerable place) but that commitment to Christian communities and beliefs is not to be taken for granted anymore. More than one-quarter of Americans have changed their faith allegiance or ended up as confessing no faith,[3] and in Europe the numbers are even more dramatic.[4] Both religious diversity and pervasive secularism have transformed American and European cultures in dramatic ways. In the Global South religious diversity is taken for granted and is a matter of fact in many areas; secularism is doing much more poorly therein. Consequently, "we do our theology from now on in the midst of many others 'who are not . . . of this fold.' Our own faith, if only we are aware of it, is a constantly renewed decision, taken in the knowledge that other faiths are readily available to us."[5]

This final section introduces the challenge of interfaith engagement and religious plurality. Thereafter, careful comparative theological exercises will be conducted with Jewish, Islamic, Buddhist, and Hindu interpretations and assessments of Jesus Christ in relation to Christian Christology.

3. Ibid.
4. See Pew Research Center, Religion: websites on Europe, www.pewforum.org/topics/europe/.
5. Douglas John Hall, *Thinking the Faith* (Minneapolis: Fortress, 1991), 208–9.

8

Jesus among Abrahamic Traditions

Theology in a Pluralistic World and Interfaith Matrix

Whereas the term (religious) "plurality" merely denotes the existence of more than one religion side by side, "pluralism"—as in any "-ism"—is a particular take on the implications of religious diversity. Approaches to religious diversity among Christian theologians were briefly discussed above (in chap. 5 with regard to Hick and Rahner). There, a brief reference to comparative theology was also mentioned: whereas the (Christian) theology of religions is occupied with the wider issues of ways Christianity may relate to and live among other faith traditions, comparative theology—the focus of this last part of the book—delves into particular beliefs and doctrines between two (or among many) faith traditions in order to facilitate comparison. As mentioned, comparative theology utilizes the results and insights of comparative religion, which attempts a more "neutral" account of religious differences and similarities.

Comparative theological work is based on the idea of honoring distinctive features, beliefs, and practices of religions. It makes room for religions to issue claims to ultimate truth. While common sense tells us that it is not possible to assume that numerous such claims are equally correct—or incorrect—it does not have to lead to the modernist pluralistic denial of truth in general or the right for any particular religion to argue for its own views. Comparative theology is not saying that because there is a number of competing truth claims, none can be true. It rather looks for ways for a peaceful interaction among competing traditions, comparing notes and giving distinctive testimony to what each tradition honestly believes.

A great challenge to Christian theology and theological education is the embarrassingly low level of knowledge of other religions even among the best-trained theologians. Rightly, Timothy Tennent, an expert in Hindu-Christian issues, notes, "In the West, it is rare to find someone who has more than a cursory knowledge of the sacred texts of other religions. In contrast, because Christians in the Majority World are often in settings dominated by other religions, it is not uncommon to meet a Christian with a Muslim, Hindu, or Buddhist background who has an intimate knowledge of another sacred text."[1] Hence, a careful and well-informed tackling of religious diversity "here at home" and "out there" is an urgent task for any theology for the third millennium worth its salt.

When doing comparative theological exercises, one must be careful about potential dangers. Even a casual acquaintance with world religions raises the question of whether comparing notes on key christological beliefs such as Christology is an appropriate and useful way of proceeding in the first place. To take up the most obvious example: how could a Christian confession of the divinity of Jesus Christ be in any way compatible with Theravada Buddhism's non-theistic views? On the other hand, in support of the comparison is the fact that while Theravada Buddhism—unlike Mahayana and particularly its branch, Japanese and Chinese Pure Land—intentionally seeks to shift the focus in religion away from the deities to highlight the primacy of each person's ethical pursuit toward enlightenment, the Buddhist view does not entail atheism in the way the term is understood in the post-Enlightenment Global North. There are very few, if any, Buddhists—and certainly Gautama, a former theistic Hindu, would not belong to that group—who deny the *existence* of deities à la modern/contemporary Western secular/scientific atheism.

At the heart of comparative theology is the acknowledgment of a deep dynamic tension concerning religions. On the one hand, "religions generate infinite differences." Attempting to water down or deny real differences among religions, as the "first generation of pluralism" seeks to do, is a failing exercise on more than one account. In this context, just consider how useless and uninteresting a task it would be to compare two items that are alike! On the other hand, "there is a tradition at the very heart of [many living] . . .

---

1. Timothy C. Tennent, *Theology in the Context of World Christianity: How the Global Church Is Influencing the Way We Think about and Discuss Theology* (Grand Rapids: Zondervan, 2007), 55.

faiths which is held common. It is not that precisely the same doctrines are believed, but that the same tendencies of thought and devotion exist, and are expressed within rather diverse patterns of thought, characteristic of the faiths in question."[2] Add to this the obvious fact that religions are living processes that develop, reshape, and reconfigure over the years and that within any major living tradition differences and diversities are sometimes as dramatic as between some religions.

What makes comparative theological work dynamic and exciting is that, differently from comparative religions, it does not aim for a disinterested, "neutral" investigation. Comparative theology is a theological discipline and as such, rightly understood, confessional by nature. As leading Catholic comparativist Francis Clooney succinctly puts it,

> Dialogue must permanently shape the whole theological environment, but dialogue is not the primary goal of theology, which still has to do with the articulation of the truths one believes and the realization of a fuller knowledge of God (insofar as that is possible by way of theology). Both within traditions and across religious boundaries, truth does matter, conflicts among claims about reality remain significant possibilities, and making a case for the truth remains a key part of the theologian's task.[3]

Confessionalism in academic study does not mean dogmatism. Indeed, comparative work calls for and hopefully cultivates the spirit of hospitality. It makes room for the religious Other—on both sides of the dialogue. Postcolonialist feminist Mayra Rivera reminds us that we "constantly fail to encounter the other as Other. Time and again we ignore or deny the singularity of the Other—we don't see even when the face stands in front of us. We still need, it seems, 'eyes to see and ears to hear'—and bodies capable of embracing without grasping."[4] What makes hospitality such a fitting metaphor for interfaith relations is that it "involves invitation, response and engagement."[5] Hospitality reaches out, makes room, and facilitates dialogue.

The investigation of the role and meaning of Jesus the Christ among some living faith traditions is divided into two chapters. This chapter delves

2. Keith Ward, *Images of Eternity: Concepts of God in Five Religious Traditions* (Oxford: Oneworld, 1998), 1.

3. Francis X. Clooney, SJ, *Hindu God, Christian God: How Reason Helps Break Down the Boundaries between Religions* (Oxford: Oxford University Press, 2001), 173.

4. Mayra Rivera, *The Touch of Transcendence: A Postcolonial Theology of God* (Louisville: Westminster John Knox, 2007), 118.

5. George Newlands and Allen Smith, *Hospitable God: The Transformative Dream* (Surrey, UK: Ashgate, 2010), 32.

into Christologies among two other Abrahamic traditions, Judaism and Islam, which naturally are close allies to Christianity. Chapter 9 highlights perspectives on Jesus Christ in two major Asian traditions, Hinduism and Buddhism.[6]

Jesus in Jewish Estimation

The Late Emergence of Interest in Jesus among Jews

Jewish expert on Christian faith and Jewish-Christian relations Pinchas Lapide puts the dialogue (or lack thereof) in proper perspective: "When one asks the basic question of what separates Jews and Christians from each other, the unavoidable answer is: a Jew. For almost two millennia, a pious, devoted Jew has stood between us, a Jew who wanted to bring the kingdom of heaven in harmony, concord, and peace—certainly not hatred, schism, let alone bloodshed."[7] Related, "Jews rejected the claim that Jesus fulfilled the messianic prophecies of the Hebrew Bible, as well as the dogmatic claims about him made by the church fathers—that he was born of a virgin, the son of God, part of a divine Trinity, and was resurrected after his death."[8]

No wonder it took eighteen hundred years for Jewish theologians to develop any meaningful interest in the study of Christology. Until that time, "Jews' perceptions of Jesus were predominantly disparaging."[9] Just consider the radical alterations of the Gospel narratives and a highly polemical and mocking presentation of Christian claims about Jesus in the most important early Jewish source on Christ, *Toldot Yeshu* (fifth or sixth century?). (A more positive counterexample is the claim of thirteenth-century Jewish philosopher Moses Maimonides that not only Christianity but also Islam are part of the divine plan to prepare the world for the reception of the message of the biblical God.)[10]

---

6. Part 4 of this book as a whole is based on the detailed comparative theological investigation in Kärkkäinen, *Christ and Reconciliation: A Constructive Christian Theology for the Pluralistic World* (Grand Rapids: Eerdmans, 2013), chaps. 9 and 15. Interested readers are referred to those chapters with detailed documentation and discussion.

7. Pinchas Lapide, *The Resurrection of Jesus: A Jewish Perspective* (Minneapolis: Augsburg, 1983), 30.

8. Susannah Heschel, "Jewish Views of Jesus," in *Jesus in the World's Faiths: Leading Thinkers from Five Religions Reflect on His Meaning*, ed. Gregory A. Baker (Maryknoll, NY: Orbis, 2008), 149.

9. Michael J. Cook, "Jewish Perspectives on Jesus," in *The Blackwell Companion to Jesus*, ed. Delbert Burkett (Oxford: Wiley-Blackwell, 2011), 215.

10. This paragraph is based on Heschel, "Jewish Views of Jesus," 149–51.

In the rabbinical writings—the formative theological tradition after the fall of Jerusalem, AD 70—there is a definite rebuttal of the claim to the divine sonship of Jesus, "a blasphemy against the Jewish understanding of God." The Christian doctrines of the incarnation, atonement through the cross, and of course the Trinity similarly are rejected.[11] That said, it is significant that even with the harshening of tone in later levels of Talmud—the "scripture" of Rabbinic Judaism—the opposition was targeted less against the historical figure of Jesus of Nazareth and more against what was considered to be Pauline Christology and the subsequent patristic and creedal tradition.[12]

Concerning Jesus's miracles, they are routinely considered to be "magic"—a highly interesting assessment in light of the fact that according to Talmud, for the Sanhedrin, men are chosen who not only are wise but also "are well versed in magic."[13] What concerns Jews about Jesus's miracles is suspicion about an effort to establish one's credentials on the basis of miracles since, as Deuteronomy 13 reminds us, a (Messianic) pretender may excel in miraculous acts and yet lead astray the people of God.

No earlier than during the aftermath of the Enlightenment did interest in Jesus emerge, particularly among educated European Jews. For leading modern intellectual Moses Mendelssohn, Jesus was a thoroughly Jewish religious figure, so much so that, "closely examined, everything is in complete agreement not only with Scripture, but also with the [Jewish] tradition."[14] Some other contemporary intellectuals echoed similar sentiments. They were also encouraged by the quest of the historical Jesus and subsequent classical liberalism's interest in the "historical, real" Jesus, divorced from the layers of dogmatic and creedal traditions. The first modern study on Jesus written in Hebrew, by Joseph Klausner, *Jesus of Nazareth: His Life, Times, and Teachings*, is a landmark work but also deeply Zionist in nature.[15] One of the main tasks of the modern Jewish investigation into Jesus was to correct misrepresentations of the past: "The modern Jewish scholarly reassessment . . . restored respectability to Jesus' image, and then reclaimed him as a Jew who *could* have merited a rightful place in Jewish literature

11. Pinchas Lapide, *Israelis, Jews, and Jesus*, trans. Peter Heinegg (Garden City, NY: Doubleday, 1979), 76–77.

12. Ibid., 77.

13. *Babylonian Sanhedrin* 17a; see Lapide, *Israelis, Jews, and Jesus*, 89.

14. Moses Mendelssohn, *Jerusalem; or, On Religious Power and Judaism*, trans. Allan Arkush (Hannover, NH: University Press of New England, 1983), 134, cited in Heschel, "Jewish Views of Jesus," 151.

15. Joseph Klausner, *Jesus of Nazareth: His Life, Times, and Teachings*, trans. Herbert Danby (New York: Macmillan, 1925).

alongside those of other ancient Jewish sages."[16] At the same time, the Jewish search for the Jewish Jesus also wanted to develop "a counterhistory of
the prevailing Christian theological version of Christianity's origins and
influence."[17]

Whether Christology Is Inherently Anti-Semitic

Over against the resurgence of interest in Jesus among Jewish scholars
looms large the shadow of the horrors and crimes of the Holocaust. The
Christian church and her theologians have shown attitudes of imperialism in
terms of political hegemony and committed crimes against the Jewish people
(as happened under the Nazi regime).

In light of the long and painful track record of Christian anti-Semitism,
many wonder whether Christology per se is anti-Semitic. It is argued that the
New Testament itself and the way Christian theology considered Jesus have
led to and fostered negativity and violence toward Jews. A vocal advocate
of that thesis is Christian feminist Rosemary Radford Ruether in her *Faith
and Fratricide: The Theological Roots of Anti-Semitism*.[18] "Theologically,
anti-Judaism developed as the left hand of christology."[19] Ruether wonders
whether it is possible to confess Jesus as Messiah without at the same time
saying that "the Jews be damned."[20]

Without in any way downplaying the severity of the history of anti-Semitism, many scholars, including Jewish scholars, greatly doubt the adequacy
of Ruether's argument. It seems like the accusations are sweeping and unnuanced, including the acknowledgment of great diversity in the New Testament (to which we paid attention in part 1). Interestingly, Jewish scholar
Thomas A. Idinopulos and Christian scholar Roy Bowen Ward have offered
a careful investigation of Ruether's claims and conclude that "the appearance of anti-Judaic thought in certain documents in the New Testament
does not lead to the conclusion that anti-Judaism is necessarily the left hand
of Christology." They are looking carefully at the parable of the vineyard in
Mark 12, which Ruether considers a showcase for inherent anti-Jewishness
and the beginning of anti-Semitism in the New Testament, and they contest

16. Cook, "Jewish Perspectives on Jesus," 224.
17. Heschel, "Jewish Views of Jesus," 152.
18. Rosemary Radford Ruether, *Faith and Fratricide: The Theological Roots of Anti-
Semitism* (New York: Seabury, 1974); chap. 2 focuses on the anti-Jewish materials in the New
Testament.
19. Rosemary Radford Ruether, *To Change the World: Christology and Cultural Criticism*
(New York: Crossroad, 1981), 31.
20. Ruether, *Faith and Fratricide*, 246.

Ruether's interpretation.[21] Similarly, they have subjected to critique Ruether's claim that "Judaism for Paul is not only *not* an ongoing covenant of salvation where men continue to be related in true worship of God: it never was such a community of faith and grace." Consider that Paul himself boasts of his Jewishness and can even say that "as to righteousness under the law [he was] blameless" (Phil. 3:6 RSV).[22]

Scholarly criticism of the unnuanced attribution of anti-Jewish attitudes to the New Testament is not to deny the "hardening of attitudes"[23] toward Jews in the Gospel of Matthew or the quite negative presentation of Jews in the Gospel of John (however the dating of these documents go). This criticism of the Jewish people—usually their religious leaders—must be put in a proper perspective. The Matthean critique of the Jewish people, especially in chapter 23 of his Gospel, is not necessarily different from or untypical of the harsh criticism of one Jewish group by another Jewish group at the time.[24]

Has the Messiah Come?

Among all the theological differences concerning the figure of Jesus Christ, the most deeply contested among the two sister faiths is the question of Messiah—even when, ironically, what unites Jewish and Christian theologies is the conviction that salvation comes through the Messiah. It is with the vastly different interpretation of the meaning of the Messiah that the deepest differences among the two traditions come to the fore. Rightly, Moltmann notes, "The gospels understand his [Jesus Christ's] whole coming and ministry in the contexts of Israel's messianic hope. Yet it is the very same messianic hope which apparently makes it impossible for 'all Israel' to see Jesus as being already the messiah."[25]

The main reason for the Jewish rejection of Jesus as Messiah has to do with the obvious fact that when looking at the state of the world (including God's own people), there is no evidence of the coming of the Messiah. As noted Jewish philosopher Martin Buber memorably put it, the Messiah could not possibly have come because "we know more deeply, more truly, that world

---

21. Thomas A. Idinopulos and Roy Bowen Ward, "Is Christology Inherently Anti-Semitic? A Critical Review of Rosemary Ruether's *Faith and Fratricide*," *Journal of the American Academy of Religions* 45, no. 2 (1977): 196.

22. Ibid., 198–99; citation in the text from Ruether, *Faith and Fratricide*, 104.

23. Ruether, *Faith and Fratricide*, 75.

24. Raymond E. Brown, *An Introduction to the New Testament* (New York: Doubleday, 1997), 222.

25. Jürgen Moltmann, *The Way of Jesus Christ: Christology in Messianic Dimensions*, trans. Margaret Kohl (Minneapolis: Fortress, 1993), 28.

history has not been turned upside down to its very foundations—that the world is not yet redeemed. We *sense* its unredeemedness."[26] Differently from Christian messianic hopes, Jewish theology anticipates the coming of Messiah as the fulfillment of all hopes for redemption, whereas Christian tradition came to understand the coming of Messiah in two stages.[27]

In Judaism the role of Messiah has to do with serving as the *agent* of reconciliation rather than acting as the one who reconciles; only Yahweh can do that.[28] The rejection of Christian claims by Jewish counterparts is thus understandable in light of the vastly differing views of messianism that go back to Second Temple Judaism. In order to facilitate dialogue, Moltmann poses this question to the Jewish counterpart, the "gentile" question to the Jews: "Even *before* the world has been redeemed so as to become the direct and universal rule of God, can God already have a chosen people, chosen moreover *for the purpose of this redemption?*"[29]

What about incarnation, an essential Christian belief about Christ? Is the idea of God taking human form absolutely unknown to Jewish faith? Yes—and no! Yes, in the sense that any idea of incarnation is missing in Jewish messianism. But that the idea of divine embodiment in itself is not totally irrelevant to Jewish theology can be argued from the presence of the following types of occurrences in Jewish Scriptures: "God walking in the garden" (Gen. 3:8 RSV), or the Lord appearing to Abraham in the form of the angel sharing a meal (Gen. 18), or Jacob's wrestling match with a man of whom he says, "I have seen God face to face" (Gen. 32:30 RSV), or Israelite leaders under Moses claiming that they "saw the God of Israel" on the mountain (Exod. 24:9–11). Jewish Michael S. Kogan argues, "For Jewish believers, then, the thought may come to mind that, if God can take human form in a series of accounts put forward in one's own sacred texts, one would be unjustified in dismissing out of hand the possibility that the same God might act in a similar fashion in accounts put forward in another text revered as sacred by a closely related tradition."[30] This is of course not to push the similarities too far; the differences are obvious, particularly in light of Christian creedal traditions that speak of the permanent "personal" (hypostatic) union of the human and divine in one particular person, Jesus of Nazareth.

---

26. Martin Buber, *Der Jude und Sein Judentum: Gesammelte Aufsätze und Reden* (Cologne, 1963), 562, cited in Moltmann, *Way of Jesus Christ,* 28–29.

27. See further Moltmann, *Way of Jesus Christ,* 30.

28. John C. Lyden, "Atonement in Judaism and Christianity: Towards a Rapprochement," *Journal of Ecumenical Studies* 29, no. 1 (1992): 50–53.

29. Moltmann, *Way of Jesus Christ,* 30 (emphasis original).

30. Michael S. Kogan, *Opening the Covenant: A Jewish Theology of Christianity* (Oxford: Oxford University Press, 2008), 115.

The Messiah of Israel and the Savior of the Nations

As much antagonism and opposition as Jesus of Nazareth caused in his lifetime, it is also true what Pannenberg states, namely, that with his announcement of the imminence of God's righteous rule dawning in his own ministry, "Jesus came to move the covenant people to conversion to its God."[31] Doing so, Jesus, the faithful Jew, did not do away with the first commandment but rather radicalized it. Most ironically, in light of Christian theology one has to conclude that it was only after the rejection of his own people that Jesus's death on the cross made him the "Savior of the nations."[32] The Messiah of the covenant people died for the people outside the covenant, in other words, the gentiles. Some few Jews have come to acknowledge the significance of the Christian church's preaching of the gospel to the gentiles; one is influential Jewish philosopher of religion Franz Rosenzweig, in his mature work, *The Star of Redemption*.[33]

Critical in this discussion, hence, is the view of the cross of Jesus. The cross as a cultural-religious symbol is highly offensive to Judaism.[34] "If the church has developed an interpretation of the cross that sees it as the point of God's rejection of Israel, of Israel's rejection of Jesus, of the loss of Israel's inheritance, and of transference to the church, then it must reckon with the fact that Jesus died for the Jewish nation before he died for the scattered children of God beyond Israel's boundaries."[35] Ironically, had not the messianic people rejected her Messiah, "Christianity would have remained an intra-Jewish affair."[36] However many Jews rejected the Christian Messiah, it is also true that according to the New Testament hope, eventually "all Israel will be saved" (Rom. 11:26).

Behind the different takes on the Messiah are highly diverse views between the two traditions about what is wrong with humanity and what makes for salvation. The idea of vicarious atonement after the Christian interpretation, with a view for the salvation of the world, "seems strange and foreign to Jews who believe that the problem of sin had already been dealt with in the Torah."[37] This is not only because Jewish theology does not endorse

31. Wolfhart Pannenberg, *Systematic Theology*, trans. Geoffrey W. Bromiley (Grand Rapids: Eerdmans, 1994), 2:311.

32. Ibid., 2:312; so also Moltmann, *Way of Jesus Christ*, 34.

33. Franz Rosenzweig, *The Star of Redemption*, trans. from the 2nd ed. of 1930 by William W. Hallo (New York: Holt, Rinehart & Winston, 1970).

34. D. Cohn-Sherbok, *The Crucified Jew* (London: HarperCollins, 1992).

35. John G. Kelly, "The Cross, the Church, and the Jewish People," in *Atonement Today*, ed. John Goldingay (London: SPCK, 1995), 166–67.

36. Carl E. Braaten, "Introduction: The Resurrection in Jewish-Christian Dialogue," in Lapide, *Resurrection of Jesus*, 18.

37. Kogan, *Opening the Covenant*, 116.

the Christian tradition's view of the fall, which necessitates divine initiative such as with the death on the cross, but also because the otherworldly goal of salvation in the afterlife is not at all as central in Judaism. Following the Torah and its commandments as the chosen people, and thus testifying to God's unity and holiness, is the way of "salvation" in Judaism.[38] For these and related reasons, the conception of atonement as the one-time, finished self-sacrifice of Jesus differs markedly from the continuing sacrificial cult administered by the priesthood in Judaism. Not only the finality of the sacrifice of Jesus but also its universality marks its difference from the understanding of the Jewish tradition. That is true even when it is also the case that Christian views of atonement and salvation are based on the Old Testament atonement traditions.

In light of the common themes and dramatic differences in their interpretations between the two sister faiths, it is useful for Christian Christology to mind Jewish theologian Michael S. Kogan's admonition "to be faithful to the New Testament command to witness for Christ to all peoples and to convert all nations, while, at the same time, affirming the ongoing validity of the covenant between God and Israel via Abraham and Moses."[39] At the center of this tension lies the obvious but important fact that "historically Christianity has been theologically exclusive and humanistically universal, while Judaism has been theologically universal and humanistically exclusive." Christian theological exclusivism, however, is qualified by the equally important conviction that Christ died for all and that therefore all people from all nations can be beneficiaries of this salvific work.[40]

Islamic Jesus

The Prominence of Jesus in Muslim Spirituality

The Roman Catholic document on other religions, *Nostra Aetate* of Vatican II, says of Muslims that "though they do not acknowledge Jesus as God, they revere Him as a prophet. They also honor Mary, His virgin Mother; at times they even call on her with devotion."[41] Ironically, Jesus is held in high honor among Muslims—notwithstanding the rampant caricaturing by Christians of Islam's founder, the Prophet Muhammad. Indeed, it can be said that

38. Ibid., 11–13.
39. Ibid., xii.
40. Ibid., xii–xiii.
41. *Nostra Aetate*, par. 3, www.vatican.va/archive/hist_councils/ii_vatican_council/documents/vat-ii_decl_19651028_nostra-aetate_en.html.

in "the Islamic tradition, Jesus ('Isa) was a Muslim."[42] Hence, we have titles such as *The Muslim Jesus* for an anthology of sayings and stories about Jesus in Islamic tradition.[43] Unknown to most Christians, in the Qur'an alone about one hundred references to Jesus and his mother can be found.[44]

The Qur'an contains nothing like the New Testament Gospel narratives. Instead, there are a number of references to key events in Jesus's life from conception to earthly ministry to death/resurrection to his eschatological future. Even the virgin birth of Jesus is affirmed in the Qur'an (21:91).[45] That said, the assessment of Jesus's meaning among Muslims continues to be a sensitive and debated issue. Behind this uneasiness is the principle of the "self-sufficiency" of the Islamic canonical tradition, according to which only the Islamic tradition presents a correct picture of Jesus. There is also the long-term debate and conflict with Christian Christology. Both sides accused each other of truncated, false, and deviant interpretations of who Jesus Christ is and what is his meaning. A typical Muslim engagement for a long time was to add to the existing references in the Qur'an (and Hadith, the main source of traditions) materials from extracanonical apocryphal writings, especially the *Gospel of Barnabas*, whose influence even today is immense in anti-Christian polemics.[46]

Titles of Jesus in Muslim Christology

Islam considers Jesus one of the prophets, a highly respected title in that tradition. Indeed, Jesus stands in the long line of Old Testament prophets beginning from Noah, Abraham, and Moses. Jesus as prophet is second only to the Prophet himself, Muhammad, who is the "seal" of the prophets. Interestingly, Jesus's role as teacher is marginal in the Qur'an when compared to the Gospels. It is rather often the case that God teaches Jesus, and at times Jesus is rebuked for teaching erroneously.

The only title that is uniquely reserved for Jesus in the Qur'an is Messiah (4:171). It is, however, difficult to determine the distinctively Islamic

---

42. Reem A. Meshal and M. Reza Pirbhai, "Islamic Perspectives on Jesus," in Burkett, *Blackwell Companion to Jesus*, 232.

43. Tarif Khalidi, ed., *The Muslim Jesus: Sayings and Stories in Islamic Literature* (Cambridge, MA: Harvard University Press, 2000).

44. In addition to over thirty references, Sura 19 is named after Mary.

45. Among a number of accessible English translations of the Qur'an, the one used here is *The Holy Qur'ān: A New English Translation of Its Meanings* (Amman, Jordan: Royal Aal al-Bayt Institute for Islamic Thought, 2008). This version of the Qur'an is also available online at http://altafsir.com.

46. For a useful discussion, see Oddbjørn Leirvik, *Images of Jesus Christ in Islam*, 2nd ed. (London: Continuum, 2010), 132–44.

interpretation of that term. What is clear is that it does not denote anything divine, after Christian tradition.

Jesus's miracles are enthusiastically affirmed by Islamic traditions. The Qur'an recounts several miracles of Jesus, such as healing the leper and raising the dead. The Qur'an also knows miracles such as shaping a living bird out of clay based on apocryphal Gospels (5:110).[47] A remarkable miracle is the table sent down from heaven spread with good food as divine proof of Jesus's truthfulness as the spokesperson for God and divine providence (5:112–15). Muslim commentary literature, poetry, and popular piety contain many different types of accounts and stories of Jesus's miracles, which lead to a high regard for the person and prophethood of Jesus. For the most well-known Muslim poet, thirteenth-century Persian Sufi Jalaluddin Rumi, the miraculous birth and life of Jesus with a ministry of miracles, including healings and resuscitations, also become the source of inspiration for spiritual rebirth. His highly influential *Mathanawi*, also called the Qur'an in the Persian language, praises Jesus for his power to raise the dead and for his wisdom.

The ample record of miraculous acts attributed to Jesus, however, does not imply that therefore he should be lifted up higher than the Prophet of Islam; the miracles wrought by Jesus are similar to those performed by Moses and other such forerunners of Muhammad. The purpose of miracles is to confirm prophetic status but not divinity. Even the fact that Jesus is described as sinless in Hadith and legendary tradition does not make him superior. Kenneth Cragg's observation is accurate: "It is clear that the Qur'an's attribution of unprecedented miracles to Jesus is not a cause of embarrassment to the Muslim commentators. On the contrary, from their point of view, since Jesus is a prophet the miracles which God vouchsafes him must be sufficiently great to convince those to whom he is sent. Hence in common with popular Muslim piety the commentators tend to exaggerate the miraculous rather than play it down."[48]

As much as Jesus and his ministry are revered in Islamic theology, it is essential to note that it is not useful to compare Jesus Christ to Muhammad. Unlike Christian faith, which is determined by belief in Christ, Islam is not based on Muhammad but rather on the Qur'an and Allah. Muhammad is the mediator (through the angel Gabriel) of divine revelation, but he—no more than Christ—is not divine; only God is. The closest parallel to Christ in Islamic faith can be found in Christ's role as the living Word of God, in

---

47. For a useful discussion of Jesus's miracles in the Qur'an, see Neil Robinson, *Christ in Islam and Christianity* (New York: State University of New York Press, 1991), chap. 14.

48. Cited in ibid., 154.

relation to the divine revelation of the Qur'an.[49] That said, the high status of Jesus is attested by the following oft-cited Qur'anic statement: "Prophets are brothers in faith, having different mothers. Their religion is, however, one and there is no Apostle between us (between me and Jesus Christ)."[50] As is well known, Muhammad's own relation to Christianity and Christian tradition in general, especially in the early phases of his career, was fairly positive and constructive.

In order to deepen the portrait of Jesus and his meaning in Islamic tradition—and its radical deviation from the Christian interpretation—let us take a closer look at the three most contested issues between Islamic and Christian Christologies: divinity, incarnation, and crucifixion.

The Islamic Rebuttal of Christian Theological Claims about Christ

As mentioned, Muhammad has no divine connotations in Islam—even less Jesus or other prophets. Only Allah is God. Islam's strict monotheism stands at the heart of the confession of faith. No wonder, "Jesus the 'Christ,' the 'eternal logos,' the 'Word made flesh,' the 'Only Begotten Son of God' and second person of the trinity has been the barrier separating the two communities [Muslim and Christian]."[51]

No wonder debates about Jesus's divinity have been conducted since the rise of Islam in the seventh century. One of the ablest Christian apologists and polemicists in the exchange was leading eighth-century Eastern Orthodox theologian John of Damascus. In his *On Heresies*, John shows an accurate awareness of the Qur'an's portrait of Jesus and provides a theological rebuttal of its claims that deviate from the Christian confession.

The Qur'an denies bluntly and strongly all Christian claims for the deity of Jesus Christ (4:171; 5:17; 9:30; 19:35). A related Qur'anic denial is the idea that Allah had a son (2:116; 4:171; 10:68; 17:111). The main arguments in these passages for not having a Son are God's transcendence and the fact that Allah already possesses everything that is in the world (10:68). In general the idea of God begetting is denied at the outset (37:152; 112:3).

Similar rebuttals of incarnation abound in Muslim theology. On the contrary, the Qur'an often speaks of the mere humanity of Jesus, and Muslim

49. Hence the heading "The 'Christ of Islam' Is the Koran," in Josef Imbach, *Three Faces of Jesus: How Jews, Christians, and Muslims See Him*, trans. Jane Wilde (Springfield, IL: Templegate, 1992), 87.

50. *Muslim, Kitāb al-Fadā'il*, quoted in Leirvik, *Images of Jesus Christ in Islam*, 38.

51. Maḥmud M. Ayoub, "Jesus the Son of God: A Study of the Terms *Ibn* and *Walad* in the Qur'ān and *Tafsīr* Tradition," in *Christian-Muslim Encounters*, ed. Y. Y. Haddad and W. Z. Haddad (Gainesville: University of Florida Press, 1995), 65.

scholars often refer to New Testament passages referring to his humanity, including ignorance, temptation, hunger, thirst, and so forth. Furthermore, Jesus's physical conception and birth as part of the doctrine of incarnation were seen as incompatible with both Christian and Muslim teachings. A related concern among Muslim commentators is the incompatibility of incarnation with God's transcendence. The idea of God becoming flesh violates in Muslim sensibilities the principles of God's glory and greatness.

Along with deity and incarnation, the most hotly contested issue between the two traditions has to do with what happened to Jesus in his final moments. The two Christologies differ sharply in the interpretation of the crucifixion: "The cross stands between Islam and Christianity. Dialogue cannot remove its scandal, and in due course a Muslim who might come to believe in Jesus has to face it."[52] One of the reasons the suffering Messiah does not appeal to Muslims is that "paragons of success and vindication" such as Abraham, Noah, Moses, and David are much more congenial with the vision of God's manifest victory on earth.

Although Muslim tradition does not speak with one voice about crucifixion, it is safe to say that almost all Muslims believe that the crucifixion did not occur or that a substitute was executed in Jesus's place (popularly, Judas Iscariot fills this role). Jesus, then, did not die. Instead of dying, rising, and ascending as in the Christian sequence of events, he was "born, lived . . . then was raised to heaven like Enoch and Elijah in the Bible, without dying."[53] Furthermore, the whole of Muslim theology unanimously "denies the expiatory sacrifice of Christ on the Cross as a ransom for sinful humanity."[54] Similarly to Jewish tradition, Islam does not endorse the traditional Christian idea of the fall and sinfulness (although no less than three accounts of the fall of Adam can be found in the Qur'an alone).

Hans Küng helps put in perspective the Islamic appreciation of Jesus and its different context from Christian interpretation. He advises Christians not to read Christian meanings into the Qur'an:

> The Qur'an should be interpreted *from the standpoint of the Qur'an*, not from that of the New Testament or the Council of Nicaea or Jungian psychology.

52. George H. Bebawi, "Atonement and Mercy: Islam between Athanasius and Anselm," in *Atonement Today*, ed. John Goldingay (London: SPCK, 1995), 185.

53. Clinton Bennett, *Understanding Christian-Muslim Relations: Past and Present* (London: Continuum, 2008), 51. The Qur'an contains only one explicit reference to the alleged crucifixion of Jesus, in 4:156–59.

54. Mahmoud M. Ayoub, "Towards an Islamic Christology, II: The Death of Jesus, Reality or Delusion (A Study in the Death of Jesus in Tafsīr Literature)," *The Muslim World* 70, no. 2 (1980): 94.

For the Qur'an, Jesus is a prophet, a great prophet, like Abraham, Noah, and Moses—but nothing more. And just as in the New Testament John the Baptist is Jesus' precursor, so in the Qur'an Jesus is the precursor—and highly encouraging example—for Muhammad.[55]

On the other hand, Küng advises Muslims to evaluate Jesus on the basis of the historical sources of the Gospels: "If we on the Christian side make an effort to reevaluate Muhammad on the basis of Islamic sources, especially the Qur'an, we also hope that for their part the Muslims will eventually be prepared to move toward *a reevaluation of Jesus of Nazareth on the basis of historical sources* (namely the Gospels) as many Jews have already been doing."[56]

The last chapter of this book will continue investigating the role of Jesus among religions by focusing on two major Asian traditions, Hinduism and Buddhism. It is clear without saying that with them we move into a different religious, philosophical, and spiritual environment from that of the Abrahamic faiths.

---

55. Hans Küng, *Christianity and World Religions: Path to Dialogue* (New York: Doubleday, 1986), 110 (emphasis original).
    56. Ibid., 111 (emphasis original).

9

Jesus among Asian Traditions

Hindu Accounts of Jesus

Although Christianity and Hinduism are no foreigners to each other when considered historically—it is likely that as early as in the first century there was a Christian presence in India—there is no record of Hindu perceptions of Jesus surviving from those early days.[1] We have to wait until (almost) the nineteenth century to have firsthand Hindu responses to and interpretations of Christ. In chapter 6 above, in the context of Asian Christologies, there was discussion of the neo-Hindu renaissance and its interest in the "modern" Jesus for India; that treatment will not be repeated here.

The earliest modern Hindu interpretation of Jesus, offered by Raja Ram Mohun Roy in the early nineteenth century, focused on Jesus's ethical meaning but with denial of divine incarnation.[2] Many other Hindu writers were attracted to the social teachings of Christ (without necessarily involving a

1. It has become a commonplace to begin studies on any aspect of Hinduism by pointing out that such a thing never existed! "Hinduism" is a fairly late scholarly (and popular) construction, in many ways misleading or at least something in need of many qualifications. A useful guide and discussion for theological purposes is Julius J. Lipner, "Ancient Banyan: An Inquiry into the Meaning of 'Hinduness,'" *Religious Studies* 32 (1996): 109–26.

2. For a useful survey and discussion of the main figures, see R. Neufeldt, "Hindu Views of Christ," in *Hindu-Christian Dialogue: Perspectives and Encounters*, ed. Harold Coward (Maryknoll, NY: Orbis, 1990), 162–75.

personal commitment to him). Swami Prabhavananda's *Sermon on the Mount according to Vedanta* considers this sermon to be the "essence of Christ's Gospel."[3] Not surprisingly, for Mahatma Gandhi Jesus is an ethical teacher who expresses the ideal of a new community and way of life in the Beatitudes and other teachings. In those teachings, Gandhi saw the same principles that guided his own pacifistic fight for the liberation of the Indian people.

By and large—with few exceptions, often related to the colonialist history—Hindu perceptions of Jesus are positive. This is similar to Buddhist views and different from a number of Jewish and Islamic views. With sweeping generalizations, Hindu perceptions, including twentieth-century ones, can be described in this way: "(1) Jesus is a rational teacher of universal values; (2) Jesus is an incarnation of God among other incarnations; and (3) Jesus is a spiritual teacher. These positions are not, of course, mutually exclusive."[4]

The Divinity and Incarnation of Jesus in Hindu Interpretations

Hindu assessments of Jesus's divinity vary considerably. Some of them consider him merely a respected teacher and reject the belief of Jesus as the incarnation of God. There are also those such as Keshub Chunder Sen, who, replacing the doctrine of the Trinity with the Biunity of Father and Spirit, fell short of regarding Jesus as the divine incarnation but did highly regard his "son-ship" as an embodiment of the ideal of God's son. Hence, Jesus provided for us a perfect example of "Divine Humanity."[5]

Many, perhaps the majority of contemporary Hindu interpreters of Jesus are willing to grant divine status to Jesus Christ, something parallel to Krishna, the avatar of Vishnu. That, however, is very different from the traditional Christology of the creeds. It is commonplace in Hindu thought to believe that some dimension of the human being is divine. The possibility of realization of the divine lies within the reach of any human being (even if with most humans that may never come to fruition). In that context, Jesus is one among those in whom the realization of the divine came to happen. Hence, Jesus's importance lies in his role as the symbol of the potential of the realization of the divine in the human person. In that outlook, even the cross may be appropriated as the form of an ultimate self-sacrifice, "in the

3. Swami Prabhavananda, *Sermon on the Mount according to Vedanta* (Hollywood, CA: Vedanta Society of Southern California, 1992 [1963]), 7.

4. Gavin Flood, "Jesus in Hinduism: Closing Reflection," in *Jesus Beyond Christianity: The Classic Texts,* ed. Gregory A. Barker and Stephen E. Gregg (Oxford: Oxford University Press, 2010), 202.

5. The editors' explanation, an introduction to Keshub Chunder Sen, *Keshub Chunder Sen's Lectures in India* (London: Casssell, 1904), 2:25–27.

metaphysical sense of the sacrifice of the ego to the all-pervasive divine."[6] Chakravarthi Ram-Prasid goes so far as to make this summative statement of contemporary Hindu christological estimations: "It is probably right to say that the aspect of earlier Hindu views of Jesus that retains influence now is the recognition of Jesus as unquestionably divine in some way. There is hardly any systematic theorization of Jesus in which he is dismissed as a charlatan or as a 'mere' human being or as having no spiritual significance whatsoever."[7]

If possible, even higher status is granted to Jesus in *The Gospel of Sri Ramakrishna*, written by nineteenth-century Bengalian guru Ramakrishna Paramahansa. He claimed to have a number of mystical encounters with Jesus and that he shared deep union with Christ.

A key belief in theistic Hinduism has to do with *avatars*, embodiments of the divine beings/deities. The best-known among them are the ten (or so) incarnations of the Vishnu deity (one of three main deities, along with Brahma and Siva). The main task of Vishnu, the "Preserver-Deity," is to make sure the universe and its order will not be destroyed in an undue manner. Through various forms of avatars, Vishnu intervenes in the affairs of the world. This "descent," as the word literally means, can be expressed in terms of the word "incarnation." The well-known passage in Bhagavad Gita (4.7–8), the "Bible" of the common folks in India, puts it this way:

> 7. Whenever, O descendant of Bharata, there is decline of Dharma, and rise of Adharma, then I body Myself forth

> 8. For the protection of the good, for the destruction of the wicked, and for the establishment of Dharma, I come into being in every age[8]

Rather than atonement after a Christian interpretation, the purpose of the "coming down" of the divine is the establishment of Dharma, the right order (or "righteousness"). Rather than the sacrificial death of Jesus, the *avatara* Krishna and others help men and women attain "enlightenment," right insight into the nature of reality. Not sin but rather "ignorance" is the main diagnosis of the human situation. Hence, "avatars come then to bring a new or renewed revelation of Truth, expressed through the example of

6. Ram-Prasad, "Hindu Views of Jesus," in *Jesus in the World's Faiths*, 85.
7. Ibid., 86.
8. Trans. Swami Swarupananda. All Hindu scriptural references, unless otherwise noted, are from the Sacred Texts website, www.sacred-texts.com (which includes the standard scholarly English translations).

their lives. This enables people to know that they can change and become like the avatars."[9]

Unlike a one-time, historical "Word becoming flesh," Hindu mythology includes numerous accounts of incarnations, as mentioned above. Of the multiplicity of incarnations, an illustrative example is the possibility of multiple avatars of the one and same figure, such as Krishna. Furthermore, unlike Christian tradition, it is customary for Hindu thought to conceive of avatars in degrees, from a partial to fuller to fullest measure of incarnation.

What about the Uniqueness of Jesus Christ?

Most Hindu traditions have a strong inclusivistic orientation, as expressed in the famous vedic saying "To what is One, sages give many a title."[10] Recall that most Hindus would be ready to affirm the divine status of Jesus Christ. The truthfulness and beauty of other traditions is often openheartedly affirmed. Yet there is also the awareness that, say, the value of Jesus, as high as it is, in some sense may be inferior—or at least is not superior—to the Hindu religion. In some sense, the typical Hindu view resembles the Roman Catholic fulfillment theory of religions but perhaps in a more radicalized form: everything good and true is being affirmed, yet with the expectation that the "fullness" may be found in one's own religion.

For the Christian theologian it is of utmost importance to mind that finding parallels between the incarnation of Jesus and Hindu avatars, and even granting divine status to Jesus, does not make him unique in the Christian sense. Rather, Hindus believe that the divine intervenes in human life in various ways and constantly. Over against the Christian view of "God-as-human" (the Word made flesh), the Hindu formula is "God-in-human." In this Hindu outlook, "the divine and human are ultimately identical, or the divine is the spark of potential in the human, or something else. . . . In all of them, everyone is potentially divine, and Jesus is an outstanding . . . embodiment of the human who has realized his divinity."[11]

The only way in the Hindu framework to speak of the "uniqueness" of Jesus is to link it with oneness, the underlying oneness of all, as explained in the often-cited formula from *Chandogya Upanishad* (6.2.1): "In the beginning . . . there was that only which is . . . one only, without a second. Others say, in the beginning there was that only which is not, . . . one only, without

---

9. Sandy Bharat, "Hindu Perspectives on Jesus," in *The Blackwell Companion to Jesus*, ed. Delbert Burkett (Oxford: Wiley-Blackwell, 2011), 255.

10. *Rig Veda* 1.164.46.

11. Ram-Prasad, "Hindu Views of Jesus," 88.

a second; and from that which is not, that which is was born."[12] This kind of uniqueness, however, is not the same as the traditional Christian "exclusive" uniqueness of Jesus Christ. Hindu thought makes Jesus "unique" among other "unique" manifestations of the divine.

Buddhist Accounts of Jesus

Jesus and the Buddha

Interaction between Jesus traditions and Buddhist traditions has not been wide until the twentieth century. The reasons are many and variegated. By the time of the birth of the Christian faith, Buddhist movements were locating themselves in areas of the world distant from Christian mission. Before the twentieth century, by far the most significant interaction between the two religions took place in China during the Tang Dynasty, in the latter part of the first millennium, in the form of Nestorian Christianity.

In terms of life history, there are obvious similarities between Shakyamuni (Gautama) Buddha and Jesus of Nazareth. This much can be said even if the historical details of Gautama's life are very scarce, including the lack of precise dating of his birth. Both founders of religions have miraculous elements attached to their birth, including cosmic signs and phenomena, as well as ominous threat; both of them face temptations, one in the forest, the other in the desert; both become itinerant preachers and teachers who also are considered to be miracle workers; both are men of prayer and meditation; and so forth.[13]

Undoubtedly the most significant features of the person and ministry of Jesus in Buddhist interpretation are his teaching and compassion. Many recent Buddhist interpretations consider Jesus an enlightened teacher.[14] Theravada Buddhist monk Ajarn Buddhadasa considered Jesus an apostle or prophet on par with Gautama. He opined that Jesus's message is enough for "salvation." Vietnamese Master Thich Nhat Hanh went so far as to say that "we are all of the same nature as Jesus," even though the manifestation of that nature takes a lot of study and effort.[15]

All traditions of Buddhism highly value the teacher's role; this is in keeping with the three original vows of the tradition: to take refuge in Buddha, *sangha*

12. Trans. Max Mueller, www.sacred-texts.com/hin/sbe01/sbe01120.htm; see Ravi Ravindra, "Jesus Is Not an Idol," in *Jesus in the World's Faiths*, 96–97.

13. See Leo D. Lefebure, *The Buddha and the Christ: Explorations in Buddhist and Christian Dialogue* (Maryknoll, NY: Orbis, 1993), chap. 2.

14. See, e.g., Gregory A. Baker, introduction to *Jesus in the World's Faiths*, 3.

15. José Ignacio Cabezón, "Buddhist Views of Jesus," in *Jesus in the World's Faiths*, 16.

(community), and *dhamma* (teaching). The aspects of Jesus's teaching most highly valued by Buddhists include the Beatitudes, love of enemy, the admonition to repay evil with kindness, and stress on charity and equanimity. Where Buddhists find omissions in Jesus's teaching are the lack of focus on living beings other than humans as well as on wisdom and spiritual praxis. What is not only foreign but also repulsive to Buddhist views is Jesus's emphasis on the kingdom and eschatological rule of God, as well as particularly the "*utter finality* of the Christian apocalypse" in terms of sealing one's destiny once and for all.[16]

In sum, as long as Jesus as Teacher stands alone, so to speak, without reference to the transcendent, absolute God the Father, Buddhists are able to admire his teaching. As Zen Buddhist Daisetsu Teitaro Suzuki puts it succinctly, "Jesus said, 'When thou doest alms, let not thy left hand know what thy right hand doeth; that thine alms may be in secret.' This is the 'secret virtue' of Buddhism. But when the account goes on to say that 'Thy Father who seeth in secret shall recompense thee,' we see a deep cleavage between Buddhism and Christianity."[17]

Although the original Theravada tradition teaches that one should not be too active in intervening in another person's suffering, in order to avoid interrupting the *karma* and *samsara*-nature of reality, particularly in the Mahayana traditions there is an emphasis on the extraordinary compassion of Gautama toward not only all sentient beings but also all other beings. In Mahayana, Gautama is known not only as the teacher of wisdom but also as magical healer and miracle worker, with acts including passing through walls, flying, and walking on water. The Mahayana tradition also knows of self-sacrificial acts of healing and alleviation of other people's pain, such as the story of Vimalakīrti. A virtuous Boddhisattva, he made himself sick, and in the presence of Shakyamuni (Gautama) and his disciples explained that there is sickness because of ignorance and thirst for existence. In order to help fellow men and women realize it, he tied his own healing to the healing of others. Still, Christians should not read into these Mahayana accounts any kind of atonement theology.

The Divinity and Incarnation of Jesus Christ in Buddhist Estimation

Similarly to Hindus, the Christian claim to the unique divinity of Jesus Christ is a stumbling block to Buddhists as well. Indeed, with all their ap-

16. Ibid., 20–21 (emphasis original).
17. D. T. Suzuki, *An Introduction to Zen Buddhism*, ed. Christmas Humphreys (London: Rider, 1995), 101.

preciation of Jesus's ethical life, ministry, and teaching, "the single most problematic aspect of Jesus' identity is his portrayal by Christians as God," says leading Tibetan Buddhist scholar and practitioner José Ignacio Cabezón. He specifies the problem in this way: "The problem lies not in the claim that Jesus is the incarnation or manifestation of a deity. What I find objectionable is (a) the Christian characterization of the deity whose incarnation Jesus is said to be, and (b) the claim that Jesus is unique in being an incarnation."[18]

That the idea of incarnation in itself is not a problem for Buddhists is based on the belief (prevalent among Mahayana Buddhists) that the universe is populated by enlightened beings. They have attained the buddhahood and have the capacity to incarnate for the welfare of others. In Mahayana Buddhism, the Boddhisattva—differently from the Theravada *Arhat*—is willing to postpone his own entrance into *nirvana* to help others reach the goal. Even that, however, is not the function of a "savior" but rather of a "good neighbor," even when the Boddhisattva may grant his own merit to help the other. In that light it is not necessarily difficult for the Buddhist to grant to Jesus the status of the manifestation of a deity, as long as the Christian interpretation thereof is not followed.

Along with the Buddha himself—and in some sense even more closely—the Mahayana understanding of the Boddhisattva bears a similarity with Jesus the Christ. The Bodhisattva is "Buddha-in-the-making," who for the sake of others is willing to suffer and postpone one's own enlightenment. A special and unique case in this regard is (Mahayana) Pure Land tradition, with its idea of the Bodhisattva as a manifestation of Amitabha, the God of the "Infinite Light," who has prepared a paradise-type existence of bliss for his followers. Between the Theravada tradition and Christian interpretation of Jesus there are even wider differences, as Theravada does not emphasize the idea of enlightened manifestations of the divine incarnating for the benefit of others.

Behind the Buddhist refusal to grant a salvific role to Jesus lie a number of doctrinal presuppositions. In that tradition, every sentient person is responsible for his or her destiny. Suffering (technically *dukkha*, a word with various meanings), the ultimate cause that necessitates "salvation," is caused by each and every person, and consequently one cannot refer to another source of deliverance apart from one's own efforts. Indeed, the "Savior has no place in the Buddhist worldview. An individual must control and be responsible for his or her own destiny."[19] The idea that salvation of men and women would

---

18. Cabezón, "Buddhist Views of Jesus," 21.

19. Satanun Boonyakiat, "A Christian Theology of Suffering in the Context of Theravada Buddhism in Thailand" (PhD diss., School of Theology, Fuller Theological Seminary, 2009), 114.

be dependent on any historical event such as the cross is totally unknown to Buddhism. Even Buddha is not the Savior but rather the template to follow on the way to enlightenment. Buddhist Rita M. Gross makes the insightful observation that Christian tradition tends to "locate truth in the messenger, whereas Buddhism tends to focus on the message." This is linked with the fact that Christian tradition has a tendency "to personify the ultimate while Buddhists tend toward nonpersonal metaphors about ultimate reality."[20] Further complications for Buddhist acknowledgment of Jesus as divine come from Christian trinitarian teaching. If Christ is divine, then it means one has to acknowledge the God of the Bible.

No wonder any idea of the death on the cross of the Savior for the sins and salvation of others is an idea totally unknown in all traditions of Buddhism, although the generic idea of redemptive or "vicarious" suffering on behalf of others is not unknown in Buddhism, as mentioned above.[21] Nevertheless, any notion of somebody suffering (death) to atone for sins or even taking up another person's suffering onto himself is utterly foreign to the Theravada tradition.[22] A resort to such a vicarious act done by another person, even a divinity, would mean shrinking from one's own responsibility to deal with one's *karma*.

These last two chapters have briefly engaged four living faith traditions with regard to the meaning and role of the Christian confession of Jesus Christ. Much work awaits in this area, as it is currently being picked up slowly by doctrinal theologians. A major challenge for the theologian has to do with the knowledge of other faith traditions. Doing comparative Christology in the religiously pluralistic world calls for a sustained and patient study of scriptural, doctrinal, and spiritual traditions of other faiths.

20. Rita M. Gross, "Meditating on Jesus," in *Buddhists Talk about Jesus, Christians Talk about the Buddha*, ed. Rita M. Gross and Terry C. Muck (New York: Continuum, 2000), 44.

21. Just think, e.g., of the commonly known story in Thai (Theravada) Buddhism of sixteenth-century Queen Srisuriyothai's self-sacrifice to save her people under threat from the king of Burma.

22. See further Judith Simmer-Brown, "Suffering and Social Justice: A Buddhist Response to the Gospel of Luke," *Buddhist-Christian Studies* 16 (1996): 107–9 particularly.

Epilogue

The Future of Christology

Many and varied have been the challenges facing Christian theology in its painful yet exciting task of accounting for the person and work of the founder and center of the faith, Jesus of Nazareth. None, however, can compete with the urgency and seriousness of the question of the theology of religions, namely, the relation of Christianity to other religions. This question, of course, focuses on Jesus Christ and his role with regard to religion in general and to concrete forms of religions in particular. Great Christian novelist of the seventeenth century John Bunyan struggled with the devil, who assailed him with painful questions about the truth among religions and the role of Christ with regard to other savior figures:

> How can you tell but that the Turks had as good Scriptures to prove their Mahomet the Saviour, as we have to prove our Jesus is; and could I think that so many ten thousands in so many Countreys and Kingdoms, should be without the knowledge of the right way to Heaven . . . and that we onely, who live but in a corner of the Earth, should alone be blessed therewith? Everyone doth think his own Religion rightest, both Jews, and Moors, and Pagans; and how if all our Faith, and Christ, and Scriptures, should be but a thinks-so too?[1]

Long before Bunyan's struggle, Christian theology faced the question of who Jesus Christ is in relation to other saviors. Christianity was born and

1. John Bunyan, *Grace Abounding to the Chief of Sinners*, ed. Robert Sharrock (New York: Oxford University Press, 1962), 31.

took its initial form in a polytheistic environment, as did its Old Testament predecessor, the Jewish faith. Therefore, the excitement of theologians and students of religions over the newness and freshness of this challenge is not always historically well informed. Early apologists spoke of the "seeds of *Logos*" sown in the rich soil of religions, and several medieval heroes, such as Peter Abelard, who wrote *Dialogue of a Philosopher and a Jew and a Christian*, and Ramon Llull, who wrote *Book of the Gentile and the Three Wise Men*, challenged the limits of Christian exclusivism.

It seems uncontested that "the future of Christian theology lies in the encounter between Christianity and other faiths."[2] That is not only a challenge or a problem. Indeed, as Alan Race puts it, Christian theology "ought to rejoice at being at the frontiers of the next phase in Christian history."[3] Some students of Christian theology who have spent considerable time living among other religions even see pluralism as an integral part of Christian faith. Such is the dream of one theological moderate, Catholic Jacques Dupuis, SJ, who wants to see a shift toward a Christian theology of religious pluralism.[4] Not insignificantly, his earlier book is titled *Jesus Christ at the Encounter of World Religions*.[5]

Indeed, of all the turns in Christian theology in general and the study of Christology in particular, the "turn to other religions" will be the scariest but at the same time potentially the most fruitful with regard to the continuing mission of the Christian church. No doubt, it will add to the fragmentation and divisions of both Christian churches and Christian theologies; yet the challenge is to be faced.[6]

Another challenge for the study of Christology and Christian theology concerns the question of contextual theologies. As this book has shown, Christian theology has already begun to tackle this issue. An exciting, rich array of contextual or global—sometimes ironically yet fittingly called "local"—interpretations of Jesus Christ are emerging in various contexts of our world. These interpretations not only add to the mosaic of christological traditions and so speak to varying needs and desires but also have the potential to correct one-sided classical Western views. They have also helped classical

2. Alan Race, *Christians and Religious Pluralism: Patterns in the Christian Theology of Religions* (Maryknoll, NY: Orbis, 1982), xi.

3. Ibid.

4. Jacques Dupuis, SJ, *Toward a Christian Theology of Religious Pluralism* (Maryknoll, NY: Orbis, 1997).

5. Jacques Dupuis, SJ, *Jesus Christ at the Encounter of World Religions* (Maryknoll, NY: Orbis, 1991).

6. For starters, see Kärkkäinen, *Christian Theology of Religions: An Introduction* (Downers Grove, IL: InterVarsity, 2003).

theology to acknowledge its own dependence on context. All theologies are shaped and conditioned by their intellectual, social, psychological, and religious environments.

The challenges of both contextualization and other religions raise anew the question of the relationship between Christ's work and his person, in other words, the relationship between soteriology and Christology proper. Here, as in any other area, the necessity of speaking to the various and changing needs of specific contexts is urgent. Addressing that challenge requires a continuous dialogue between biblical and historical traditions and contemporary contexts.

The development of a distinctively Christian Christology in all its various colors and shades—we do not want to suppress plurality, for the simple reason that the Bible, the foundational source of all Christian theology, embraces a variety of approaches to who Christ is and what he has done—requires painstaking dialogue among biblical texts, historical developments, and varied current contexts. There is no easy way, no miracle solution. Doing Christian Christology is a global, intercultural exercise, transcending ecclesiastical and theological boundaries. The end result is not one Christology but a variety of rich voices, not unlike the Gospels, yet voices that share a common focus.

The study of Christology has yet another dimension. Great Catholic theologian of beauty Hans Urs von Balthasar, in his spiritual reflections on the Creator Spirit, issued a warning that has to do not only with pneumatology; it is also appropriate for the study of the Second Person of the Trinity: God, the source of life and beauty, is never an "object" to be studied but rather a Subject who grants us the needed, albeit necessarily limited, lenses to look at him. If the Spirit, according to the vision of von Balthasar, is the "seeing eye of grace," the Third Unknown who turns our eyes to the Son and the Father in the blessed Trinity, then "in the same way the Son neither wishes nor is able to glorify himself but glorifies only the Father (John 5:41; 7:18)."[7] What von Balthasar reminds us of is twofold. First, everything we say about Jesus Christ is conditioned by and related to the doctrine of the Trinity, the specifically Christian understanding of the Godhead. Consequently, though for pedagogical reasons this introductory text has focused on Jesus Christ alone, we cannot disassociate the person and work of Jesus Christ from the Christian understanding of God as triune. Second, von Balthasar underlines the ancient—albeit too often forgotten—conviction that the study of theology in general, and Christology in particular, is always an exercise in "spiritual things." Despite all that a careful, painstaking study gains, much is always

---

7. Hans Urs von Balthasar, *Explorations in Theology*, vol. 3, *Creator Spirit* (1967; repr., San Francisco: Ignatius, 1993), 111; see also 106–7.

left unexplained. More importantly, the "kernel" lies somewhere behind the "husk" of scientific inquiry. Even if it is neither feasible nor desirable to go back to the pre-Enlightenment idyllic mind-set, students of Christology need to remember that Christian theologians have always approached their task of inquiring into Christ with reverence and anticipation.

At the end of the day, Jesus of Nazareth, whom Christians confess as Lord and Savior, searches the depths of our lives and hearts. When the dilemma of faith and history is overcome—so the Christian church confesses—the "seeing eye of grace" will allow us to behold the beauty of the Savior. With Melanchthon and a host of other witnesses, we will grasp the depths of the dictum "To know Christ means to know his benefits."[8]

---

8. Philipp Melanchthon, *Loci communes theologici*, in *Melanchthon and Bucer*, ed. Wilhelm Pauck (Philadelphia: Westminster, 1969), 21.

Subject Index

Scripture Index